VERLAINE
A Study in Parallels

On doit voir sous mes vers

le ... *gulf-stream* de mon existence,

où il y a des courants

d'eau glacée et des courants d'eau bouillante,

des débris, oui, des sables, bien sûr,

des fleurs, peut-être ...

VERLAINE TO JULES HURET, 1891

UNIVERSITY OF TORONTO ROMANCE SERIES 14

UNIVERSITY OF TORONTO PRESS

VERLAINE
A Study in Parallels

A. E. Carter

Illustration on title page:

Paul Verlaine,

a woodcut by Felix Vallotton

To J. W. Hassell Jr.

UNIVERSITY OF TORONTO ROMANCE SERIES

Preface

NO POET'S WORK is more intimately bound up with his life than
Paul Verlaine's. All his best verse and much of his worst was the
result of direct experience. He seldom wrote in obedience to a
theory, not even in his youth, when he was trying to be a Parnassian. For this reason I have tried to bring into as sharp a focus as
possible the circumstances from which his poetry grew: the "parallels" as he called them between thought and action, mystic aspirations and devouring sensuality. "L'œuvre de Verlaine," his ex-
wife noted, "est obscure pour ceux qui ne sont pas très au courant
de sa vie, puisque, la plupart du temps, il fait allusion à des événe-
ments tout personnels." (*Mémoires de ma Vie*, 281)

A book of this sort is easier to write now than ten or fifteen
years ago. A proper edition of the *Œuvres complètes*, both prose
and verse, has recently been published (Le Club du Meilleur Livre
1959), and a number of brilliant studies have shed a flood of light
on hitherto obscure episodes: V. P. Underwood's *Verlaine et l'Angleterre*, Georges Zayed's *Lettres inédites de Verlaine à Cazals*, etc.
Lack of information is no longer our problem; the difficulties
arise when we begin to present and explain the material before us,
based, as it is, on those same "parallels." It allures and repels, leading off in opposite directions at the same time. Verlaine was an
alcoholic who abused his mother and beat his wife, lived in squalor
and liked it, lied his way out of difficulties, refused all responsibility for his behaviour. And he was also a lyric poet of the first order

– insinuating, seductive, intimate, personal: a man whose genius inspired not only admiration but a sort of complicity. Critical judgment hesitates. We oscillate between contradictions, fascinated by the reprobate and neglecting the writer, or turning appalled from the man and exalting his verse. In either case we cut him in two. What Verlaine thought of this method is well known:

> Ce Monsieur crut plaisant de me couper en deux,

he wrote of one such critic in *Invectives*:

> Le poète, très chic, l'homme, une sale bête.
> Voyez-vous ce monsieur qui me coupait en deux?
>
> Rentre, imbécile, ton "estime" pour mes livres.
> Mais ton mépris pour moi m'indiffère, étant vil.
> Garde, imbécile, ton "estime" pour mes livres.

I have often had the lines in mind. They are both a guide and a warning: we have to take Verlaine on his own terms. His verse is the all-important fact about him, and if we exaggerate his defects we are obviously in error; but to imagine him without his vices is to imagine him something he was not, and in that case he might very well have been no poet, and it would not be necessary to write books about him at all. The unedifying scenes in the rue Nicolet are a case in point: we must know something of them before we can appreciate the poetry he wrote at the time, its beauty and its hypocrisy, its blending of lucidity and self-deception.

To quote him once more, he was a *homo-duplex*, a merging of antitheses. Modern psychiatry would probably add a few terms, but this explanation is as good as any. It allows us to understand many things. Internal conflicts for which the sufferer finds no satisfactory therapy usually result from hereditary or environmental factors, and in Verlaine's case both were present. Recollections of his first years – the paradise of his mother's affection – pursued him until death, and this psychic lesion was further exacerbated by the alcoholic taint he got from his father's line. He lived in perpetual evasion, both of himself and of reality. Sensation, exquisitely attenuated or frankly brutal, was his only contact with the world; and when time dulled his perceptions and he could no longer feel intensely, his verse lost its edge: the subtle harmonies of his first books became the clogged prosody of his last. Both as man and artist he had every fault of the emotionally retarded.

The violent drama of such a personality almost forces us to take sides. We blacken or whiten Verlaine according to personal bias; we praise or blame unduly the secondary characters: Mathilde, Rimbaud, Elisa, etc. On this point I have nothing to say except that neither praise nor blame was ever my intention. Mathilde was prudent, courageous, affectionate, well-bred; she had all sorts of excellent qualities except one: the ability to hold Paul Verlaine. As for Rimbaud, I have tried to show him as he was; and during the four or five years that Verlaine knew him he was all but a juvenile delinquent: insulting, pig-headed, mercenary, sadistic, ready for anything, even blackmail, provided he got what he wanted. A thoroughly unpleasant character – and so much the better for literature! When later he reformed, began to save money, became a tender son and a loving brother, he wrote no more verse. His influence on Verlaine was good or bad depending on how we view it. From the standpoint of ordinary living he was a disaster; from the standpoint of poetry he was not merely beneficial but starkly necessary. Verlaine would have been a minor writer had they never met. He forced Paul to choose: was he to be a worthy civil-servant, with a wife, children, and one or two pretty volumes to his credit, or a great poet whose work, at its best, touches the very summits of the art? The answer required a frank and outrageous departure from convention and normality. It was the crucial point of Verlaine's life: everything led up to it, all subsequent events resulted from it. This is why even the minor details are important and worth recording. Until we have understood that, we have not understood him.

During the course of my work, the University of Georgia supplied me with generous research grants, without which nothing could have been done. I wish particularly to thank Mrs. Christine

Burroughs of the library for her pertinacity in obtaining inter-library loans, and my friend Pierre Guyénot who spent an after-noon at the Préfecture de la Seine ferreting out information on Charles Floquet which helped explain the failure of Verlaine's civil-service application in 1882. M. Yvan Christ put at my dis-posal certain unpublished documents concerning Verlaine's son Georges; Dr. Oscar Haac, Dr. J. W. Hassell, and Dr. Maxwell Smith supplied advice or criticized my manuscript. I also owe a considerable debt to the readers of the University of Toronto Press, whose perspicacity detected many blemishes of style and meaning which would otherwise have escaped me. This work has been published with assistance from the Publications Fund of the University of Toronto Press.

AEC

Athens, Georgia
September 1968

Contents

VERLAINE
A Study in Parallels

All quotations from Verlaine are taken either from
Œuvres poétiques complètes (Pléiade 1962),
referred to as "Verlaine, Pléiade," or from
Œuvres complètes de Paul Verlaine,
édition présentée dans l'ordre chronologique
(Le Club du Meilleur Livre, 2 vols. 1959),
referred to as *CML.*
All Rimbaud quotations are from
Œuvres complètes (Pléiade 1963),
referred to as "Rimbaud, Pléiade."

1 / The child and
the family

ABOUT THE YEAR 1850 two children, a boy of seven and a girl of
eight, played together every afternoon on the Esplanade at Metz.
It was the town's fashionable promenade above the Moselle River,
and especially on Thursdays and Sundays, when there were band
concerts, local society turned out in force. The Esplanade offered
more than an airing; it was a function, almost a rite, a way of
meeting friends and exchanging gossip to the brassy lilt of waltzes
and polkas. The little girl was less pretty than charming: "Blond-
ardent très près d'être fauve," her companion recalled later, "aux
yeux d'or brun parmi le teint moucheté de taches de rousseur
comme autant d'étincelles dans cette physionomie de feu ...
et, dans la démarche, un bondissement, un incessant élan ..."[1]
Their affection had been sudden, with all the directness children
put into such relationships. They even had their tiffs and their
jealousies, particularly if some other child tried to join them and
one or other showed too much interest in the new arrival. The
throng of idlers watched this romance with good-natured amusement. Smiling officers from the garrison nicknamed the tiny pair
"Paul and Virginie" or "Daphnis and Chloe" – symbolic names,
evoking childish innocence in a garden. The Moselle flowed time-
lessly among its vineyards; day waned; the old cathedral turned
black against the sunset. Flocks of crows drifted slowly in the
violet light. Nothing existed for the children beyond this charmed

1 *Confessions, CML,* II, 1107.

circle of sky, river, and benevolent crowd, enclosed in its own beauty as in a bland prism.

We usually recall the past as a series of pictures, and this was the first Paul Verlaine remembered when he wrote his *Confessions* at the end of his life. Its Edenic quality is obvious. With the passage of forty years, the Esplanade represented his childhood, a paradise where evil could not enter. And just as interesting, the very perfection of the image suggested another in direct contrast, representing the shock of a first contact with reality.

His father, an army officer, had resigned his commission and moved the family to Paris. In 1853, at the age of nine, Paul was entered as a boarder at the Institution Landry, an establishment which prepared students for secondary school and university. It was a dark October afternoon. The rooms were gloomy; in the refectory, the tables had black marble tops and there were no cloths. Dinner consisted of watery soup, boiled beef, and tough red beans; as drink there was a mixture of wine and water, so weak that it tasted like the rinsings of bottles. A normal child, interested in finding playmates, would scarcely have noticed such things. But to Verlaine (and the fact shows how unlike a normal child he was) the other boys were the worst detail of all: boisterous savages, probably hostile: "comme d'instinct ... j'eus horreur, pas peur, horreur ... des camarades." The idea of spending the night in such a place was intolerable. Profiting by the confusion in the yard, where some day-boys were leaving, he escaped through the gate and ran home. The family was at dinner. "Je tombai ... dans les bras de ma mère et puis de mon père ... Dans les yeux ... dans les bras tendus presque d'avance ... dans les baisers doux et longs de ma mère ... je perçus bien vite toute indulgence sinon quelque approbation ..."[2]

At first glance the episode seems irrelevant, the panic of a frightened child. And we could dismiss it as such, if it were not

2 *Ibid.*, 1122, 1127. Verlaine returned several times to these two episodes, the Esplanade and the school room: *Les Poètes maudits*, 1888 (*CML*, I, 884), *Souvenirs d'un Messein*, 1892 (*CML*, II, 551-52). He also mentioned them to Ernest Delahaye, who speaks of the matter in *Verlaine*, 2; and to Charles Donos, *Verlaine intime*, 8 *sqq.*

repeated again and again throughout Verlaine's adult life. He never learned to accept reality; he was forever running away from it in pursuit of the security he had lost. Both memories, the luminous Esplanade and the doleful school-room, reveal a fundamental maladjustment; we can trace it through the incidents of his career and the pages of his books. Everything he wrote is escapist in some way or other, just as each of his passionate attachments was an evasion of himself. In the terrified boy, dashing home through the October mist and the damp light of the gas-jets, we see already the poet of *Romances sans paroles* and *Sagesse*, the future lover of Mathilde Mauté and Arthur Rimbaud.

The family took its name from the hamlet of Verlaine in what is now Belgian Luxemburg, and was perhaps of noble origin. Records exist of a Gilles *de* Verlaine in 1577, who claimed bastard descent from a feudal house, the D'Ochains, and a Charles de Verlaine was *primus* at the University of Louvain in 1722.[3] By mid-eighteenth century, however, all claims to gentility had been dropped. The Verlaines were coarse peasants, and sometimes worse. There was an unbalanced streak in the line, a tendency to drink and violence. Paul's great-grandfather, Jean, a wagoner known as an unpleasant drunk, was fined six gold florins in 1742 for intemperate cursing. The personality of his son, Henry Joseph (born 1769), showed other complications as well: he thought for a time of studying for the priesthood, but changed his mind, married, and settled as notary in the village of Bertrix. There is nothing unusual about an abortive vocation. But Henry Joseph was not content merely to abandon the idea: he became a violent anticlerical as well, and joined an advanced literary circle, "Le Club des Baudets." When the armies of the French Revolution invaded the province in 1795 he was one of the radicals who applauded the destruction of the crucifix on the village church. He still held the same ideas ten years later, although Napoleon's concordat with Rome had made atheism unfashionable. One Sunday in 1804 he got drunk in a bar, saw the congregation leaving church after

3 See the *Chronologie* in the Verlaine, Pléiade, xv-xliv,

Mass, and gave vent to such anti-clerical and anti-Napoleonic sentiments that he was summoned to appear in court. At this point he died suddenly and the matter lapsed.

Rips of his kind often have an attraction for nice women, and his wife Anne Grandjean came from one of the best families of the district. After the scandal of his death, she left Bertrix with her three children (two daughters and a son, Nicolas Auguste, born in 1798) and moved in with her parents at the neighbouring town of Jehonville. Like Mathilde Mauté, Paul's wife eighty years later, she probably thought that she had a right to a second try at matrimony, and remarried shortly afterwards. Her parents brought up Henry Joseph's children. They were too young to remember much about their disreputable father and he was soon forgotten; doubtless a conspiracy of silence was maintained on the subject. The Grandjeans were strict, traditional, very pious; the family and its branches had given no fewer than nine priests to the Church, and close relations were maintained with the clergy. This was an important fact in Paul's childhood. Whenever he visited his relatives in the country he was in contact with priests: the Church was as much a part of his adolescence as the rambling country-houses where he spent his holidays and the forests and prairies where he learned to hunt – not to mention the village dram-shops where he learned to drink, and where the ghosts of two previous generations lay in wait. A heavily charged ancestry, that much is obvious: drink and bad temper on one side; stability, order, piety on the other.[4]

Under the influence of one of the Grandjean sons (a lieutenant-colonel in the French Army), Nicolas Auguste enlisted in 1814, saw Napoleon's last campaigns, and obtained a commission, eventually rising to the rank of Captain Adjutant Major in the Engineers. When his native province was handed over to the Kingdom of the Netherlands by the Vienna treaties, he chose French nationality and continued his career in France. He was a typical soldier

---

4 Léon Le Febve de Vivy, *Les Verlaine* 23; J. H. Bornecque, *Etudes verlainiennes, les Poèmes saturniens*, 14-15. The alcoholic tendency emerged disastrously in Verlaine's son Georges. See the Appendix.

of the period: conscientious, capable, rather inarticulate. The dark heredity of his father's stock had skipped him: he took after his mother, a well-balanced Grandjean. "J'étais si fier ... de son port superbe ... visage martial et doux, où néanmoins l'habitude du commandement n'avait pas laissé de mettre un pli d'autorité qui m'imposait," his son Paul remembered.[5] Everything we know about him suggests a well-regulated mind, even his marriage. He waited until he was thirty-three and then chose Elisa Stéphanie Dehée, daughter of rich sugar-refiners at Fampoux, in the Pas-de-Calais. They were married on December 15, 1831.

She was a pretty woman – regular features and large dark eyes: the sort of face one sees in the keepsakes of the period. Till the end of her life her manners were ceremonious, even a bit stiff, though she could unbend with people she knew and liked to mother her son's friends.[6] But beneath this correct exterior lurked some strange characteristics. She was twenty-one when she married, a fairly late age in those days; and although she loved the handsome Captain, she was one of those women whose passion for mother-hood dwarfs her affection for her mate. During the first twelve years of marriage, as she followed her husband from one garrison town to another, she had three miscarriages. The experience was not uncommon in those days of primitive gynaecology, but Elisa could not accept it without protest. She had the foetuses preserved in alcohol and kept the jars in a cupboard; and these lugubrious mementoes accompanied her for over thirty years.[7] As time passed, she despaired of bearing a living child. After her third mis-carriage, in 1842, she persuaded the Captain to adopt her niece, Elisa Moncomble, whose father (another alcoholic) had died leav-ing his family in difficulties. The little girl grew up with Verlaine and played an important role in his life.

5 *Confessions, CML,* II, 1096.
6 Delahaye, *Verlaine,* 324-25.
7 Le Febvre de Vivy, *Les Verlaine,* 67. Delahaye detected something unbalanced in her. He says that the Dehée family was *émotive,* and that Elisa was "curieuse jusqu'à la nervosité, jusqu'aux témérités folles," *Verlaine,* 5-6. P. Bougard, how-ever, in "La Famille maternelle de Verlaine d'après les archives du Pas-de-Calais" (*Revue des Sciences humaines,* avril-juin 1952) found nothing very un-usual about the Dehées. By 1947 the family was extinct in the region.

It is clear from all this that Paul's birth on March 30, 1844, while the Captain was stationed at Metz, was the answer to a prolonged frustration. He became his parents' main concern as they moved from garrison to garrison. His father trembled whenever he fell sick. Measles was a crisis; a cold looked like bronchitis; when cholera appeared in Metz (where the household returned in 1849) Nicolas Auguste rushed his wife and baby out to the country. As for Elisa, her love verged on the neurotic. From the moment of her son's birth she surrounded him with an exaggerated care which continued until long after he had reached maturity. "Honnête femme ... mais si aveuglée par sa tendresse maternelle qu'elle en perdit tout sens moral," writes his wife Mathilde, who was the astounded witness of the relations between the pair when the child had become a man of twenty-seven. "A table, elle servait son fils le premier et lui donnait les meilleurs morceaux, prétendant qu'il avait besoin d'être fortifié. Elle l'avait habitué à coucher avec des bonnets de coton comme un vieux ou un malade d'hôpital ... Elle lui mettait du coton dans les oreilles pour éviter les maux de dents ... elle l'emmitouflait de cache-nez très laids. Quand il sortait, elle lui recommandait de faire attention aux voitures, de ne pas passer près des maisons en construction, ni dans les rues trop désertes. En somme, elle le traitait comme un enfant de six ans, et le rendait ... pusillanime, égoïste et ridicule."[8]

The sketch has all the lucid venom of a daughter-in-law whose marriage has ended in divorce. But it is not overdrawn; it corresponds too well with other things we know about Paul Verlaine and his mother. The rearing she gave him is the worst preparation for life – not because it produces a tough egotist, forever demanding more than his due. On the contrary. Over-indulgence is just as likely to create a divided personality, troubled by a sense of unworthiness and an obscure desire for atonement. The boy's whole nature is warped, and as he matures his sexual instincts take on a subtle depravity. Dominated by the mother-image, he turns love

8 Mathilde Verlaine, *Mémoires de ma vie* (henceforth Mathilde, *Mémoires*), 122, 148-49. These details are confirmed by Edmond Lepelletier, *Paul Verlaine, sa vie, son œuvre*, 48.

into a search for protection; becomes diffident, unassertive, maso-chistic, swallowing insult and putting up with treatment the aver-age man would never tolerate. A normal sexual relationship is seldom his goal; he wants defenders to shelter him or long-suffering martyrs to carry his burdens. And when people turn him down (few men and women enjoy pandering to a moral invalid) he bears suffering with voluptuous resignation: suffering is a way of expiating his guilt-feelings. He may even court it, as Verlaine courted Rimbaud's sadism or the sluttish abuse of Eugénie Krantz. And at the same time, with another side of his mind, he is resent-ful. He endures to a point and then, when he cannot have what he wants, he drops the situation and runs away. The two things com-plement each other: intolerance of restraint and search for a van-ished Eden. In each of Verlaine's adventures (Mathilde, Rimbaud, Létinois, Philomène, and Eugénie) he was trying to find a substi-tute for his mother. Each failed him and finally he was left with nothing but her memory. "Elle vit dans mon âme," he wrote when she had been nearly ten years in her grave, "et je lui jure ici que son fils vit avec elle, pleure dans son sein, souffre pour elle et n'est jamais un instant, fût-ce dans ses pires erreurs ... sans se sentir sous sa protection, reproches et encouragements, toujours!"[9] He never matured emotionally: until the end of his life he suffered from the vulnerable sensitivity of a child. It was the immediate source of all his misfortunes, and a direct result of Elisa's remorse-less tenderness.

His father may have suspected what was happening, which ex-plains why he sent Paul to school as a boarder instead of as a day-boy. With more clairvoyance than Elisa possessed, he saw that his son was becoming morbidly sensitive in the hot-house atmos-phere of home and needed toughening. He refused to be impressed by the first night's escapade: the child was taken back to school next day and continued as a boarder the following year at the Lycée Bonaparte (now Condorcet) where he remained until he graduated at eighteen in 1862. "Mon fils ne sera quelqu'un qu'à Paris," the Captain used to say in family circles,[10] which sug-

9 *Confessions, CML*, II, 1119.   10 Le Febvre de Vivy, *Les Verlaine*, 51.

gests that he gave up his commission partly at least for Paul's sake and had no intention of being thwarted. For much the same reason he had been watching expenses and was a moderately rich man. Thanks to his wife's dowry and his own savings, he had about 400,000 francs by the time he left Metz. It is difficult to estimate this sum in modern terms, but if we put it at $400,000 we shall not be far wrong.[11] During the next ten or fifteen years it was somewhat reduced by unwise speculation. In 1851 the Second Empire was just beginning; Napoleon III's *coup d'état* took place on December 2, shortly after the Verlaine family reached Paris, and it was an era of frantic stock-jobbing. The Captain, like a good many men of strictly regular life, had an itch for gambling, provided it was disguised behind the Corinthian façade of a stock exchange. Just how much money he lost is uncertain, perhaps about half his original fortune,[12] but enough remained to allow Paul to grow up as what the French call *un fils de famille*, the son of parents in easy circumstances who would leave him a good income. And this was a further source of weakness. The Captain wanted to spare his son the penny-pinching he had known himself. The only result was that Paul never learned to handle money. Until the day he died it slid through his careless fingers like water.

He never ran away from school again, but his career as a student was hardly brilliant. The grades indicate a slow loss of interest: at the end of his first year at the lycée he ranked sixth out of seventy-one students, and just a year before graduating he was fiftieth in a class of fifty-nine. As he says in a letter written in August 1862, he had to "travailler comme un nègre" to get his bachelor's degree

---

11 The franc was worth 20¢ in contemporary American money. What was the purchasing power of 20¢ in the United States of 1850?

12 Lepelletier, *Paul Verlaine, sa vie, son œuvre* 46-47. The ruin of the original fortune can be traced with some certainty. The Captain had to sell stock in Algerian railroads at a 50 per cent loss, and Mathilde (122) says that between 1872 and 1886, Verlaine squandered 250,000 francs. (The figure is perhaps a bit too high, but we have no way of correcting it.) Since Elisa was then reduced to indigence, she must have inherited between two and three hundred thousand from her husband, which means that his unlucky stock-jobbing cost him about two hundred thousand. It is ironic that, during a period of fourteen years in each case, the son's extravagance was hardly more ruinous than his prudent father's investments.

that autumn.[13] Such details, however, are unimportant; mere surface phenomena. The real Verlaine was being formed obscurely, in the physical and moral tensions of adolescence. As is often the case, school was less important for the learning he acquired than for the friends he made.

Three stand out: Charles de Sivry, Lucien Viotti, and Edmond Lepelletier. Through Charles he met his future wife. Viotti deserves a chapter to himself, if we had the material to write it. His role in Verlaine's life was obscure but crucial: I shall return to him shortly. Lepelletier became that indispensable comrade who often appears by the side of a genius. Their friendship lasted until the poet's death. For over thirty years, Edmond noted down anecdotes, kept letters, helped Verlaine find publishers, and did his best to obtain favourable reviews, some of which he wrote himself. His *Paul Verlaine, sa vie, son œuvre* (1907) is the first and most important biography of the poet. Without it a mass of valuable information would be lost. But it is not complete. Lepelletier was far from knowing the whole truth about Verlaine. He was so well balanced and normal that he never understood his friend's basic problems: the disordered sexual tendencies and the need for religious faith. As far as possible he ignored the former: like every man who writes somebody's life within a few years of the funeral he had no wish to shock the survivors. And as for religion, he was a tranquil agnostic, intelligent enough to appreciate the splendid verse of *Sagesse* and one of the few men of his time who did, but quite unable to understand the faith which inspired it.

Christian mysticism played such an important role in Verlaine's poetry that even his earliest contacts with the Church deserve attention. He could probably never remember a time when religion – its ceremonies and its priests – had not been part of his life. The abbés he met when he visited his relatives were more than mere acquaintances: they were members of the family, men to whom he could turn for advice and consolation. A priest appeared at every crisis of his life – from the curés of his childhood to the vicar in the Latin Quarter who administered extreme unction.

13 Verlaine, Pléiade, XVII.

And although his parents were not devout, their religious attitude was "correct": they raised him as a practising Catholic. He was eleven when he took his first communion: "Ma première communion fut 'bonne'. Je ressentis alors, pour la première fois, cette chose presque physique que tous les pratiquants de l'Eucharistie éprouvent, de la Présence absolument réelle ... Dieu est là, dans notre chair et dans notre sang."[14] We need not attach too much importance to this statement: he wrote it at fifty, after the tremendous experience of conversion: in retrospect his first communion naturally assumed a significance out of all proportion to anything the boy of eleven may have felt. At school he dropped religious practices altogether: his first communion was also his last – for over twenty years.[15] The atmosphere among the lycée students was irreverent and anti-clerical, and Paul began imitating his friends before he had been among them six months. But he never forgot his first contact with God. It corresponded too intimately with his thirst for security and enduring love. For some years he made a parade of free thinking, read materialistic philosophy, and trifled with Parnassian neo-paganism; but he was never a genuine pagan, much less an atheist, and his return to the faith was inevitable in the long run.

The religious eclipse of adolescence (if eclipse there was) grew from the disorders of puberty: and here a number of factors, acting on his latent internal conflicts, were significant. One of them – upon which Lepelletier dwells at some length – was his strange physical ugliness. By the time he reached his teens, the chubby baby of his early photographs had turned into a gangling adolescent, flat-nosed and hollow-eyed, with an overslung jaw and bushy eyebrows. "Mon Dieu!" exclaimed Mme Lepelletier, when her son brought Verlaine to the house for the first time, "Ton ami m'a fait l'effet d'un orang-outang échappé du Jardin des

14 *Confessions, CML,* II, 1130.
15 Le Febve de Vivy (*Les Verlaine,* 48), however, suggests that during his holidays with the Grandjeans he fulfilled all his religious duties. Against this must be placed Verlaine's own statements, that at the time he met Mathilde "il ne croyait plus en Dieu depuis belle lurette" (*Confessions, CML,* II, 1167), and that his conversion in 1874 brought him back to a religion he had "oubliée depuis sa première communion." *Les Hommes d'aujourd'hui, CML,* II, 593.

Plantes!"[16] He was quite conscious of the impression he made, and adopted the defence-mechanism of ridicule: he often made fun of his appearance in conversation and drew ape-like sketches of himself in the margins of his letters, a habit which remained with him for many years. Ugliness increased his natural timidity: it was another problem for which his sheltered childhood had ill prepared him, and it deepened and sharpened the crisis of his teens. Sexual conquest is one of the first battles in which an adolescent measures his strength, and Verlaine was immediately at a disadvantage: women found him repulsive. He never had a mistress, not even when Lepelletier introduced him to the salons of the Marquise de Ricard and Nina de Callias, where a number of easygoing beauties were usually to be found. The situation was certainly unfortunate. Lepelletier paints a heart-rending picture of the young man returning home solitary and depressed after an unsuccessful courtship, and forced to look for prostitutes because he could get nothing else. But had Verlaine's case really been so tragic, it is strange that the themes of jealousy and sexual frustration are almost non-existent in his work[17]; the subject never fascinated him as it fascinated Racine and Proust or even Leopardi and Alfred de Vigny.

Judging from certain passages in the *Confessions*, his difficulty was of a very different order. Are we to see it as another result of Elisa's maternal coddling, and to define Verlaine in Freudian terms as an example of the Œdipus complex? The boy's affection for his mother was so intense that, as he matured, it made normal love appear incestuous, and he sought sexual partners as unlike her as possible. At first glance, the hackneyed formula does nicely: aside from Verlaine's brief passion for Mathilde Mauté (and even that had a very muddy side) he was less attracted by love than by vice, and by vice reduced to its lowest common denominator. As early as his seventeenth year, he began to visit brothels. His first experience of the kind was banal enough, but it made a profound im-

16 Lepelletier, *Paul Verlaine*, 88.
17 As far as I am aware, they occur only once, in "Gaspard Hauser chante" (*Sagesse*). Most of Verlaine's love poetry describes triumphant satisfaction, whether in *Chansons pour Elle, Chair, Femmes,* or *Hombres.*

pression on him, as we see from the description he wrote thirty
years later. The red and gold parlour, the obscene engravings, the
heavy beauties in pink underwear: it is very "period"; we might
be looking at a lithograph by Toulouse-Lautrec. Nor was this
sensuality mere adolescent lust, easily satisfied and soon forgotten.
It was cerebral: an intellectual as well as an emotional stimulant,
to be meditated over and explored through hours of heated dream-
ing. "Les femmes de la catégorie à laquelle pouvait juste prétendre
... mon très modeste porte-monnaie, m'enivraient ... Je les avais
dans le sang, ma peau cherchait la leur ... Je m'imagine qu'une
reine, qu'une impératrice – ou tout bonnement une femme mariée
... *honnête* ... se serait offerte à moi, je l'eusse priée de me laisser
tranquille." – "Je continuai mes expériences avec une fréquence
qui ne fit qu'accroître mes curiosités ... non encore satisfaites à
mon âge de cinquante ans passés."[18] He did not frequent whores
because they were the only women he could get, but because they
were the women he preferred; their very degradation excited him.

This was not the only sexual anomaly. Another element, even
more characteristic of the Œdipus pattern (if we must follow it)
had appeared a few years before, and coincided with his literary
awakening. "Ce fut aux environs de l'époque où se remuait en
moi la manie des vers et de la prose ... que commença de grouiller
dans mon ... coeur l'amativité dont j'ai parlé plus haut et ... il
m'arriva dès lors d'éprouver à l'endroit de plusieurs camarades
plus jeunes que moi et successifs ou collectifs ... la jolie passion-
nette de l'Esplanade à Metz. Seulement ... la puberté venant, ce
fut moins pur ... Toutefois il n'est que juste de dire ... que mes
'chutes' se bornèrent à des enfantillages sensuels ... à des jeunes
garçonneries partagées au lieu de rester ... solitaires."[19] Were anybody else but Verlaine in question, we could dismiss this confession without further comment. Such habits are common to
most adolescents, and with maturity they disappear. But in Verlaine's case they never disappeared. He was still writing about
them at the end of his life, and in greater detail. Already, in the

18 *Confessions, CML*, II, 1150-51, 1169.
19 *Ibid.*, 1142-43.

tormented adolescent of the Lycée Bonaparte we discover the first symptoms of the bisexual tendency which afflicted Verlaine as a man. It grew more and more precise as his teens passed. There was his friendship for Lucien Viotti; there was the "ardent friendship" he struck up at eighteen with a cousin by marriage, Dujardin, whom he met during his holidays in the country near Lécluze. "Il m'en fit part, dans ses lettres, septembre-octobre 1862, avec enthousiasme ... Il s'exprimait sur le compte de son jeune cousin comme un amant vantant sa maîtresse," Lepelletier says.[20] None of these letters has survived, and even if they had they would probably not give us any definite information. Lepelletier, at least, saw nothing suspect about them. But considering the later Verlaine – the companion of Rimbaud, the author of *Hombres* – these adolescent passions are somewhat dubious, and one thing appears almost certain: sex, more and more, presented itself to him in two forms and neither satisfied him entirely. But he craved both and indulged both, and this sort of semi-appeasement is the worst kind of frustration, leading as it does to an unending repetition of the same actions in a vain hope of finding release. The result is a perpetual state of tension from which, even then, he had begun to seek escape in alcohol: "la manie, la fureur de boire." He was eighteen when he acquired the dipsomania which was to blight the rest of his life.

"D'abord, j'ai bu beaucoup quand j'allais chez mon oncle, à Fampoux ... La première fois que j'ai bu, je pouvais en effet avoir dans les dix-sept, dix-huit ans."[21] From the beginning there was a sinister element in these excesses, a playing of tricks with his own personality: he used to dress like a peasant when he visited roadside taverns, and sit for hours, his bourgeois status shed with the clothes that represented it, tossing off glass after glass of *bistouille*, a potent mixture of coffee and brandy.[22] He was no longer a *fils de famille* but a drunken tramp. Alcohol has always been a symbol of anarchy, a denial of normal life and its obligations; it

---

20 Lepelletier, *Paul Verlaine*, 30.
21 *Confessions*, CML, II, 1155.
22 Lepelletier, *Paul Verlaine*, 66.

enabled Verlaine to indulge a side of his character which convention normally forced him to hide. "Ah! si je bois, c'est pour me soûler, non pour boire," he wrote many years later:

> Etre soûl, vous ne savez pas quelle victoire
> C'est qu'on remporte sur la vie, et quel don c'est!
> On oublie, on revoit, on ignore et l'on sait ...[23]

It was a never-failing triumph over reality, abolishing the present and reviving the past; a means of regaining the carefree, irresponsible world he had known as a child. The vagabondage of his last years, the deliberate herding with prostitutes and vagrants, answered a profound need, a perennial nostalgia. His wife attributed such habits to innate vulgarity: "Verlaine aimait les choses laides et vulgaires; il lui plaisait d'avoir l'air pauvre, d'être mal habillé, mal logé, de se donner des airs peuple et paysan."[24] But the truth of the matter went deeper. And at this point the Freudian interpretation no longer seems infallible. It explains the facts up to a point and after that we are left wondering. There is no easy key to a life like Verlaine's. He was one of those Baudelaire defined, "qui ont ardemment cherché à découvrir les lois de leur être, ont aspiré à l'infini, et dont les sentiments refoulés ont dû chercher un affreux soulagement dans le vin de la débauche."[25] It is the nature of criticism to try for a solution, but we have to admit that in cases of this sort the essential truth eludes us whatever theory we adopt. *Why* the "ardente recherche," the "aspirations à l'infini"? Why does any man choose drink and prostitutes and homosexuality instead of sobriety and marriage and a successful career? And how, by what obscure forces of his being does he transform the results of his choice into imperishable verse? The fact is that Verlaine did so, and there the enigma rests.

His incipient alcoholism accompanied him back to Paris, where he discovered something much more powerful than the country beverages: absinth, "l'atroce sorcière verte" – "source de folie et

23 Verlaine, Pléiade, 395-96. "Amoureuse du diable" in *Jadis et Naguère*.
24 Mathilde, *Mémoires*, 121.
25 Charles Baudelaire, "Edgar Allan Poe, sa vie et ses ouvrages" (in E. A. Poe, *Œuvres en prose traduites par Charles Baudelaire*, Pléiade 1965), 1029.

de crime, d'idioties et de honte," as he wrote in a moment of contrition.[26] His mother sat up for him with cups of herb tea, accused his comrades of leading him astray, and concealed his escapades as best she could; but Captain Verlaine took alarm. As an old army hand he knew something about drink. Lepelletier was a constant visitor at the house and often heard him express the determination to "caser Paul."[27] The boy had graduated, was a bachelier-ès-lettres, and as such eligible for law school. With a law diploma he could hope for employment in one of the ministries. He was accordingly entered at the Ecole de Droit in the autumn of 1862. The experiment was disastrous: by the following June, having spent more time in the Latin-Quarter bistros than the lecture room, he had failed his examinations and was back on his family's hands.

Echoes of this fiasco reached his relatives in the country. One of his father's sisters, Louise, had married a Grandjean and settled at Paliseul in Belgium. She had no children and took a motherly interest in her nephew. His conduct had long worried her, and during the summer of 1863 (which Paul spent at her house) she asked the Abbé Delogne, one of the priests in the family circle, to have a talk with him. Delogne wrote her an account of the interview the following September. The letter is an important revelation of Verlaine's emotional state at this moment: "J'ai longuement conversé avec lui. Sa nature est restée bonne, je crois. J'ai d'autant plus de raisons d'en juger ainsi qu'il m'a avoué certaines faiblesses et qu'il m'a confié sa peur de Paris. La grande ville convient peu à sa pauvre volonté. Servirait-il d'en parler à son père? Vous connaissez sa réponse. Il nous l'a faite à tous deux déjà: son fils ne sera quelqu'un qu'a Paris. Je n'hésiterai pas cependant à le revoir à ce sujet. En attendant, prions."[28]

Whether the Abbé saw Captain Verlaine or not is uncertain. Mme Grandjean's move was part of a pious little conspiracy to get Paul to settle in the country; she brought it up again some years

---

26 *Confessions, CML*, II, 1163.
27 Lepelletier, *Paul Verlaine*, 94.
28 Le Febve de Vivy, *Les Verlaine*, 51.

later. For the time being, he remained in Paris and his father needed no prodding from anyone to make him see that something had to be done. He had been proud when his son graduated, and the law school failure must have been a severe blow, all the more so since Paul now had no occupation of any sort, and spent the winter of 1863-64 in idleness. He had become that unwieldy object which is a source of anxiety to all parents: an above-average son who seems unable to earn a living. Six months of desperate search followed. The Captain pulled all strings, used what influence he possessed. At last an old army friend found the young man a clerkship in an insurance office (L'Aigle et le Soleil réunis), and then, in March 1864, a civil service appointment at the Hôtel de Ville, the Paris city hall. His duties consisted of sending out pension cheques to retired priests. The initial salary was 1800 francs a year; five years later, thanks to automatic increases, he was earning 3000.

It was an obscure job, and the Captain was rather disappointed: he had hoped for greater things. But at least he had the satisfaction of thinking that Paul was settled, and that after thirty or forty years of service he could retire with a pension. Fortunately for the old soldier's peace of mind, the future was hidden. Such an attempt to turn Verlaine into a bureaucrat was bound to fail: it is doubtful if any sort of regular work could have held him long. He was twenty in 1864, and his character was already fixed: sensuous, imaginative, incapable of self-control, intolerant of anything that contradicted the child's world of illusion and self-indulgent reverie in which he dwelt. It was a bad type of personality under any circumstances, and doubly so in Verlaine's case because the difficulties awaiting him were more complicated than any the average man has to solve: contradictory sexual urges, a hereditary taste for alcohol. Clearly, his tenure at the Hôtel de Ville was bound to be of short duration. In only one sense had the Captain been right, though in a different way than he supposed. Paris was indeed necessary to his son's career; the capital alone could give Verlaine the intense stimulation his poetry required. For centuries the metropolis has been a hearth where men smelt experience into art and literature: the great furnace burns them up, but without it they would be so many mute, inglorious Miltons. Even as he confessed to the Abbé Delogne his terror of the city, it had become one of his main sources of inspiration. He had "Nocturne parisien" in his pocket:

> Roule, roule ton flot indolent, morne Seine. –
> Sous tes ponts qu'environne une vapeur malsaine
> Bien des corps ont passé, morts, horribles, pourris
> Dont les âmes avaient pour meurtrier Paris ...

It was the first in date of *Poèmes saturniens*, though not the first poetry Verlaine had composed. He had been writing for some years; the awakening of his poetic genius, like his interest in sex and alcohol, was part of the crisis of his adolescence.

2 / The young poet/
Poèmes saturniens/Fêtes galantes

ON THIS POINT THE *Confessions* are definite. "Le poète naquit en
moi vers précisément cette quatorzième année si critique, de sorte
que je puis dire qu'à mesure que se développait ma puberté, mon
esprit, aussi, se formait."[1] And by an odd chance it was just then
that he met up with the great poet who immediately precedes him
in literary history, and to whose work his own is more or less a
continuation, Baudelaire. "Mes premières lectures ou pour parler
plus nettement, ma première, toute première lecture fut ... *les
Fleurs du Mal,* 1re édition, qu'on pion avait laissé traîner sur sa
chaire et que je *confisquai* sans scrupule."

The fact is curious. *Les Fleurs du mal* appeared on June 25, 1857,
and was withdrawn from circulation by court order on July 11.
Whoever the *pion* was, he must have had a keen interest in contemporary verse to procure so quickly a copy of a book which
had scarcely been on sale a fortnight; and it was a strange accident
that this volume should have lain in wait for the Verlaine of
thirteen or fourteen, at the precise moment when it was bound to
exercise a decisive influence upon him. He says, it is true, that a
good deal of Baudelaire's powerful verse was over his head: "Il va
sans dire que je n'avais aucune idée de cette poésie si éloignée de
mon âge ... et j'avais dévoré le bouquin sans y comprendre rien
sinon que ça parlait de 'perversités' ... et de ... nudités parfois,
double attrait pour ma jeune 'corruption'," and that for a long

1 *Confessions, CML,* II, 1139-40.

time he did not even understand the title, which he thought must be *Fleurs de mai*. But "a long time" for a child of fourteen is never more than a few years, and of the dozen or so poems he wrote at this period (1858-62) the most interesting – "La Mort," "Aspirations," "Fadaises," "Un Soir d'Octobre," "Nocturne parisien" – already show the influence of Baudelaire. One of them, a fragment of three lines, is an imitation of "Les Petites vieilles": like "Nocturne parisien," it shows how certain Baudelairean themes had opened new perspectives to his anxious mind.

Baudelaire has been many things to many men, and to Verlaine he was an immediate revelation; a moral, spiritual, and aesthetic guide for the rest of his life. In 1895, a year before he died, he told an interviewer that he owed the awakening of poetic feeling, and whatever was deepest in his work, to Baudelaire.[2] Their destinies had certain points in common. The older poet, though in a much more terrible way, had also lost a childhood paradise, represented by his mother; exile and remorse are two of his main themes, heightened by religious memories and a demanding sensuality. He too lived in eternal contradiction with himself, solicited by good and evil, alternately fascinated and repulsed by reality. And beneath this exhausting combat lay the perpetual seduction of death, the final solution and also the ultimate novelty: the death of beauty, of love, of civilization itself, as revealed in the swarming, evanescent solidity of the great city. By a miracle of assimilation, he transformed these destructive antitheses into verse whose alluring power is very nearly unparalleled in French poetry – or in any poetry. The impact of such a genius on a mind like Verlaine's is not hard to imagine. A child who has grown up too attached to his elders, as Paul was to Elisa, acquires a precocious experience of sorrow. He soon learns that they must leave him long before he dies himself, and the idea of death preoccupies him in a way the average child seldom knows. In the very first of Verlaine's poems, "La Mort" (December 1858), this theme appears. The lines are a remarkable achievement for a boy of fourteen, and

2 Published in *L'Eclair*, 11 janvier 1896, quoted by Bornecque, *Etudes verlainiennes*, 36.

even more remarkable is the fact that in the last of all his verse, "Mort!" (December 1895), he treated the same subject after thirty-seven years. Between the two poems stretches a thematic cord on which all his volumes are strung like beads. It added to his terror of reality and goes a long way to explaining his escapism, his emotional stasis, his craving for sanctuary – whether in art, sex, or religion. All three, in some way or other, promise refuge from death. He treated the idea in the verse he wrote between fourteen and eighteen as he handled it in later life. Sometimes it is deliberately indulged, with a sort of masochism: "Fadaises," a bitter-sweet serenade to an unnamed beauty who turns into "Madame la Mort" in the last line, or "Un Soir d'octobre," where dissolution is mirrored in the death of the year itself. Sometimes he avoids it in flight – "Aspiration," whose Baudelairean echoes "anywhere out of the world" are too numerous to mention. When he first read Baudelaire he found the death-wish stated with a seductive beauty which overwhelmed him. The fact is of interest to literary history; it demonstrates how Baudelaire's genius had begun to work on a key member of the younger generation within a short time of the publication of *Les Fleurs du mal*.

Baudelaire, of course, was not the only influence. Like most adolescents with literary ambitions, Verlaine was an avid reader. Lepelletier enumerates some of the authors they went through together; it is an impressive list – Shakespeare, Calderon, Lope de Vega, Goethe, Dickens, Thackeray, and Stendhal, not to mention the great Romantics from Rousseau and Chateaubriand onward, and the French classics like Racine, Corneille, and Molière, who, together with selections from the Greeks and Latins, were part of the school programme.[3] The resulting picture is rather confused, and ought perhaps to be entitled "readings" rather than "influences"; a man who was "influenced" by so much variety would have very little originality left. Verlaine was seeking his way, and was much more inclined to look for guides to contemporary writers like Baudelaire than to the great names of the past.

The literary current, in those mid-years of the century, was

3 *Confessions, CML*, II, 1140 *sqq.* give a general picture of these readings.

hesitating and changing its course. Romanticism was over. Its great poets – Lamartine, Musset, Vigny – had produced their best work and fallen silent; Hugo, indeed, still dominated the period as he was to dominate it until his death in 1885. His *Contemplations* appeared in 1856 (one year before *Les Fleurs du mal*) and both Verlaine and Lepelletier considered it "la Bible même de la poésie."[4] Hugo was now in Promethean exile at Jersey, in opposition to the Second Empire and not to return to France until 1870; it was *de rigueur* for all young writers to send him their works. Verlaine himself was no exception to the rule; he mailed Hugo (not Baudelaire, who did not die until 1867) the manuscript of "La Mort" in 1858, and followed it with copies of *Poèmes saturniens, Fêtes galantes*, and *La Bonne Chanson* as they appeared. But Hugo, for all his glory, was no longer a writer to be imitated and a source of poetic theory. A new generation of poets had appeared, attracted by other ideas and techniques.

Thanks to his friends, Verlaine was soon in touch with these circles. The literary world of Paris has always been small, and he had a good deal of time on his hands. His duties at the city hall were not exacting and did not take up more than four hours of the day. He reached the office at ten, lunched from noon until two at the Café du Gaz in the rue de Rivoli (where other employees with an interest in literature took their meals), and went home at four. He accepted the job with curious passivity; his father had put him there. Throughout, he was indifferent – "absent" says Lepelletier who, as a hard-working man with a future to make, could not understand his friend's total lack of ambition. Verlaine never even bothered to take the routine examinations which would have given him the right to a higher salary. More and more he was living in the conflicts and seductions of his imagination, in his friendship for Lucien Viotti (they were collaborating on a farce, *Vaucochard et fils Ier*), in his conversations with young writers. There were a number of them at the Hôtel de Ville in those days – Georges Lafenestre, Armand Renaud, Léon Valade, Albert Mérat. Their names mean nothing now, but in the late sixties it would

4 Lepelletier, *Paul Verlaine*, 76.

have been hard to say that Verlaine, with his ape's face and his hesitant speech, was the great man. They all knew the world of letters, read the latest books; they were enthusiastic and full of theories and ideas. "Là ... on entendait s'élever de bruyantes et contradictoires discussions sur la rime riche, sur l'*e* muet, sur la consonne d'appui, sur la césure libre, sur le rejet et le vers blanc, et autres questions prosodiques," Lepelletier says of the lunch-hours in the Café du Gaz. "On donnait des comptes rendus de ce qui s'était passé aux Samedis de Leconte de Lisle ... On évoquait l'étrangeté des premiers vers ... de Stéphane Mallarmé, dont Verlaine admirait la forme obscure et recherchée, et on lisait passion-nément les revues, les journaux, où les questions de littérature et de poésie étaient accueillies."[5]

Nor was the Café du Gaz Verlaine's only contact with the liter-ary world. Early in 1863, a year before he started work at the city hall, he began attending the receptions of the Marquise de Ricard. She was another indulgent mother, the wife of one of Napoleon's old generals; her son Louis Xavier had founded *La Revue du pro-grès moral*, suppressed by the police in 1864 for its anti-clerical ten-dencies. The discussions in the Ricard salon were brilliant and varied. Bright young men appeared there: Catulle Mendès, Fran-çois Coppée, Anatole France, Sully Prudhomme, Villiers de l'Isle-Adam, José Maria de Heredia, the musician Emmanuel Chabrier. As Lepelletier says, it was the cradle of the Parnassian school, and it would be difficult to over-estimate the importance of meetings of this kind to a budding writer. The obscure youths who frequent them are the masters of the future, and their work is one day uni-versally read. On the testing ground of such evenings they can advance their ideas and recite unpublished manuscripts. Such an atmosphere was of special value to a shy and diffident nature like Verlaine's; even more important, Ricard gave him an opportunity of getting into print, always a crucial problem for a young author. His first published verse, the sonnet "Monsieur Prudhomme," ap-peared in the *Revue* in August 1863.

5 *Ibid.*, 97.

It was at this moment too that he met the publisher Alphonse Lemerre, who had just opened an office in the Passage Choiseul and was willing to take a chance on unknown writers provided they paid expenses. Ricard's periodical had been suppressed, but he still had money enough for a second venture, a weekly entitled *L'Art* which Lemerre brought out. In November and December 1865 it printed articles by Verlaine on Barbey d'Aurevilly and Baudelaire, and in December two more of the *Poèmes saturniens*, "Dans les Bois" and "Nevermore." As the title of the last suggests, he had been reading Poe, doubtless in Baudelaire's translation. He was no longer an anonymous civil-servant: *L'Art* might not be widely read, its circulation was even microscopic, but it had made Verlaine an author. Finally, in March 1866 it changed its title to *Le Parnasse contemporain*, and a new school of French poetry had been born.

It is known to literary history as Parnassianism – from the title of the periodical; and since Verlaine began his poetic career under its banner, we need a definition. In 1866, "Parnassianism" meant nothing more than the poets who published in the new magazine, and on that basis Baudelaire and Mallarmé as well as Verlaine, Heredia, and Leconte de Lisle were Parnassians. This definition is obviously so broad as to be meaningless. The origins of the movement go further back than 1866. *Le Parnasse contemporain* gave a name to something which already existed. Parnassianism was a reaction against certain aspects of the Romantic school, more especially the lyric frenzy and exaggerated inspirational state which the great Romantics thought necessary for poetic composition. Hugo comes to mind, with his interest in automatic writing and his sybilline trances at the work-table, or Alfred de Musset, sitting down in a moment of ecstasy, with a bottle of brandy and all the candles in the house, to pour out a flood of lyric anguish in a single night. The poet was also a prophet; unless he spoke in sacred madness, his words were sterile. And as a prophet, he pointed the way to the future – sang, with Hugo, the glories of democracy, or, like Auguste Barbier, deplored the conditions of the working class. Excess of this kind inevitably provoked a revulsion, and we can trace its beginnings over thirty years before the appearance of *Le Parnasse contemporain*.

Théophile Gautier – to take the outstanding example – began writing as a member of Hugo's circle, and his first books (*Albertus*, *La Comédie de la Mort*) are purely Romantic. But as early as 1834, in his novel *Mademoiselle de Maupin*, he turned to what he thought to be the Greek ideal: an exaltation of beauty as revealed in external form. It was one of the first expressions of "Art for Art's sake" in French poetry, although the idea had been in the air for some time, an idea well suited to Parnassianism. He elaborated it later on, especially in the little ode "L'Art" (included in *Emaux et Camées*, 1852), which we always quote when we want a definition:

> Tout passe. L'Art robuste
> Seul a l'éternité.
> Le buste
> Survit à la cité.[6]

The same characteristics distinguish Théodore de Banville's work, as his titles suggest: *Les Caryatides* (1839-42), *Les Stalactites* (1846), *Odelettes* (1846-72), *Améthystes* (1860-61): "L'Art," in fact, was written in reply to a similar poem in *Odelettes*, composed on the same rhythm:

> Quand sa chasse est finie
> Le poète oiseleur
> Manie
> L'outil du ciseleur.
>
> Car il faut qu'il meurtrisse,
> Pour y graver son pur
> Caprice
> Un métal au cœur pur.

6 As usual with such theories, the origin of the art for art's sake idea is hard to trace. On February 11, 1804, Benjamin Constant noted in his diary: "Dîner avec Robinson, écolier de Schelling. Son travail sur l'esthétique de Kant. Idées ingénieuses. L'art pour l'art, et sans but; tout but dénature l'art. Mais l'art atteint au but qu'il n'a pas." (*Œuvres*, Pléiade, texte présenté et annoté par Alfred Roulin, 226.) This diary was not published (and then only partially) until 1887. In 1818 Victor Cousin, in a lecture on art at the Sorbonne, declared: "Il

This is the earlier side of Parnassianism: graceful, charming, not too serious, a side we sometimes forget nowadays because of the later contributions of Leconte de Lisle. In the massive verse of *Poèmes antiques* and *Poèmes barbares* (1852, 1862) he deepened and widened the light fancies of Gautier and Banville. An impeccable technique, a rather ponderous neo-paganism (which included Hindu and Scandinavian divinities as well as Greek), and much brilliant description, the whole expressed as impersonally as possible: these are the hallmarks of his poetry, and only one or two of the young men who gathered in the offices of *Le Parnasse contemporain* were really able to carry them on, notably José-Maria de Heredia. He wrote a number of sonnets which, collected in 1893 as *Les Trophées* and dedicated to the master, form the most characteristic Parnassian work of the century.

From all this a definition of sorts emerges. Parnassianism is a poetry of careful form, neo-pagan in harking back to the marble serenity of ancient Greece (as ancient Greece was then understood), and correspondingly anti-Gothic, anti-medieval, anti-Christian: epithets which show to what an extent it is also anti-Romantic; a poetry interested in plastic rather than musical effects, and therefore seeking inspiration in painting and sculpture. It is an objective art; it looks for higher significance in life than the revelations of private sorrow. The Parnassian writer is impersonal: he seeks aesthetic effects and effaces himself behind them.[7]

In the long run, these ideas were of little importance to Verlaine. Years later he admitted a technical debt to Banville and Leconte de Lisle, and sometimes referred to himself as "an old Parnassian," by which he meant that his first verse had appeared

faut de la religion pour la religion, de la morale pour la morale, comme de l'art pour l'art ... Le beau ne peut être la voie ni de l'utile, ni du bien, ni du saint; il ne conduit qu'à lui-même." The passage was printed in his *Cours de philosophie* in 1836. Gautier dwelt on the idea in his prefaces to *Albertus* (1832) and *Maupin* (1835).

7 Bornecque, *Etudes verlainiennes*, 34. Verlaine had small talent for "impassibility," but the idea haunted him for many years. In the prefaces to *Parallèlement* (1889 and 1894, *CML*, II, 31-2) he stated that he hoped to write "impersonal" works henceforth, and in his interview with Harry Graf Kessler on July 26, 1895, he said that "er wolle jetzt in seinen Werken 'impassible' werden, wie Leconte de Lisle" (Kessler, "Besuch bei Verlaine").

in *Le Parnasse contemporain*. But his whole nature was at variance with the school's basic theories. To see just what he thought poetry to be while he was nominally a Parnassian and composing *Poèmes saturniens*, we need merely turn to his article on Baudelaire, published in *L'Art* in December 1865. It is the best prose he ever wrote, and besides showing how little of a Parnassian he really was, it proves that, during the crucial years from fourteen to twenty-one, he was constantly under Baudelaire's influence. After his boyhood contact with *Les Fleurs du mal* he read all his predecessor's work – not merely the verse, but the artistic and literary criticisms as well.

Baudelaire's thought ran parallel to Parnassian theory in several ways. He admired Théophile Gautier and dedicated *Les Fleurs du mal* to him as to a "maître et ami." Without too much trouble we can even find some "impersonality" in his work, poems such as "Rêve parisien" and "La Beauté." And in his articles on Poe and his *Salon de 1859*, he rejected the Romantic theory of inspiration and declared that poetry was neither didactic nor moral and had no other end than itself. Verlaine quotes all these passages and draws from them a declaration of faith and principles: "Oui, l'Art est indépendant de la Morale, comme de la Politique, comme de la Philosophie, comme de la Science, et le Poète ne doit pas plus de compte au Moraliste, au Tribun, au Philosophe ou au Savant, que ceux-ci ne lui en doivent. Oui, le but de la Poësie, c'est le Beau, le Beau seul, le Beau pur, sans alliage d'Utile, de Vrai ou de Juste ... Une autre guitare qu'il serait temps aussi de reléguer parmi les vieilles lunes ... c'est l'Inspiration, – l'Inspiration – ce tréteau! – et les Inspirés – ces charlatans! ... Apollon, c'est la volonté qui traduit, exprime, et rayonne! Rien de plus."[8]

This is orthodox Parnassianism, or, with a little juggling, can be made so; Verlaine was trying to adapt Baudelaire to the new school. But since in a number of other ways Baudelaire was hostile to everything the Parnassians admired (at least the Parnassians like Leconte de Lisle and Heredia), fitting him into their pattern was no easy task.

He was particularly interested, for example, in certain musical

8 *Charles Baudelaire, CML,* I, 60-61.

techniques: not the facile use of vowel sounds and alliteration, but
the repetition of thematic elements which, carried out with great
suggestive power, produce an incantatory effect. I am not anxious
to overstress this aspect of his work; he was always an intellectual,
and in everything he wrote one senses a keen intelligence, sifting
and analysing the impressions supplied by reality. But he was also
fascinated by the realm of pure sensation, which led him to experiment with alcohol, opium, and hashish; in certain poems (the
famous sonnet "Correspondances," with its parallels between colour, sound, and perfume; and "Le Balcon" and "Harmonie du
Soir," where the theory is applied), he dissolved the evidence of
the mind into a dream state, a kind of narcosis. Verlaine calls this
transposition of normal experience "unequalled": poems like "Le
Balcon," he says, bring back "un vers toujours le même autour
d'une idée toujours nouvelle et réciproquement," thus painting
an *obsession*. In selecting such pieces for special praise, he was devi-
ating from Parnassian doctrine: "Le Balcon" and "Harmonie du
Soir" have nothing in common with the plastic effects and impersonal descriptions dear to Leconte de Lisle and Heredia; it was
no accident that Leconte de Lisle hated music and never attended
a concert, and that he thought Baudelaire's poetry unimaginative,
short-winded, and awkward.[9]

Even less Parnassian was the modernism of *Les Fleurs du mal* –
what Baudelaire called "the heroism of modern life." The phrase
occurs in his *Salon de 1845*, a review of the year's painting; it was
aimed at the artists who obstinately chose ancient or medieval subjects for their canvases. In retrospect, the last half of the nineteenth century appears as the age of the great Impressionists, and
we think at once of Manet, Monet, Renoir, Cézanne, the sun-
drenched groups on the banks of the Seine or the dancers at the
Closerie des Lilas. But this was not the official art of the time. The
official art specialized in "Joan of Arc at the Siege of Orleans,"
"Nero in the Golden House," "Cleopatra Poisoning Slaves," etc.
A good deal of Leconte de Lisle and nearly all Heredia is verse
treatment of subjects like these. Hence the bric-a-brac effect of so

9 Quoted by Bornecque, *Etude verlainiennes*, 68–69.

much Parnassian verse, as though one were visiting the flea-market at Clignancourt. Baudelaire's poetry is a resolute effort to break with this convention. He especially had small patience with the neo-paganism of Gautier and his friends, even dared turn it to ridicule in an article (*L'Ecole païenne*, 1852). The ancient legends were beautiful; he could see that and sometimes used them himself. But they were only fairy tales, with no more reality than Puss in Boots, and were singularly ill adapted to express the mighty tensions of nineteenth-century man. This effort to come to grips with his age, to invest it with tragic grandeur, has made Charles Baudelaire one of the greatest poets of his time; it was the thing about him which impressed Verlaine most. Modernism inevitably meant the modern city; since the Renaissance, western civilization has been urban. The huge accumulations of men and stone fasci-nated both Baudelaire and Verlaine; he had followed the master's lead through the streets and byways of Paris, less utilized until then by poets than by novelists: "Et pourtant quel thème poéti-que, quel monde de comparaisons, d'images et de correspondan-ces! Quelle source intarissable de descriptions et de rêveries! C'est ce qu'a compris Baudelaire, génie parisien s'il en fut ..." Verlaine's greatest talent lay in depicting modern man in these metropolitan surroundings: "La profonde originalité de Charles Baudelaire, c'est ... de représenter puissamment et essentiellement l'homme moderne ... l'homme physique moderne, tel que l'ont fait les raf-finements d'une civilisation excessive, l'homme moderne, avec ses sens aiguisés et vibrants, son esprit douloureusement subtil, son cerveau saturé de tabac, son sang brûlé d'alcool ... Cette indivi-dualité de sensitive ... Charles Baudelaire ... la représente à l'état de type, de *héros* ..."[10]

In all these passages, Verlaine was outside Parnassianism. He was defining his own poetic art, and in doing so he came within mea-surable distance of the two schools of poetry at the end of the cen-tury – Symbolism and Decadence, with which his name is linked; they both claimed him as a precursor.

Poèmes saturniens, his first volume, grew out of these fruitful years

10 *CML*, I, 57, 54.

of discussion and experimentation. Issued by Alphonse Lemerre in mid-November 1866, it is a complex affair, as might be expected from the varied influences which went into its making. "Du Leconte de Lisle à ma manière, agrémenté de Baudelaire de ma façon," he called it later.[11] At the end of his life, precocity was part of his legend, and he used to maintain that he wrote the poems while he was still at the Lycée Bonaparte: "J'avais seize ans ... et j'avais déjà fait ... tous les *Poèmes saturniens* tels qu'ils parurent, en 1866."[12] This can hardly be so. The earliest poem appears to be "Nocturne parisien," which Lepelletier says Paul handed him in a book during class, in the winter of 1861-62;[13] the other pieces were written during the next four or five years, the greatest number probably dating from 1863 to 1866, when eleven out of a total of forty appeared in *La Revue du progrès*, *L'Art*, or *Le Parnasse contemporain*. The "Parnassian" items were almost certainly composed after 1864 – after Verlaine made contact with Leconte de Lisle and his circle. In discussing such a book, the first production of a great poet, we have to distinguish between the poems of the young man (Verlaine was only twenty-two in 1866), imitative like all young men, docile to the teachings of his masters, and the durable, personal note, the "Verlaine" note, which only he could have struck.

Everything considered, the Parnassian items are surprisingly few, seven poems out of forty; they can be dropped without damaging the collection; indeed it is rather improved by their omission. "L'Heure du berger" and "Un Dahlia" are pieces of "impersonal" description. "Çavitri" is a Hindu legend in Leconte de Lisle's style; "César Borgia" and "La Mort de Philippe II" are Romantic themes parnassianized: the Romantics were always interested in Philip and the Borgias because they provided high colour, stylized horror, a facile anti-clericalism, and references to priestly debauchery and the rigours of the Inquisition. Verlaine's Philip owes as much to Hugo's "Rose de l'Infante" as to any poem by Leconte de Lisle. As for the "Prologue" and the "Epilogue," they are expositions

11 *Confessions, CML*, II, 1166-67.
12 *Ibid.*, 1143.
13 Lepelletier, *Paul Verlaine*, 77-78.

of Parnassian doctrine: quite in line with some of the ideas set forth in the article on Baudelaire. The poet should express beauty, a reflection of the ideal world; and to this end he must remain master of himself, distrusting inspiration and all the disorders to which it leads:

> Ce qu'il nous faut, à nous, c'est, aux lueurs des lampes,
> La science conquise et le sommeil dompté ...
> C'est l'Obstination et c'est la Volonté!
>
> C'est la Volonté sainte, absolue, éternelle ...
> C'est l'effort inouï, le combat nonpareil,
> C'est la nuit, l'âpre nuit du travail d'où se lève
> Lentement, lentement, l'Œuvre, ainsi qu'un soleil! ...
>
> L'Art n'est pas d'éparpiller son âme:
> Est-elle en marbre, ou non, la Vénus de Milo?

The echoes of Gautier and Leconte de Lisle are so clear that it has been suggested that Verlaine was writing a good-humoured parody of Parnassian theory.[14] This, I think, is giving him credit for a degree of aesthetic independence he did not possess. He was an obscure young man in 1866, and he looked up to Leconte de Lisle as to a master. Parnassianism could not hold him long, but he took it very seriously for a while. The "Prologue" and "Epilogue" open and close *Poèmes saturniens* and give it the tone of a manifesto. As he said in one of his Belgian lectures in 1895, he was *impassible*, "mot à la mode en ces temps-là," and he thought his "Epilogue" was "la crème de l'esthétique."[15] Into the bargain, there is nearly as much Baudelaire as Leconte de Lisle in the two poems. Verlaine was trying to combine the contradictory ideas of his masters, and the fact that he stressed, if only for a short time, the Parnassian elements in Baudelaire is perhaps the strongest proof he ever gave of adhesion to the school.

Parnassianism, in any case, is much the least interesting side of *Poèmes saturniens*. "L'homme qui était sous le tout jeune homme un peu pédant que j'étais alors, jetait parfois ou plutôt soulevait le

---

14 In Jacques Borel's opinion. Verlaine, Pléiade, 49.
15 *Conférence sur les poètes contemporains, CML*, II, 930.

masque et s'exprimait en plusieurs petits poèmes, tendrement," he says in the same lecture. The volume is divided into a number of sections, *Melancholia, Eaux fortes, Paysages tristes, Caprices*; it now appears that the mask fell most completely in *Melancholia*. It contains eight poems (seven of them sonnets) which are among the loveliest in the book, and most of which are addressed to an unnamed woman. According to the latest theory (advanced by M. Jacques Bornecque),[16] she was Verlaine's cousin, Elisa Moncomble, for whom these pieces reveal a hidden passion.

What are the facts? Elisa was eight years Paul's senior and was adopted by the Captain and his wife two years before Paul was born. It might have been expected that the little girl would be jealous of the new baby, who became at once the centre of the family's life, but not at all; she idolized him as much as his parents did. "Elle fut la particulière douceur de mon enfance dont elle partagea et protégea longtemps les jeux," he writes in the *Confessions*. "C'était une petite mère sous la grande, une autorité non plus douce, non plus chère, mais comme de plus près encore." [17] She fitted perfectly into the childhood paradise, being as much a part of it as the good-natured father, the indulgent mother, and the hours of play on the Esplanade. And in 1866, since Lemerre expected his authors to bear the expenses of publication, she found the money for *Poèmes saturniens*. Verlaine evoked her phantom often in later years, notably in *Amour*, when he called her "presque une sœur aînée"–"d'abord guide, puis camarade, puis ami."[18] In 1861 she married Auguste Dujardin, a sugar-refiner at Lécluze, near Douai. Paul spent the summer of 1862 with them, and wrote Lepelletier several interesting descriptions of the countryside which resemble the landscapes of *Melancholia* and *Paysages tristes*, with their pools, poplars, and water-lilies. In 1865 he returned for a second visit, which seems to have been the decisive moment. The memories and impressions of three years before crystallized out into the sonnets of *Melancholia* (one is even entitled "Après trois

16 Bornecque, *Etudes Verlainiennes*, 87.
17 *Confessions*, CML, II, 1097.
18 The fourth poem of the Lucien Létinois cycle. Verlaine, Pléiade, 445.

ans"); they all evoke the summer of 1862, and the dominant note is one of wistful nostalgia. Something, it is clear, had changed during the interval. Was Elisa, if not less affectionate, more on her guard? Possibly. They may have loved each other, and Elisa, in every way a better-balanced character than Paul, with a sense of her responsibilities as a married woman, may very well have drawn back when she discovered the nature of his sentiments, and perhaps of her own. And again, we may be reading too much into the episode. It is just as likely that his affection for her was nothing more than an intenser form of the love he felt for his mother:

> Si que me voilà seul à présent, morne et seul,
> Morne et désespéré, plus glacé qu'un aïeul,
> Et tel qu'un orphelin pauvre sans sœur aînée.
>
> O la femme à l'amour câlin et réchauffant,
> Douce, pensive et brune, et jamais étonnée,
> Et qui parfois vous baise au front, comme un enfant![19]

The terms he uses, *sœur*, *enfant*, suggest that this was the case.

However this may be, a disconcerting fact emerges: the sonnets deal with the 1862 visit, and it was just then that Verlaine first met the Dujardin boy of whom, even as he stayed at Elisa's house, he was writing to Lepelletier "with the enthusiasm of a lover boasting about a mistress." In other words, his love for Elisa (supposing him to have loved her) and his love for Dujardin both flourished at the same time. What is the explanation? If we had an answer to that we could solve the problem of Verlaine and of a good many other men as well. Was this a precocious example of *parallèlement*, as he used the adverb in the title of his 1889 volume? Or was he, like so many weaklings, solicited in several ways at once and yielding to them all? The last two sonnets of *Melancholia* show him in the toils of a violent spiritual struggle, apparently of a sexual nature:

> A vous ces vers ...
> Ces vers du fond de ma détresse violente ...

19 *Poèmes saturniens*, "Voeu."

C'est qu'hélas! le hideux cauchemar qui me hante
N'a pas de trêve et va furieux, fou, jaloux ...
Oh! je souffre, je souffre affreusement ...

Lasse de vivre, ayant peur de mourir, pareille
Au brick perdu jouet du flux et du reflux,
Mon âme pour d'affreux naufrages appareille.[20]

There is a good deal of "literature" in the verse: Verlaine adapts from Baudelaire phrases and images which, written for the context of *Les Fleurs du mal*, give his adolescent crisis a more lurid colouring than it perhaps had in reality. Nevertheless, he was going through an intense emotional experience, and it is difficult to say just what it was. The "nightmare" may have arisen from the knowledge that Elisa was in the sexual possession of another man. We know that her conjugal life was active; she was frequently pregnant and finally died of a miscarriage. And on the other hand, since Verlaine was in close contact with her and with Dujardin at the same time, it is possible that we are dealing here with an early manifestation of the conflict between normal and abnormal which emerged again in 1869 – when his passion for Lucien Viotti clashed with his love for Mathilde – and yet again in 1871, when Rimbaud appeared on the scene.

This emotional turmoil, however we explain it, produced the best verse of *Poèmes saturniens*. "Mon Rêve familier," the sixth of the Elisa cycle, is one of the finest sonnets in French; Verlaine produced more of the same but none better. The "Verlaine" note is already there: the deliberate imprecision, the hesitant, musical stammer:

Je fais souvent ce rêve étrange et pénétrant
D'une femme inconnue, et que j'aime, et qui m'aime
Et qui n'est, chaque fois, ni tout à fait la même
Ni tout à fait une autre, et m'aime et me comprend.

The poem is a slow incantation, a result achieved partly by the fluidity of the verse (in certain key lines, 1, 7, 8, 9, and 14 the tra-

20 *Ibid.*, "A une femme" and "L'Angoisse." Compare with Baudelaire: "Je te donne ces vers" and "Les Sept Vieillards."

ditional caesura after the sixth syllable is slipped past with rather
the effect of water overflowing a barrier); partly by the lingering
repetition of detail – just as Chopin strikes again and again the
same chord in a prelude. A dream state is induced, infinitely prolonged by a final echo:

> Son nom? Je me souviens qu'il est doux et sonore
> Comme ceux des aimés que la Vie exila ...
> Et, pour sa voix, lointaine et calme, et grave, elle a
> L'inflexion des voix chères qui se sont tues.

The half-rhyme "exila" and "elle a" is an early example of Verlaine's interest in assonance; by its very attenuation, it reinforces
the effect of reverie.

This sonnet is the high point of the book, but some of the other
poems are of great interest, if only because of the hints they give
of the later Verlaine. Two pieces, "Nuit de Walpurgis classique"
and "Sérénade," point directly to *Fêtes galantes*, and show that he
had that volume in mind some years before it was composed.
There is the same ominous gaiety, the same keen, neurotic music,
lit up and subtly distorted by moonlight. In "Crépuscule du soir
mystique" and "Chanson d'automne," the Baudelairean lesson is
utilized to produce fragments of pure harmony; we are already
in the atmosphere of what thirty years later was known as Symbolism. Verlaine pointed this out in a preface he wrote for *Poèmes
saturniens* when the volume was republished in 1890: "Plus on me
lira, plus on se convaincra qu'une sorte d'unité relie mes choses
premières à celles de mon âge mûr: par exemple les *Paysages tristes*
ne sont-ils pas en quelque sorte l'œuf de toute une volée de vers
chanteurs, vagues ensemble et définis, dont je suis peut-être le premier en date oiselier?"[21]

Poèmes saturniens, on the whole, is the volume of a young man.
He was beginning his career and imitated his masters: Gautier,
Banville, Leconte de Lisle, and Baudelaire. But since he had genius even his imitations are beautiful, and when we have purged
the collection of all its borrowings, it still contains great poetry.

---

21 "Critique des *Poèmes saturniens*", *CML*, II, 301.

And once at least, in "Mon Rêve familier," he wrote verse which none of his predecessors could have written; verse entirely his own, uneasy, exquisite, nostalgic, and obsessive, the sort of verse we think of whenever we pronounce his name.

The book's originality escaped the notice of contemporaries. Hugo, Leconte de Lisle, and Banville replied to the copies Verlaine sent them with the good-humoured benevolence of established poets congratulating a young one on his first volume.[22] Sainte-Beuve (he was usually inept when it came to judging contemporary work) preferred "César Borgia" and "Philippe II" to the other poems, criticized the technical experiments and, noting the sombre tone of the volume, advised against taking "poor good Baudelaire" as a point of departure. The published reviews (there were seven, usually very brief) were nearly all harsh. Barbey d'Aurevilly ridiculed "Mon Rêve familier"; Anatole France said that the volume showed great promise, but then he was a friend and frequented Parnassian circles. Another contributor to *Le Parnasse*, Stéphane Mallarmé, thanking Verlaine for a copy, detected the novelty of the verse – "virgin metal" he called it. Apart from this, criticism was mute. Five hundred and five copies were printed; twenty years later they had not yet been sold.

Verlaine, however, was not discouraged. He knew the world of letters too well to have any illusions about producing a best-seller. His volume had achieved favourable if vague attention from those who counted, and as for the severe reviews, they touched him so little that he started work on a new book before *Poèmes saturniens* had been in circulation three weeks. On February 20, 1867, *La Gazette rimée*, another artistic little periodical, printed "Clair de lune" and "Mandoline," two of the best pieces of *Fêtes galantes*. Six more appeared in July 1868, and the volume was finished and published by February 1869, though not put on sale until July.

Between November 1866 and February 1869, then, we have the problem of its genesis. As always with Verlaine, there is the personal factor, the moral and psychic struggle from which his

22 Bornecque, *Etudes verlainiennes*, 49-61.

books grew, and the aesthetic question – the influence of his age, his friends, and all the complicated poetic and artistic forces which played on him and explain why he chose one subject instead of another. Untangling this confusion is not easy, the more so as *Fêtes galantes*, with its eighteenth-century setting, is more detached in tone – more Parnassian – than anything else he wrote.

Outwardly his life continued as before. He went every day to the city hall, lunched with friends at the Café du Gaz, and in the evenings visited the Marquise de Ricard or Nina de Callias. His acquaintance with Nina began early in 1868. Like Mme de Ricard, she was one of those admirable Frenchwomen whose sole (but immense) contribution to her age consisted of opening her house to young writers and artists. They could always count on a meal and (if necessary) a bed, and her doors never closed. The parties were more or less chaperoned by her mother; a grim lady in black, who sat all night without speaking or moving, a pet monkey on one shoulder, while the talk raged on around her. Nina's husband, Count Hector de Callias, was a pleasant alcoholic who seldom appeared, and she lived entirely for the contemporary Bohemia. We can guess what she meant to her friends by looking at the portrait Manet painted of her, "La Dame aux éventails," now in the Louvre. She stares quizzically from the canvas, intelligent, ugly, and charming, the sort of person who could read Verlaine's poetry with appreciation and give him self-confidence. Lepelletier says that he recited a good deal of verse at her house.[23] Years later, in 1875, when he was spattered with scandal and very nearly ostracized, his work refused by publishers, his friends cutting him in the street, she sent him a piece of excellent advice: "À la place de Verlaine, je reviendrais carrément à Paris, me passerais fort bien d'aller au Voltaire et de revoir les camaraux (peu drôles en somme) d'autrefois, et devant le succès (journal ou théâtre) on reviendrait bien si toutefois j'y tenais."[24] Compare this with the thick-headed prejudice of an Anatole France, who refused Verlaine's contribution to a new issue of *Le Parnasse contemporain* on the grounds that

23 Lepelletier, *Paul Verlaine*, chap. VI, *passim*.
24 Quoted by V. P. Underwood, *Verlaine et l'Angleterre*, 274.

the author was immoral and his verse bad. Mme Nina had the brains and the critical faculty; the others were fools.

On the surface, Verlaine in the sixties was a civil servant who had begun to make a name for himself in literature. He had written one promising book and was about to produce another. But what was going on beneath this banal exterior? We know very little (there is a gap in his letters), but what we do know is disquieting.

His drinking, which until now might have been dismissed as youthful ebullience, was becoming habitual and sottish. Only the strictest self-control could have kept it from degenerating into frank alcoholism, and not only was Verlaine will-less and unruly, but just at this moment he lost the one being who exercised some measure of command over him: his father died on December 30, 1865. Deprived of that steadying influence, the mechanism of his personality lacked an essential part. It could still function, but there was a subtle loss of equilibrium, as we see from certain events of the next few years. In February 1867, Elisa Dujardin died in childbirth. The catastrophe was so sudden that Verlaine only reached Lécluze in time for the funeral; and "Les deux jours qui suivirent, je ne mangeai pas, je bus."[25] His conduct was so obstreperous that it scandalized both the village and his relations. Mme Grandjean's suspicions that he was in a very bad way were confirmed: she decided that something must be done. When she herself died on March 22, 1869, she made the attempt, posthumously, as it were, for like Elisa she was dead by the time Verlaine arrived on the scene. But she had discussed matters with her confessor, and, together with Elisa Verlaine and Paul's aunt Rose Dehée, he got Verlaine to promise that he would leave Paris, settle in the country, and marry. An Amazonian cousin was proposed, one of his mother's nieces: it was hoped that her energetic character would bring the young poet round.

He agreed to everything; it was a weak man's way of shutting people up, but the results of this touching scene were not immediately apparent. Mme Grandjean's funeral was another excuse for a

25 *Confessions, CML,* II, 1161.

bender. We have a record of part at least of what he consumed during two days at Paliseul: a hundred glasses of brandy, one every thirty minutes. Once again there was a family scandal.[26] His sorrow for Elisa and his aunt was sincere enough, but he was in a tense neurotic state which made it impossible for him to bear any kind of suffering without the panacea of alcohol. And the results of his father's death are obvious; he would never have dared behave in such a way had the Captain been present. Meanwhile, he did not leave Paris, and the country project remained a project until 1880, when it was realized (but in every different circumstances) with Lucien Létinois at Juniville. At the time of Mme Grandjean's death, literature claimed all his attention. He had written a number of other poems besides *Fêtes galantes*; like his growing alcoholism, they provide strange clues to his mental and moral state at the time.

In December 1867, he published a little book of Lesbian sonnets, *Les Amies*, at Brussels.[27] Lesbianism was not a new subject by that time. Both Balzac and Gautier had treated it; Gautier's *Maupin* is almost a glorification of the anomaly. It had long provided painters like J. R. Auguste and Gustave Courbet with an excuse for luscious nudes; and there were Baudelaire's two "Femmes damnées" in *Les Fleurs du mal*, probably Verlaine's main source of inspiration. Other Parnassians were interested in the theme, notably Catulle Mendès, who later treated it in several very long and bad novels (*La Première Maîtresse*, 1887; *Méphistophéla*, 1890). Verlaine's sonnets have a lascivious charm. Like most works of the kind, they are voyeuristic: the spectacle of two sprigs of girlhood in amorous abandon is of high erotic potency. Although the result is pretty enough in an exhibitionist way, it cannot compare with Baudelaire's verse which, as in everything he wrote, invests the subject with an intense and tragic grandeur. *Les Amies* is provocative; Verlaine was young enough to want to be shocking, and perhaps too he found in Lesbianism a convenient mask for his

26 François Porché, *Verlaine tel qu'il fut*, 72.
27 It was printed by Baudelaire's old friend, Poulet-Malassis. Verlaine had a peculiar regard for these sonnets, republishing them in *Parallèlement* and in *Femmes*.

own bisexual tastes. On the whole, the book is chiefly interesting as an early example of his skill in handling erotic themes. In this respect he was to become one of the most remarkable poets on record: with *Les Amies, Parallèlement, Femmes,* and *Hombres,* he beat the writers of the Greek Anthology on their own ground.

The slim volume caused a storm. The Second Empire had always posed as a champion of morality. One of the charges against Baudelaire ten years before was based on "Femmes damnées," and *Les Amies* was duly seized at the frontier and condemned by a Lille court when copies were sent to Paris.

Even more revealing of the poet's mental and moral state are a number of other compositions, both in verse and in prose, dating from this period. Most of them were not printed until much later.[28] The literary merit is small, there being an abundance of ill-digested Romanticism – the poet is a "fatal" creature, born under an evil star, condemned by his age – some rather callow satire on the bourgeois society of the nineteenth century and a certain amount of immature musing on death and dissolution. The overall impression is that Verlaine was handling subjects too heavy for him. But throughout there are clear indications of a permanent moral crisis, particularly in "Un Monstre," an account of a nightmare which, this once at least, certainly lends itself to a Freudian interpretation.[29]

Seen against this sombre background, the nimble elegance of *Fêtes galantes* appears in a new light. The book creates a dream world as smooth and iridescent as a soap bubble, floating isolated in a dark sky. At first glance it looks like an example of Parnassian impersonality. But this is deceptive. The poet's neurotic state had grown too intense for such detachment. The poems are pure escapism; Romantic posturing and Parnassian theory are alike abandoned for an illusive state of attenuated shades and harmonies, quite divorced from reality; here Verlaine was in his own element and nobody could equal him.

---

28 "Poèmes contemporains des *Poèmes saturniens* et des *Fêtes galantes*," Verlaine, Pléiade, 125-31.
29 See Jean Richer's analysis of "Le Monstre" in his *Paul Verlaine*, 19.

By a singular paradox this book, containing some of his lightest and most exquisite verse, has inspired the heaviest commentaries. The setting alone (a *fête galante* was what the eighteenth century called a garden party) has given rise to a maniacal hunt for sources; so many have been found that a well-annotated edition produces the effect of a chained butterfly. Some, it is true, are beyond dispute: the volume has a pictorial side, inspired by eighteenth-century painting – particularly the canvases of Antoine Watteau, to whom there is a reference in the "Nuit de Walpurgis classique" of *Poèmes saturniens*. During a feverish career of some twenty years (he died in 1721), Watteau executed nearly eight hundred works, and his popularity continued unabated throughout the old régime. The neo-classic schools of the Revolution and the First Empire, however, were interested in Spartan, Greek, and Roman subjects; they despised the frivolous elegance of the fallen monarchy. For years Watteau's beautiful "Embarquement pour Cythère" hung in David's studio, where the master's pupils used it as a target for spit-balls. A reaction began in the 1840s. The reign of Louis xv was no longer old-fashioned, it had become historic, and studies appeared rehabilitating its art.[30] Presumably Verlaine read some of them or heard them discussed. By 1860 the expression *fête galante* was current to describe the peculiar atmosphere of eighteenth-century painting, and he would also have found a favourable comment on Watteau in Baudelaire's *Salon de 1846*, not to mention the well-known stanza in "Les Phares." Banville and Gautier were also attracted by eighteenth-century themes:

> Près de ce rocher blanc taillé comme un autel,
> Ainsi qu'un lévrier l'eau folâtre et se dresse.
> Pardieu! c'est la marquise, avec son air cruel,
> Qui se baigne là-bas en nymphe chasseresse.

> Il manque un Actéon, ce sera le mari:
> Il a tout ce qu'il faut, et pourrait en revendre.

30 Notably Arsène Houssaye, *Watteau et Lancret* (1841), *Galerie de portraits du* xviiie *siècle* (1845-8, where he calls Watteau "le peintre des fêtes galantes"), *Histoire de l'art français au XVIIIe siècle* (1860); Charles Blanc, *Les Peintres des Fêtes galantes, Watteau, Lancret, Pater, Boucher* (1854); E. and J. de Goncourt, *L'Art au dix-huitième siècle* (1860).

Abbé! votre musique est un charivari!
Vous soupirez, Eglé! Que vous a fait Silvandre?

The stanzas might come from *Fêtes galantes*: in fact, they are by Banville ("L'Arbre de Judée," *Les Stalactites*). Albert Glatigny, another poet Verlaine knew and admired, had utilized the same kind of material, especially the poem "Cythère" in *Les Vignes folles*.[31] Finally – and here we are on firmer ground – there was Victor Hugo's "Fête chez Thérèse" in *Les Contemplations* (1856). "Peut-être aussi devons-nous *les Fêtes galantes* à une impression très forte produite par 'la Fête chez Thérèse', pour laquelle Verlaine éprouvait une admiration telle que c'est la seule poésie d'un auteur connu que je lui entendis réciter par cœur."[32] Hugo describes a Louis-Quinze reception: it is easy to see what Verlaine borrowed from the poem.

In addition, the museums of Paris contained a large number of pictures, not only by Watteau, but by other pre-Revolutionary painters, both French and Italian: Nattier, Lancret, Pater, Van Loo, de Troy, Boucher, Tiepolo, La Tour, Guardi, and Canaletto. They all evoke the seductive elegance of their period, and could have supplied Verlaine with whatever local colour he needed. There were literary influences as well, a good number of which exist in *Fêtes galantes*. Poems like "Cortège" and "Les Coquillages" owe as much to the libertine writers of the eighteenth century as to any painter: "Lettre" reads like a mild version of one of Valmont's epistles to his Présidente in *Les Liaisons dangereuses*.

When we have piled up all this documentation, however, we have to admit that it proves very little. The more one reads *Fêtes galantes*, the more the eighteenth century tends to disappear. What eighteenth-century artist ever painted moonlight? Certainly not Watteau.[33] Yet in several of the most successful poems, "Clair de

---

31 Pierre Martino has a useful summing up of these sources in his *Verlaine*, chap. IV. See also *Confessions*, *CML*, II, 1152 *sqq.* for Verlaine's own remarks.
32 Lepelletier, *Paul Verlaine*, 162.
33 Anatole France pointed this out in 1867 (quoted by Bornecque, *Lumières sur les Fêtes galantes de Paul Verlaine*, 153). It used to be thought (on the strength of Lepelletier's testimony, 161-62) that *Fêtes galantes* owed something to the Lacaze collection of eighteenth-century painting in the Louvre. But this exhibition was not opened until after the book had been written.

lune," "Mandoline," and "Fantoches," moonlight is the main theme, Verlaine's theme, the essential magic which transforms reality into illusion: insubstantial reflections, flashes of muted colour, echoes. A comparison of some of these pieces with their immediate predecessor, the "Nuit de Walpurgis classique" of *Poèmes saturniens*, shows the progress he had made in handling effects of this sort. The "Nuit" is Romantic and somewhat hackneyed: in a setting of statues, fountains, and clipped yews (a garden by Le Nôtre – Versailles or Trianon) a horn summons ghosts to dance to the moonlight. There is nothing very original about the poem but the setting; witches' sabbaths usually took place on lonely heaths or in Gothic ruins. But in "Clair de lune" and "Mandoline," this heavy diabolism vanishes; only the lighting and the décor remain – Verlaine's contribution. Maskers and clowns, abbés and powdered fops replace the pallid spectres; the poems are nostalgic and internal. "Votre *âme* est un paysage choisi" we read in the first line. And the net result has nothing much to do with the robust sensuality of the eighteenth century. What would a contemporary of Louis xv have thought of *Fêtes galantes*? The world of the poems is Verlaine's own; he may have conceived it as he looked at a canvas by Watteau or Boucher, but his fantasy has little more resemblance to the eighteenth century of history than Leconte de Lisle's ponderous Hellenism has to the true Greece. This impression grows stronger every time the book is read and ends as a certainty. "Les Ingénus," for example, begins with an evocation of high heels and long petticoats: "Les hauts talons luttaient avec les longues jupes." But what of the conclusion?

> Le soir tombait, un soir équivoque d'automne;
> Les belles, se pendant rêveuses à nos bras,
> Diraient alors des mots si spécieux, tout bas
> Que notre âme depuis ce temps tremble et s'étonne.

Where, in the whole body of eighteenth-century literature, is there anything like the accent of these lines? And if we seek a parallel effect in the paintings of the time, and end by finding it, we are probably finding too much. The two last poems, "En

Sourdine" and "Colloque sentimental" are even more conclusively Verlaine and only Verlaine. In "Colloque" only one word is genuinely eighteenth century, the "parc" of the first line: "Dans le vieux parc solitaire et glacé …" The reader's mind is switched in a Louis-Quinze direction and the rest follows: the two figures, evoking a dead love in a winter landscape of bare trees, avenues, and icy fountains. But had Verlaine written something else, "bois" for example, the scene could take place anywhere – could be a memory, suitably transposed, of one of his promenades with Elisa Dujardin at Lécluze in 1865 when, if M. Bornecque's thesis is correct, he might well have asked her: "Te souvient-il de notre extase ancienne?" As for "En Sourdine," it is reality translated into pure sensation: trees, silence, deepening twilight, the sudden note of a bird. All this harks back to "Mon Rêve familier" and forward to "La Lune blanche" of *La Bonne Chanson* and to certain pieces in *Romances sans paroles* and *Sagesse*: verse so light, so purely musical, that all other poetry seems awkward by comparison.

Ever since its publication, *Fêtes galantes* has become increasingly popular, partly because composers like Debussy and Fauré later set some of the poems to music. Its full magic is apparent in their harmonies: the half-light, the nostalgia, the hidden depths beneath the glimmering surface. The content is a bit uneven at times; here and there a poem is less poetic than flippant, a neatly turned bit of bric-a-brac ("Pantomime," "Sur l'herbe," "Dans la grotte," "Les Indolents"), but on the whole *Fêtes galantes* marks a clear advance over most of *Poèmes saturniens*, even though it contains no single poem as fine as "Mon Rêve familier." It is less derivative, more original. Provided nothing intervened to prevent him, Verlaine was on his way to becoming a great poet. It was just at this moment, within three months of the publication of *Fêtes galantes*, that he took, if only temporarily, the wrong road. The mistake was to have a dramatic effect on the rest of his life.

3 / Mathilde Mauté /
La Bonne Chanson

LATE ONE AFTERNOON in June 1869, Verlaine dropped in for a drink with Charles de Sivry, who was living with his mother and her second husband, Théodore Mauté de Fleurville, at their house in the rue Nicolet near Montmartre. The two men were talking literature when a girl of sixteen came into the room. It was Charles's half-sister, Mathilde Mauté, and her entry was almost certainly deliberate; she knew Verlaine was there and wanted to meet him. We often provoke fate in just this way. She had read *Poèmes saturniens* and *Fêtes galantes*, which so impressed her that she learned some of them by heart. She nourished literary ambitions of her own and had even written some verse (all of it very bad). The effect of the introduction was immediate. To Verlaine, with years of coarse debauchery behind him, she appeared like virginity itself – untouched and unsullied; and the impression he made on Mathilde was no less deep. "J'avais remarqué un changement complet dans sa physionomie pendant qu'il me parlait ... son regard, habituellement luisant et noir, était devenu câlin et doux en me regardant, sa bouche, souriante; il paraissait à la fois ému et heureux. En ce moment, il cessa d'être laid."[1] By the time the interview was over they were both half in love.

  She was certainly the worst possible wife for Verlaine. We know a good deal about her, thanks to the *Mémoires* she wrote at the end of her life. Her book has no literary merit, but its value as

---

1 Mathilde, *Mémoires*, 89.

a document is very great. Reading it, one regrets that a host of other dishevelled women, victims of poets, have not left us their reminiscences; the resulting collection would not lack piquancy. Mathilde, of course, is not always veracious. She had an axe to grind which was, briefly, that Rimbaud's evil genius broke up an ideally happy marriage. But apart from this, and one or two other discrepancies, her account of her life with Verlaine has a ring of truth about it which cannot be denied.

Perhaps nobody would have questioned her story at all if she had not been such a snob. This was her most unpleasant characteristic; it sheds a false glamour over the first part of her memoirs and irritates the reader into quibbling about much of the rest, even when she is obviously telling the truth. The "de Fleurville" in her name was purely ornamental, added by her father or grandfather for reasons of prestige. Théodore Mauté was a notary. Lepelletier first revealed this awful truth in his biography of Verlaine; it was one of the things that led Mathilde to write her own book. She reacts to the statement as though it were an insult. Her father, she insists, was independently wealthy, a sort of landed aristocrat, who never had to work for a living and spent his time in a round of hunting, travel, and high society. Everything else about her family is similarly bedizened. Mme Mauté, widow of a first marriage with the Marquis de Sivry, was a good musician. But this is not enough; Mathilde must have her a former pupil of Chopin and an intimate friend of the Wagners, in whose box she attended the Paris première of *Tannhäuser*. As for the De Sivrys, they descended from Jean, Duc de Brienne, Emperor of Constantinople... In keeping with so much distinction, she herself was raised "in the society of the Faubourg Saint-Germain." For fifteen years she spent every winter with her parents on the country estates of noble friends. It is an account of dinners, balls, and hunting-parties, liberally sprinkled with aristocratic names, some of them the best in France.

Obviously the woman is not telling a pack of lies; she had some sort of entrée to these circles. Her account is so detailed that François Porché, taking Lepelletier's hint, suggests that Mauté, as a notary, was a kind of estate manager and legal adviser to members of the gentry – something between a friend and a servant.[2] This is probably the truth. Not to mention that Mme Mauté's talents as a pianist were an asset in the days before stereo and television; at a house-party she could always be counted on to amuse the company. Whatever the truth of the matter, Mathilde's connection with the aristocratic world came to an abrupt end when she married Verlaine, which is surprising if her relations with the great were as intimate as she pretends. She was perhaps aware of this discrepancy, and hints more than once that out of pure love she made a misalliance and sacrificed her social position. In 1907, when she sat down to write, her ex-husband was world-famous, and she probably felt a very human desire to enhance her own importance. She even tells us that she refused a number of good offers in his favour: one was a viscount, another had 50,000 a year. "J'avais déjà donné mon cœur."[3]

A more preposterous marriage never was planned. Both the principals misread each other. Mathilde saw herself marrying a literary man with a future, and marriage, as such, was of no interest to Verlaine. He was not seeking a wife, the worthy helpmate of a successful author, but a new toy, a plaything, a virgin, something he had never had before. Thirty years afterward he still recalled the episode with a sort of lubricious relish: "Je ne pensais guère qu'à mon but, me préparer une facile et délicate pourtant nuit de noces, aussi peu pénible pour les deux intéressés, par le fait!"[4] And there was another element as well. The truculent cynicism of the *Confessions*, the accent of a man with a bad case who does his best to minimize his faults by laughing them off, while true as far as it goes, is not the whole truth about the Verlaine of June 1869. He does not mention the climactic state in which he was living when he met Mathilde.

He had been working at the Hôtel de Ville for nearly five years, and although he took his duties lightly enough, he must have

2 In his introduction to Mathilde's book, 18–19.
3 *Ibid.*, 113.
4 Confessions, *CML*, II, 1195.

found them tiresome. Even more serious, his bisexual tendency had become increasingly acute. By the summer of 1869, his friendship for Lucien Viotti had reached a point of open passion. We have no proof that Lucien returned it, but the possibility that he did so is very strong, for reasons I shall mention. Like most men suffering from this anomaly (the type is commoner than usually supposed), Verlaine was never able to make a satisfactory adjustment – or at least not until his last years when, having broken with regular society and his proclivities notorious, he produced the verse of *Hombres*. We know that he wrote that strange collection during one of his sojourns at the Hôpital Broussais in 1891, but the moment of its conception is still in dispute.[5] Whatever its date, it throws a sinister glow over this whole aspect of his life. If we attribute it to his late twenties, we see that he was an experienced homosexual when he married, and if we date it from his last years, we are obliged to admit that he had an extraordinary knowledge of sexual inversion, a knowledge so complete that it could only have been acquired by long experience. And in either case, when a man is acknowledged as the greatest living French poet, and one of the greatest religious poets (thanks to *Sagesse*), he does not write such lines unless he judges the matter of great personal importance. One argument in favour of a later date is the tone of the volume; the homosexual tendency is accepted frankly and without misgivings, and in 1869 Verlaine was not yet ready for this. His passion for Viotti inspired him with a sort of terror.

He reacted to the difficulty, as to all difficulties, by flight – into the paradise of absinth. His excessive drinking during 1866 and 1867, reaching peak force whenever he had an excuse (as at the funerals of his aunt and cousin) was a sure sign; and night after night, during the winter of 1868-69, even before he met Mathilde, he came home so drunk that he could not undress and slept in his boots, once even in his hat. His mother, always adoring, said nothing, and Captain Verlaine was no longer on hand with a stern rebuke. But Paul's friends learned to dread his drunken rages; on one occasion he chased Lepelletier among the trees of the Bois de

5 Written in 1891 but not published until 1904.

Boulogne with a sword cane. The scene is not unlike the later episode with Rimbaud in Brussels, even down to the intervention of the police (the two men had some difficulty evading a constable). Had the friend been anybody else but Lepelletier, who treated the whole thing as a joke, matters might have ended very badly.[6] There was something like desperation in the Verlaine of 1869.

In such a situation, marriage, with all its social and legal security, seemed a veritable life-raft. Verlaine felt that it would cure him of his ambiguity. He did not understand (and this too is characteristic of the bisexual) that once his craving for a woman was satiated, the other thing would come back with redoubled force. He decided to sacrifice Lucien to Mathilde. Lucien's immediate reaction is unknown, but a year later, at the beginning of the war of 1870, he enlisted and disappeared in a skirmish under the walls of Paris, either killed or wounded; his exact fate remains obscure.[7] All this would give us little to build on were it not for the sequel. After the war, Lepelletier told Verlaine's mother (and later repeated in his biography of Paul) that Lucien had been in love with Mathilde. The old lady passed the information on to her daughter-in-law adding, "Lepelletier m'a raconté que Viotti était amoureux de vous, et ne s'est engagé que par chagrin de vous voir épouser mon fils." Mathilde was astonished. She had known Viotti ever since her girlhood; he was another of Charles de Sivry's school chums and often came to the Mauté house. "Nos relations amicales durèrent des années," she says, "et rien ne put jamais me faire supposer qu'il eût pour moi un autre sentiment que cette simple amitié que je ressentais pour lui." However, she accepted the story. Her knowledge of Viotti appears to have been very limited. She was not aware of his collaboration with Verlaine on *Vaucochard*; as she understood the relations between the pair, Verlaine had offered to help Lucien prepare the civil service examinations with a view to a job at the Hôtel de Ville. But their interviews usually ended in a bistro where the poet overdrank himself, and Viotti, who disliked alcohol, grew tired of the pretended les-

6 Lepelletier, *Paul Verlaine*, 184.
7 *Ibid.*, 337, 415, 450-51.

sons and left abruptly for Le Havre without giving Verlaine his address. Paul was offended, wrote De Sivry that the young man was *sans cœur* and *homme en bois*, and from that moment (the summer of 1869 when the marriage was under discussion) Lucien's visits to the Mautés ceased.[8]

Everything in this tale indicates a stifled passion, of a quite different kind than Mathilde ingenuously believed. Verlaine told Lucien of his matrimonial intentions by letter; it was a safe way of avoiding an unpleasant interview. Shortly afterwards Lucien wrote a carefully worded note to Charles de Sivry, asking for information: "Comment ta famille a-t-elle pris la proposition – enfin le consentement est-il donné – Je lui ai répondu sans faire aucune allusion à tout cela mais ... je serai curieux d'en connaître le résultat ..."[9] De Sivry doubtless answered that Verlaine's suit had been favourably received; Lucien's abrupt disappearance and subsequent enlistment and death require no other explanation. Lepelletier seems to have believed the story of the young man's love for Mathilde. He repeats it in his life of Verlaine: "Ce ne fut que beaucoup plus tard que nous apprîmes qu'un amour secret et douloureux, pour celle qui allait devenir la femme de son ami, avait surtout motivé son enrôlement." But he must have got it from Verlaine himself; it smacks of Verlaine's invention, reads like the plots he later used in such short stories as "Pierre Duchatelet." They are quite as hackneyed and sentimental. And the very fact he thought it necessary to make up such a yarn indicates that there was something to hide. Lucien's dislike of Verlaine's drinking habits is pure Mathilde. By the time she wrote her memoirs she was quite ready (and with some justification) to paint her ex-husband as an incorrigible drunk. Twelve years after his friend's death, Verlaine evoked their long bistro conversations in a tone of poignant regret: "A cette même table de café, où nous avons causé si souvent face à face, après douze ans ... je viens m'asseoir et j'évoque ta chère présence ... Tes yeux me luisent vaguement

8 Mathilde, *Mémoires*, 150-52.
9 Quoted in Verlaine, Pléiade, 1070. A complete photostat of the letter appears in *CML*, II.

comme jadis, ta voix m'arrive grave et voilée comme la voix d'autrefois. Et tout ton être élégant et fin de vingt ans, ta tête charmante (celle de Marceau plus beau), les exquises proportions de
ton corps d'éphèbe sous le costume de gentleman, m'apparaît à
travers mes larmes lentes à couler ... Hélas! ... ô moi imbécile de
n'avoir pas compris à temps! ... Tu t'engageas ... tu mourus atroce-
ment, glorieux enfant, à cause de moi qui ne valais pas une goutte
de ton sang ..."[10] It is a confession of remorse, for something more
than mere friendship.

Mathilde had won the day, although she was unaware that a
battle had been fought. But it was inevitable that this smothered
affection should return to life once Verlaine's love for her began
to wane. And the whole episode is of great importance in explaining the sudden violence of his sentiment for Rimbaud. There was
more than mere inverted sexuality in his feelings for the young
poet from Charleville; there was rancour, and something like revenge.

Immediately after the meeting in De Sivry's rooms, Mathilde
left for a summer in the country. Forty years afterward she could
still remember one of her dancing partners, "M. Léon de Janzé, un
excellent valseur."[11] Verlaine remained at Paris, in a state approaching frenzy. Mathilde had become a symbol (he says) of that
"mystérieuse candeur ... qui est à la fausse, à la coupable sécurité
du libertinage ... la sécurité même." – "Ma souffrance ... était ... le
besoin ... de 'changer de vie'." But the past still held him: "Ce
m'eût été ... un gros crève-cœur que de rompre avec ce délice, que
de ne plus connaître la saveur des lèvres, des seins, de toute la chair,
l'énervement, l'excitement ... des inoubliables caresses de tant de
femmes, pour ne parler que de ce délice-là!"[12] The last phrase

---

10 Lepelletier, *Paul Verlaine*, 451. Verlaine, *Mémoires d'un veuf*, CML, I, 701, where
   the title is "À la mémoire de mon ami ***." When first published (*Lutèce*, 1-8
   février 1885), the title read "À la mémoire de mon ami Lucien Viotti." Lepelletier discusses Verlaine's affection for Lucien several times, notably on pages 30
   and 415, where he groups it with Verlaine's other "sentiments homo-sexuels":
   Dujardin, Rimbaud and Létinois, sentiments, he insists, which were of a "caractère purement cérébral, platonique." But see *infra*, chap. IV, note 12.

11 Mathilde, *Mémoires*, 99.

12 *Confessions*, CML, II, 1168-69.

suggests that he was fighting his sexual dualism; it was one of those terrible moral struggles all the worse since it has to be fought alone. The victim dares not confide in anyone.

Was it at this moment (in June or July 1869) that he underwent a brief but intense religious crisis? Four years later, lunching with Rimbaud and Delahaye, he told them how, "quelques années auparavant," he had felt a sudden desire for faith: "Un jour, Verlaine se trouve devant une église, entre soudain, va vite, cherche, et voit des femmes à genoux, le blanc surplis d'un prêtre qui disparaît dans l'étroite loge d'un confessionnal. Notre impulsif s'y jette, s'y prosterne. Le pénitent quitte l'église indiciblement heureux, un peu inquiet. Cela tiendra-t-il? Cela tient."[13] The episode is certainly authentic. It reveals Verlaine's thirst for security and reassurance, the main sources of his subsequent conversion. But when did it occur? Just after he met Mathilde? Or at some other time altogether – when Mme Grandjean died, or at the moment of his conversation with the Abbé Delogne? We have no way of knowing; it would fit into any one of those contexts. Personally, I am inclined to place it after his interview with Mathilde, when, in his own words, he felt an urgent need to change his life. Whatever its date, it did not resolve his difficulties, particularly during the summer of 1869. His drinking remained as bad as ever, even grew worse, and some appalling incidents occurred.

A full account of them exists in letters written by Victoire Bertrand, Mme Verlaine's maid. After Paul's shocking conduct at his aunt's funeral in March, there had been a kind of family council. It included Hector Pérot, the mayor of Paliseul, an old friend and relative. Victoire had been Mme Grandjean's servant; since she was now jobless, Mme Verlaine took her on. The family had long since despaired of learning the truth about Paul from his mother, and it was agreed that Victoire should write M. Pérot accounts of what she saw in the Verlaine household. Her letters must have caused a sensation when they reached Paliseul. The first is dated from Paris, July 18, 1869, about a month after Verlaine first met Mathilde. "Je viens vous dire sa triste et exécrable conduite. Au

13 Delahaye, *Verlaine*, 75, and Louis Morice, *Verlaine le drame religieux*, 113.

bout de trois ou quatre jours que j'étais arrivée un jour il rentre à cinq heures du matin ... ensuite j'ai entendu du tapage dans sa chambre; au même instant Mme Verlaine arrive et me crie: Vite, levez-vous il veut me tuer! Je suis accourue de suite et j'ai aperçu ce misérable tenant à sa main un poignard, un sabre et un grand couteau, disant qu'il voulait tuer sa mère et lui après. Je ne voulais pas croire mes yeux. Il était dans un état effroyable, sa mère me disait: 'Il est malade, et il se trouve parfois très agité.' Mais il était agité par la boisson ... Il y a eu hier huit jours, tout à coup j'entends du bruit pendant la nuit. C'était lui qui rentrait; il était une heure ... Il a commencé un tapage, qu'il y a une pauvre femme qui a dû se relever, pensant que le plafond tombait ... Tout à coup on crie ... Je cours vite dans sa chambre et là, je le vois armé de son sabre. Il voulait se jeter sur sa mère ... Il voulait que sa mère lui donne deux cents francs ... Une fois il a renversé sa mère et il la tenait par la gorge en disant qu'il allait la tuer et lui après ... Il disait à sa mère: 'Tu ne sortiras pas vivante de cette maison.' ... Nous avons été depuis une heure jusqu'à huit à lutter avec ce malheureux. De ma vie je n'ai vu une personne plus redoutable à voir. J'aurais un fils pareil, je demanderai à Dieu de me le reprendre à l'instant ... Je crois que s'il continue, un jour ou l'autre, *il fera un crime.*"[14]

Next day Mme Verlaine took her son to Fampoux; she intended to stay there for a month or six weeks, but within four days she was back in Paris, and despite her denials, Victoire was convinced that there had been another scene. A sleepy country town like Fampoux was no cure for Verlaine's state; he had scarcely arrived there than he reached breaking-point. He tells us that he took a train to Arras, went from café to café drinking absinth, and ended the night in a brothel. The following day he awoke with a physical and moral hangover, and without hesitation or reflection he wrote De Sivry asking for Mathilde's hand. The answer arrived three days later; it was not a definite acceptance, but there was reason to hope. Transported with joy, Verlaine set to work on a poem for Mathilde, "Le soleil du matin doucement chauffe

14 Le Febve de Vivy, *Les Verlaine*, 64 *sqq*. The italics are Victoire's.

et dore"; it was to be the first of *La Bonne Chanson*, the record, he says, of a "purified heart."

So far the *Confessions*. The scene is pretty: a libertine reclaimed by "pure" love. Indeed it is much too pretty to be true: it includes no reference to the tail-end of this spiritual tornado, which reached peak force precisely during those three days of suspense. Waiting, uncertainty, and the self-discipline they require were intolerable to Verlaine: "Il y a un ami de M. Paul qui avait promis de lui écrire et il ne l'a pas fait," says Victoire in a second letter, "et je réponds qu'il aura fait une scène et que sa mère aura dû revenir." This can only refer to De Sivry's expected reply. Elisa had scarcely reached Paris when Paul followed. He came to the house in the middle of the night, drunk and shouting for money. When she refused to give him any, he broke open the cupboard in which she kept the foetuses of her miscarriages. The bottles crashed to the floor and burst; he stood whacking the debris with his cane: "Au diable les bocals! donnez-moi des argents!" In tears Mme Verlaine gathered up the remains and buried them in the courtyard; then, accompanied by Victoire, sought refuge with friends. It took Paul three days of repentance and persuasion to get her back.[15] It was apparently after this that he returned to Fampoux and received de Sivry's letter. The whole episode forms a ghastly prelude to the sugary lines of *La Bonne Chanson*. Mathilde was not aware of the fact, but the story of her life with Verlaine was being acted out in advance as she waltzed with M. de Janzé.

The main opposition to the marriage came from M. Mauté. He did not like what he had seen of Verlaine, thought him eccentric and unstable (he was later to conclude that he had been only too right). Mathilde portrays him as an aristocrat yielding reluctantly to his daughter's caprice and allowing her to marry beneath her. When both families got back to Paris in the autumn, visits were exchanged. The Mautés were not impressed. Elisa, in her black dress, looked poverty-stricken, provincial, and not very intelligent, and her apartment was "deplorable" – four gloomy rooms full of shabby furniture. M. Mauté thought that Paul was trying to marry

15 *Ibid.*, 67.

his daughter for her dowry, and in hopes of bringing the whole business to an end, declared that he would not give her one. Here he got a surprise. Elisa Verlaine replied that money did not count since her son was in love; he had 3000 francs a year from the city hall, one of his aunts would provide a lump sum of 20,000, and she herself would add 40,000. This was a handsome settlement. M. Mauté had to withdraw his objections and agree to give the young couple an income equal to what such capital would bring in. The matter was thus settled.[16]

This is Mathilde's story, and it needs some qualification. Lepelletier, who got his information from Verlaine, says bluntly that the Mautés gave no dowry at all, and were delighted to settle their daughter without financial inconvenience – a statement which naturally led Mathilde to protest: "S'il vous a dit que son contrat de mariage avait été onéreux pour lui, il vous a induit en erreur. Allez lire mon contrat chez Maître Taupin."[17] Rash advice. We do not know whether Lepelletier acted on it, but others have done so since, and it now appears that although the Mautés did not actually "sacrifice" their daughter, they must have found Verlaine's proposal extremely advantageous. A dowry was of great importance in those days, and M. Mauté was living up to the last franc of his income and perhaps beyond. Nowhere does Mathilde, so verbose in other matters, give any concrete details about her father's fortune. And it is strange that, had there really been money in the family, she should have ended her life (in 1914) running a boarding-house at Nice. Nor was she the only child: there was a sister who would have to be provided for. M. Mauté, for all his pretensions, would have had difficulty finding anything like the 60,000 francs Elisa produced so quickly. It is doubtful if he ever gave his daughter an income approaching Verlaine's. According to the contract, Mathilde put up 4206 francs in cash, a 50 franc bond at 3 per cent, and some furniture.[18] This was not much. Financially, the marriage settlement was a potential source of friction and recrimination.

16 Mathilde, *Mémoires*, 110-11.   17 *Ibid.*, 265.
18 This contract is reproduced in *CML*, I, 1405-13.

At the time, of course, money was the last thing Verlaine had in mind. As Mathilde's fiancé he now visited her regularly. He was in a state of "calm joy" as he calls it; he worked regularly at the city hall and became such a model employee that his supervisor complimented him. His friends missed him at the usual cafés; he went directly home after work and he stopped drinking.[19] The winter of 1869-70 was probably the happiest moment of his life if we define happiness as "calm joy" and the accomplishment of a rational desire. His state of mind is clearly revealed in *La Bonne Chanson*. Mathilde had freed him from terrible obsessions – from his inverted love for Lucien Viotti, from drink, and from the homicidal frenzy drink induced.

But such benefits had to be paid for and the price was high; they cost him the best of his talent. Mathilde received the first of *La Bonne Chanson*, "Le soleil du matin," in July 1869, immediately after Paul's proposal had been more or less accepted. The following eleven reached her during the rest of her holiday in the country, and the last eight were written during the happy winter of 1869 and the spring of 1870. The results are charming enough; *La Bonne Chanson* is Verlaine's "safe" volume. But charm is about all it has. Nowhere, except in one poem, vi, "La lune blanche," do we find the unearthly accent of *Poèmes saturniens* and *Fêtes galantes*, where the dream, going beyond reality, opens infinite perspectives of emotional adventure. This was inevitable; in *La Bonne Chanson* Verlaine was not thinking of a sublimated universe of poetry, but of a bourgeois marriage, with all the humdrum trappings of dowry, family, and a steady job. Or rather   and this was serious – he mistook this dead end for the ideal world of music and suggestion he had glimpsed and partly expressed in his earlier work. Poems ii and iii are little more than glamorized descriptions of Mathilde, and iv comes within measurable distance of banality:

> Je veux, guidé par vous, beaux yeux aux flammes douces ...
> Oui, je veux marcher droit et calme dans la Vie ...
> Sans violence, sans remords et sans envie ...
> Et vraiment je ne veux pas d'autre Paradis.

19 Mathilde, *Mémoires*, 97-98.

The Baudelairean echoes – "Ils passent devant moi, ces yeux pleins de lumières" – only make the weakness of such verse the more apparent. The greater poet, gifted with impeccable intuition, never allowed sentiment to degenerate into sentimentality, but this was a reef on which Verlaine very nearly foundered. The whole conclusion of the volume, XIII-XXI, is insufferably hackneyed:

> Le foyer, la lueur étroite de la lampe ...
> L'heure du thé fumant et des livres fermés ...
>
> Et je tremble ...
> A penser qu'un mot, un sourire
> De vous est désormais ma loi ...
>
> Sans nous préoccuper de ce que nous destine
> Le Sort, nous marcherons pourtant du même pas,
> Et la main dans la main, avec l'âme enfantine
> De ceux qui s'aiment sans mélange, n'est-ce pas?

No cliché is spared, not even the confession of a reformed rake:

> J'allais par des chemins perfides,
> Douloureusement incertain.
> Vos chères mains furent mes guides.
>
> Votre regard fut le matin ...
>
> Mon cœur crantif, mon sombre cœur
> Pleurait, seul, sur la triste voie;
> L'amour, délicieux vainqueur,
>
> Nous a réunis dans la joie.

We are no longer in the shimmering, suggestive world of "Mon Rêve familier" and "Clair de lune." Even the best pieces (always excepting "La lune blanche") such as v, "Avant que tu ne t'en ailles," are concrete descriptions: morning, dew, the inevitable birds in the first light of dawn; the only thing that saves them from disaster is the style. Verlaine was always a poet, even at his worst, but it is not the eerie style of his first books. If it were not for "La lune blanche," which echoes the "En sourdine" of *Fêtes galantes* and the "Chanson d'automne" of *Poèmes saturniens*, *La*

Bonne Chanson would indicate a serious decline, a drying-up of inspiration. Fortunately, it only amounted to a halt. Verlaine was marking time; he had given up his visions, but only temporarily. The faun had left the forest and allowed himself to be tamed. The experiment was to fail, and in any case it only lasted for two years.

Since the marriage was now settled, Mathilde went house-hunting and found an apartment at 2 rue du Cardinal-Lemoine, on the corner of the Quai de la Tournelle. The house still exists, just across the street from the Tour d'Argent restaurant, with the balcony facing the river on which the young couple, for a few short months, used to take their coffee. In view of the grotesque catastrophe that overtook the marriage, there is something almost pathetic about Mathilde's smug description of the home she created: she obviously thought she was getting settled for life. The bedroom was furnished with "meubles anciens authentiques ... pur Louis xv laqué blanc à filets roses"; there was a Pleyel grand piano in the sitting-room, and a suite of red plush.[20] The wedding was set for June 1870, but had to be postponed. Smallpox was raging in Paris and Mathilde caught the disease. She had barely recovered when it attacked her mother, who had nursed her; and by the time Mme Mauté was back on her feet an even more serious impediment confronted the lovers.

While Verlaine, in Mathilde's phrase, was "cooing out the *Bonne Chanson,*" the international situation had taken a fatal turn. France opposed the candidacy of a Hohenzollern prince to the Spanish throne, the famous Ems telegram was sent, and Bismarck manoeuvered the ailing Napoleon iii into declaring war on Prussia (July 19). The first disasters occurred and on August 10, 1870, the Empress Eugénie, as Regent, signed a decree conscripting all un-married men of the class of 1864, to which Verlaine belonged. Theoretically he could not now marry; and if the ceremony was nevertheless performed on August 11, it was doubtless because, the confusion being so great, the Regent's orders were no longer obeyed. Crowds shouting "Vive la République!" were already parading through the streets; Verlaine, like most of his friends,

20 *Ibid.*, 121.

had long been in opposition to the Second Empire, and nearly got arrested for a similar demonstration on the terrace of the Café Tortoni. He only escaped the police when a crowd of sympathizers intervened. The Second Empire, like so many French régimes since the Revolution, had an impressive façade and no foundations. It collapsed when the news reached Paris that Napoleon III had surrendered at Sedan with his last army, and the Republic was proclaimed on September 4.

Despite this catastrophic background the marriage began well enough. Verlaine got his wedding night; he ruminated over it long afterwards, like a man digesting truffles. "Elle fut tout ce que je m'en étais promis ... tout ce que nous nous en promettions, elle et moi, car il y eut dans ces divines heures autant de délicatesse de ma part et de pudeur de la sienne que de passion réelle, ardente, des deux côtés. Elle fut, cette nuit, sans pair dans ma vie et, j'en réponds, dans la sienne ..."[21] He and Mathilde paid little attention to external events, and they were both delighted with the change in government, like a good many of their contemporaries. For over half a century France had been living on the most dangerous kind of political Romanticism – frothy memories of the Revolution and the Napoleonic wars. There was a vague idea that a republic meant a *levée en masse* and a smashing victory like Valmy which would hurl back the invaders. Unfortunately, the armies organized by Bismarck and Von Moltke were very different from the Duke of Brunswick's lumbering coalition in 1792. The Franco-Prussian War was the first modern conflict, an authentic Blitzkrieg, neglecting the old tactics of cavalry charge and dashing advance in favour of heavy strokes at key points, designed to paralyse all resistance. Nobody in France was prepared for such relentless novelty; by the end of autumn, the north was occupied and Paris under siege. The winter was exceptionally severe. Carts crossed the frozen Seine; food ran short. People ate horses, dogs, cats, animals from the zoo; hostesses cooked giraffe and zebra stew over drawing-room fires built of green wood from the boulevard trees. All this, grim as it was, would have been something

21 *Confessions, CML*, II, 1206.

of a gay adventure had Verlaine not begun drinking again. In a burst of patriotism he joined the National Guard, a kind of civilian militia, and was on duty every two days for forty-eight hours. There were too many comrades, too much idleness, too many wine-shops. Drink was as much a duty as carrying a gun. One day, and certainly not for the first time, he came home so obviously intoxicated that Mathilde could not contain her tears and re-proaches. They quarrelled, and when he left for the the office next morning she was still sulking. He returned that evening to find that she had taken refuge with her parents (since the Prussians were shelling Paris, M. Mauté had moved from exposed Mont-martre to the Boulevard Saint-Germain, a few streets from the rue du Cardinal-Lemoine). Verlaine went to fetch her – in what a state of irritation may be imagined. When they got home, dinner was bad: over-done horse and pickled mushrooms. The quarrel began again and this time it ended in blows.

From then on, relations between the pair entered that dreary stage of all ill-assorted unions headed for disaster. Mathilde insists (it was her grounds for separation and later divorce) that all was well for fourteen months, until Rimbaud's arrival. But Verlaine gives a different account in the *Confessions* and at times it is frankly brutal. He takes a sort of perverse enjoyment in describing "the first whack"; and given what Lepelletier and Victoire Bertrand tell us of his behaviour when drunk, we feel that he is telling the truth. Besides which Mathilde's own story is not always consis-tent. She admits that when in April 1871, Charles de Sivry came to the apartment for a few days Verlaine had been drinking and was in a bad mood. She gives no details of the scene, but it must have been very unpleasant. Like every woman who marries a drunk by choice, she wanted to hide the truth from her family. Next day, when she awoke after a bad night (she was three months pregnant), she found Verlaine on his knees by her bedside, im-ploring forgiveness – the usual pattern – and when Charles left she begged him not to tell her parents what had occurred, adding that it was exceptional.

In the meantime, the political situation had taken a shift that

was to modify Verlaine's career profoundly. A provisional government, led by Adolphe Thiers, had been elected; its main task was
to negotiate peace with Germany. France was prostrate, her terri-
tory occupied, her armies destroyed. There was nothing for it but
to accept Bismarck's terms, though they included a huge indem-
nity and the loss of Alsace-Lorraine. When the news of this humili-
ation reached Paris the city revolted, with more enthusiasm than
common sense. A coalition of left-wing parties, known to history
as the Commune, seized power. It has a bad reputation nowadays,
chiefly because Lenin claimed it as a political ancestor (although
only one member of the government was a genuine Marxist).
Verlaine and his friends seem to have looked on it as a form of
ultra-liberalism, with a strong humanitarian tinge – a proper reaction against the stuffy authoritarianism of Napoleon III. Matters
soon became so tense that Thiers took his government to Versailles, along with what was left of the French army. Elisa Verlaine,
with considerable foresight, wanted her son as a civil servant to
follow the administration; she understood that by attaching himself to a revolutionary clique he would lose his job once order was
restored. But he was enthusiastic and refused, and Mathilde agreed
with him. "Je considérais le traitement de Verlaine comme une
quantité négligeable dans notre budget ... Je pensais que, s'il per-
dait sa place, le mal ne serait pas grand, qu'il pourrait consacrer
tout son temps à la littérature et vivre ainsi selon ses goûts." She
knew he hated his work. He joined forces with the Commune
and was put in charge of the press bureau. His duties consisted of
reading newspapers and noting articles unfavourable to the new
government, a typical police-state job. He only exercised these
functions for about two months, but that was enough. Henceforth
he was a marked man, suspected of "subversive tendencies."

By May 22, 1871, troops of the Versailles government had
fought their way into Paris and reached the Arc de Triomphe.
The Communards were constructing barricades in the streets for
a fight to the death. When Verlaine learned that shells were falling
in Batignolles, his mother's quarter, he was panic-stricken. "L'idée

ne lui était pas venue de prendre une voiture et d'aller la chercher,"
Mathilde notes acidly; and when she proposed that they do so
together he replied that if they met a Communard patrol he ran
the risk of being arrested and forced to man a barricade. Mathilde
therefore, with his consent, set out alone, at six in the morning.[22]

Paris was now in one of those paroxysms of anarchy which
only civil war can produce. Seeing defeat inevitable, the worst
elements of the Commune seized control. The Hôtel de Ville, the
Cour des Comptes, the Tuileries Palace, and other public build-
ings were fired in an orgy of hysteric vandalism. Mathilde, a girl
of seventeen now four months pregnant, passed through smoke,
flame, and discharges of musketry, climbed over barricades, and
once at least came within an ace of being shot. Her courage is
amazing, and makes Verlaine's poltroonery all the more striking
by contrast, but it is true that he had some excuse. A man at loose
ends in the Paris streets was in great danger of being conscripted
for service on the barricades or shot outright as a possible Versailles spy. Mathilde managed to reach both her father and her
brother, and neither showed any more courage than Verlaine.
"C'est bien toi!" exclaimed Charles de Sivry when, on her second
day of wandering, she reached his house. "On se bat dans les rues
et tu fais des visites! Je ne puis sortir, *mais je vais envoyer ma femme*
prévenir ta belle-mère qu'elle aille chez vous dès qu'elle le pourra."[23]

In the light of this remark, Verlaine's cowardice appears a little
less shocking. His indifference to Mathilde's safety was odious for
quite another reason: "Je restai à la maison, ayant peut-être des
intentions sur la bonne qui était mignonne et qui commençait à
avoir si peur, qu'elle semblait ne demander, dès qu'elle se vit seule
avec moi, pas mieux que d'être rassurée."[24] This revelation, when
she read it in the *Confessions* twenty-five years later, was too much
for Mathilde's vanity to swallow. The maid, she insists, was cross-
eyed, ugly, and so stupid that she didn't even know how to use

22 Mathilde, *Mémoires*, 155, 161-62.
23 *Ibid.*, 166. The italics are mine.
24 *Confessions, CML*, II, 1213.

an egg-timer. But Verlaine's story is corroborated by Lepelletier. He had been fighting in the ranks of the National Guard, and now that the Versailles army was taking over Paris his danger was even greater than Verlaine's. He came to the rue du Cardinal-Lemoine with a friend, Emile Richard, who was still in uniform. They found that Verlaine had piled mattresses in a closet to make a bomb-shelter and was trying to lure the maid into it.[25] The girl may have been as unattractive as Mathilde declares, but she offered novelty. Verlaine was not merely drinking again; he was tired of his wife, after less than a year.

"Et tout," he writes of this period, "alla cahin caha dans ce ménage."[26] And subsequent events were not calculated to improve the situation. After the fall of the Commune, there was something of a reign of terror in Paris. Anyone who had been involved with the revolutionary government was likely to be denounced to the police. It was an opportunity for private vengeance in which politics often played no role at all; Charles de Sivry was arrested on the strength of an anonymous denunciation which later turned out to have been sent in by a jealous woman. Verlaine thought it best to leave town until things quieted down. He took Mathilde to Fampoux, where they stayed with his mother's family, the Dehées. When he heard of De Sivry's arrest, he decided that even after his return he would not go back to the Hôtel de Ville. "Il est évident que ce ne fut qu'un prétexte pour lâcher définitivement son bureau, qui l'ennuyait," says Mathilde, forgetting her previous statement that she attached no importance to his job.[27] Lepelletier agrees with her. Verlaine, he declares, gave up his position voluntarily; he could easily have returned to the office; no questions would have been asked. Perhaps so. The fact remains that two years later (April 4, 1873) when he left London for Belgium, a police spy in the British capital notified the French authorities,

25 Lepelletier, *Paul Verlaine*, 109.
26 *Confessions, CML*, II, 1217.
27 Mathilde, *Mémoires*, 174-75.

who at once requested "urgent confirmation" of the report.[28] As late as 1878, spies were sending Paris detailed accounts of Verlaine's movements, as we find from his dossier at the Préfecture de Police. The Third Republic long kept an uneasy eye on anybody who had been involved with the Commune. Had Verlaine boldly returned to the Hôtel de Ville perhaps nobody would have noticed that he had ever been absent; perhaps he was spied on and reported on precisely because he fled. The question is open. He dropped his job because he wanted to drop it, but even had he tried to resume it, he might very well have found that it no longer existed.

This cessation of regular work was a further blow to his marriage. There was still money: the 60,000 francs of the settlement had not been touched, and Elisa was always on hand, a moderately rich woman. But he was 3000 francs a year poorer, and, even more ominous, he was again living in idleness. The routine of the office, as his father understood, was a kind of discipline, however light; a barrier between his sensuous, impatient nature and the temptations around him. Now he was once more thrown back on himself, and, to further complicate matters, he allowed circumstances to manoeuvre him into an impossible situation. Partly for financial reasons, partly because he was afraid to return to his old address, he decided to abandon the apartment in the rue du Cardinal-Lemoine. Mathilde wrote from Fampoux, explaining things to her father, and he agreed to give the young couple a floor of his house in the rue Nicolet. The fact that Verlaine accepted this arrangement, if only temporarily, shows what a child he was, living heedlessly from day to day, jumping at ready-made solutions, never giving a thought to the morrow. Alcoholism had seized him once more; he was leading irregular hours and fighting with his wife. Yet he proposed to live in her parents' house. Sheer infantilism could go no further.

28 The Verlaine dossier at the Préfecture de Police, Paris, published by Auguste Martin, "Verlaine et Rimbaud," *Nouvelle revue française*, février 1943.

He had met Mathilde at a difficult moment and she had saved
him from despair, but only by imposing a solution which became
as intolerable in the long run as the ills it was supposed to cure.
The old moral lesion still existed, never properly healed. The marriage would have ended badly no matter what happened; Verlaine was "not marriageable," as his friends recognized.[29] But if
any one thing could have accelerated the catastrophe, it was this
incredible step of residence with the Mautés. And just then, as
though to make disaster doubly sure, two letters reached him
from an unknown correspondent in Charleville who signed himself Arthur Rimbaud.

29 Lepelletier, *Paul Verlaine*, 211; Delahaye, *Verlaine*, 90.

4/ Rimbaud/
The end of life in
the rue Nicolet

THE ADVENT OF RIMBAUD was the central point of Verlaine's life
and explains everything that followed. His flight from Paris, the
Brussels drama, his conversion, the squalor of his last years – each
in turn is linked to the same volcanic experience. It marked his
poetry indelibly; without it he would never have written *Roman-*
ces sans paroles and *Sagesse*.

Rimbaud has his legend, and it still makes any rational judgment of him all but impossible. He is the incredible adolescent,
half god, half demon, who ran through literature like fire in an
oil slick, produced verse now universally acclaimed and prose
hailed by writers of all nations as a revelation, and who then abandoned poetry and civilization itself for a life of filth and savagery
in Abyssinia, returning to die sixteen years later, repentant and
transfigured, from carcinoma of the knee. How can we submit
such glamour to the yardsticks of criticism? Rimbaud is one of
those strange figures upon whom no general agreement will ever
be reached; the literature on him is vast, and any proper discussion
would run to many pages. However, if only to explain his cata-
clysmic influence on Verlaine, a few details are necessary.

He was born at Charleville in the Ardennes on October 20,
1854, and was therefore not yet seventeen when he first met the
older poet. There was much of the brilliant sophomore in his
make-up: strikingly handsome in a blue-eyed, tow-headed way,
he had carried off all the college prizes when he graduated and

been composing verse for some years. He was intolerant and anti-social in the intransigent way of the young and clever, and fond of the sort of callowly outrageous paradoxes boys of his type turn out by the dozen. Similar things can still be heard in bars and cafés from Saint-Germain-des-Prés to Greenwich Village. He thought all previous literature trash, and as for painting, when Verlaine took him to the Louvre he remarked that it was a pity the Commune had not burnt the whole collection.[1] His interest in poetry fits the same pattern; it was intense but brief. He wrote in a kind of frenzy for five or six years and then stopped writing altogether. He settled down to making money with a determination which would have done credit to any bourgeois son. "Chaque notaire porte en soi les débris d'un poète," as Flaubert put it. In only one way he differed from numerous boys like him: his adolescent verse had genius.

This fact was obvious to Verlaine when he read the two letters from Charleville in September 1871. They contained poems which are now classics of French literature, such as "Les Effarés," "Accroupissements," "Les Douaniers," and "Le Cœur volé." The writer sketched himself briefly: "J'ai fait le projet de faire un grand poème et je ne peux travailler à Charleville. Je suis empêché de venir à Paris, étant sans ressources. Ma mère est veuve et extrêmement dévote. Elle ne me donne que dix centimes tous les dimanches pour payer ma chaise à l'église."[2] It was the letter of a promising youth in difficult circumstances and it also contained what Verlaine calls some *renseignements bizarres* which whetted his curiosity: Rimbaud defined himself as a *petite crasse, moins gênant qu'un Zanetto*.[3] How are we to understand the phrase? Something like "a rather dirty little guy, less of a nuisance than Zanetto"?

Possibly, for as conclusion there was a note of recommendation from Charles Auguste Bretagne, a man Verlaine had known for

---

1 Lepelletier, *Paul Verlaine*, 253; Porché, *Verlaine, tel qu'il fut*, 130.

2 Rimbaud, Pléiade, 280–81.

3 *Ibid.*, and Verlaine, "Nouvelles Notes sur Rimbaud," *La Plume*, octobre 1895, *CML*, II, 1289. Zanetto is a sentimental character, a kind of wandering troubadour, in François Coppée's play, *Le Passant*, first produced at the Odéon on January 14, 1869.

some years, and this alone was enough to arrest his attention. He was in his teens when he first met Bretagne, during his holidays at Fampoux with his Dehée cousins. The man occupied a post in the customs service and was responsible for checking production at the Dehée sugar refinery. After his retirement, he moved to Charleville and there met Rimbaud. He had a large library of esoteric works which he allowed the boy to consult; he read his manuscript poems and discerned their merit. It was he who suggested that Rimbaud (who had made two unsuccessful applications to Théodore de Banville and had even come to Paris during the siege of 1870) get in touch with Verlaine. Since Mathilde later burned all Rimbaud's letters to her husband, we cannot know what Bretagne said. He remains an enigmatic figure, playing an occult but decisive role between the two poets. It is very likely that he knew the whole truth about Verlaine's sexual problems, and that he had either received similar confidences from Rimbaud or opened the boy's eyes to tendencies which he was too young to understand for himself. In any case, the effect of the letters, with their enclosed poems and Bretagne's note, was immediate. Verlaine showed the verses to some of his friends (Burty, Cros, Valade). They were as impressed as he was; he wrote Rimbaud to come to Paris at once: "Venez, chère grande âme, on vous appelle, on vous attend."[4] He enclosed a moneyorder to cover the expenses of the trip, and an invitation to stay at the Mauté house. He had spoken of Rimbaud with such enthusiasm to his wife and mother-in-law (M. Mauté was absent on a hunting trip) that they had agreed to this arrangement.

Subsequent events were both catastrophic and obscure. We know most of the details but few of the explanations, largely because of Mathilde's destruction of letters which would have revealed the truth. The result is not unlike listening to a violent telephone conversation between unknown persons.

Verlaine and his friend Charles Cros went to the Gare de l'Est to meet Rimbaud. They missed him in the crowd, and when they returned to the rue Nicolet, they found that he had walked there.

4 September 1871, Rimbaud, Pléiade, 281

Mme Mauté and Mathilde (who was now within a month of delivery) were doing their best to make conversation and not succeeding. Rimbaud was not merely a genius, he was also a raw youth and a provincial, who had never seen anything like the Mauté drawing-room in his life before and who had no idea how to behave in regular society. He was awkward, timid, not interested in women (particularly when they were old or pregnant), and he became ill-mannered and boorish by a very simple process of self-defence. "C'était un grand et solide garçon à la figure rougeaude, un paysan," Mathilde describes him. "Il avait l'aspect d'un jeune potache ayant grandi trop vite, car son pantalon écourté laissait voir des chaussettes de coton bleu tricotées par les soins maternels. Les cheveux hirsutes, une cravate en corde, une mise négligée. Les yeux étaient bleus, assez beaux, mais ils avaient une expression sournoise que, dans notre indulgence, nous prîmes pour de la timidité."[5] Lepelletier's impression a few days later was even more unfavourable: "Un gavroche sinistre ... mince, pâle, dégingandé ... froid, méprisant et cynique, il domina rapidement le faible Verlaine. Il fut son mauvais génie ... le fatal conseiller des légendes, le satanique campagnon qui entraîne à sa perte la proie à laquelle il s'est attaché."[6]

The hostility of these portraits is not hard to explain. Mathilde had obvious reasons for disliking the young man, and as for Lepelletier, the most normal friendship is never entirely free from jealousy – or wounded vanity if you prefer. Verlaine was his great man; they had known each other for ten years or more, and now he found himself supplanted by an obstreperous boy. He admits that Rimbaud had talent, but aside from that, he could not understand Verlaine's infatuation.

To us, looking back, the matter is less obscure. Rimbaud, like Mathilde herself in 1869, arrived at a critical moment, and his combination of innocence and violence, beauty and genius, was irresistible. Verlaine has left several accounts of the impact of their first meeting; they read as though he were refuting in advance the strictures of his wife and friend. He notes the same details, the

5 Mathilde, *Mémoires*, 180.
6 Lepelletier, *Paul Verlaine*, 30-1; see also 250, 269-70.

eyes, the hair, and the demonic quality; but they meant something quite different to him than to Mathilde and Lepelletier.
Rimbaud was " 'l'Enfant Sublime' ... Un Casanova gosse mais
bien plus expert ès aventures," with "narines hardies," a "beau
menton accidenté," and a "superbe tignasse," whose whole face
seemed to cry " 'va te faire lanlaire' à toute illusion qui ne doive
l'existence à la plus irrévocable volonté." He had a virile disdain
of clothes, which for that matter were "inutiles à cette littérale
beauté du diable." "L'homme était grand, bien bâti, presque ath-
létique, au visage parfaitement ovale d'ange en exil, avec des cheveux châtain-clair mal en ordre et des yeux d'un bleu pâle
inquiétant." As for his poetry, it was "en dehors de toute littérature et sans doute au-dessus ... On pourrait ... mettre l'homme en
dehors, en quelque sorte, de l'humanité et sa vie en dehors et au-
dessus de la commune vie. Tant l'œuvre est géante, tant l'homme
s'est fait libre ... Le tout simple comme une forêt vierge et beau
comme un tigre."[7]

The tone of sensuous, masochistic adoration is obvious in every
word, and when we remember that these passages were written
ten or fifteen years after Verlaine had last seen Rimbaud, we can
understand his complete surrender to the boy's domination in 1871.
Rimbaud's destructive cynicism and novel ideas, presented through
the bewildering medium of his sulky, adolescent beauty and the
authentic genius of his verse, answered an imperious craving of
which Verlaine had been only half-aware. Stifled sexual tendencies came back to life – the memory of Lucien Viotti, sacrificed
for Mathilde – but the sorcery was much deeper and more complete than mere inverted desire. The word *libre* gives us the clue,
l'homme s'est fait libre. Verlaine's passion involved his whole vocation as a poet, and here Rimbaud (unlike Viotti) could meet him
as an equal, if not a superior. For besides the verse he had enclosed
in his letters and "Le Bateau ivre" which he brought with him to
Paris (Verlaine always considered it his best poem), he had formu-
lated a new theory of poetry. It was in complete contrast with
both Parnassianism and the sort of life Verlaine had been leading

7 *Les Poètes maudits* (1884), *CML*, I, 465-66; new edition (1888), *CML*, I, 475; *Les
Hommes d'aujourd'hui* (1888), *CML*, II, 637.

in the rue Nicolet: "Le Poëte se fait *voyant* par un long, immense et raisonné *dérèglement* de *tous les sens*. Toutes les formes d'amour, de souffrance, de folie; il cherche lui-même, il épuise en lui tous les poisons, pour n'en garder que les quintessences ... Il devient ... le grand malade, le grand criminel, le grand maudit – et le suprême Savant! – Car il arrive à l'*inconnu*! ... Donc le poëte est vraiment voleur de feu ... Baudelaire est le premier voyant, roi des poëtes, *un vrai Dieu*. Encore a-t-il vécu dans un milieu trop artiste; et la forme si vantée en lui est mesquine. Les inventions d'inconnu réclament des formes nouvelles."[8]

It was a message, in short, of complete and even anarchic liberty, and it burst on Verlaine like a revelation. Here was escape from the bog of platitude in which marriage had landed him. He had written nothing since *La Bonne Chanson*; it was the longest period of sterility in his career, and it must have weighed heavily on his mind.[9] He was smothering, wadded down and stingless, amid the upholstery of the Mauté house, and Rimbaud broke open the prison. The operation was brutal, the results no less so; Verlaine was to be a vagabond and a debauchee for the rest of his life, despite rare moments of reform. But it gave him back his genius. Of all his bonds with Rimbaud, this was the most important; it dominated their relationship from first to last. "Avec moi seul tu peux être libre," Rimbaud wrote him later. "Resonge à ce que tu étais avant de me connaître."[10]

There is a hint of contempt in the words, the keynote of Rimbaud's attitude from the moment he arrived. He had read *Fêtes galantes* while he was still at Charleville, and Verlaine was one of the few living poets he was ready to acknowledge as a seer and an inventor of new forms. Now he found him living like a bourgeois, in overfurnished rooms with a pregnant wife. Where was the seer, the sage, the *voleur de feu*? He set out to be offensive,

8 The famous letter to Paul Demeny, May 15, 1871, Pléiade, 269-74.
9 Between *La Bonne Chanson* in 1870 and the first of *Romances sans paroles* in the spring of 1872, he produced only "Les Renards," – stanzas on the Franco-Prussian War – and "Retour de Naples," a parody of Heredia (Pléiade, 213-14). Neither has any value.
10 His letter of July 5, 1873, from London. Rimbaud, Pléiade, 292-93.

smashed various pieces of bric-a-brac, stole an antique ivory cross, and infected his bed with lice, which (Verlaine laughingly told his wife) he carried in his hair to throw on any priests he met. Mathilde and her mother, realizing that M. Mauté would never put up with such an intruder, asked Verlaine to move his guest elsewhere. Other lodgings were found; he was expelled from each in turn.[11] Things were even worse when Verlaine introduced him to writers and poets. Rimbaud thought their verse bad and said so, obscenely. His behaviour was so revolting that in the end nobody would meet him, and this meant that Verlaine was now estranged from all his old friends, since he refused to go anywhere without Rimbaud.

It is impossible to say just when their relations reached an erotic stage; probably in a very short time. For almost at once, and with curious unanimity, unpleasant gossip began. They appear to have invited it themselves, frequenting the most off-beat circles and making a parade of exaggerated affection which was bound to arouse comment. At the first night of Coppée's sentimental drama, *L'Abandonnée* (November 15, 1871), their conduct was deliberately provoking. The play is an insipid piece of work – another variation of the Camille theme about a noble harlot – and, doubtless to show their contempt, Verlaine and Rimbaud appeared half-drunk in the foyer with their arms around each other's necks. It was the age of white ties and tails, low-cut gowns, and ostrich feathers. Verlaine and Rimbaud, dressed like tramps, were bad enough at any time; in a setting like this, staggering about caressing each other, they were so scandalous that next day they got into the newspapers. *Le Peuple souverain*, in a review of the evening, noted that "parmi les hommes de lettres ... on remarquait le poète Paul Verlaine donnant le bras à une charmante jeune personne, Mlle Rimbaud."

It was signed Gustave Valentin, one of Lepelletier's pseudonyms. The fact shows as nothing else could how Verlaine's new passion had alienated his friends. If the faithful Edmond could drop such a hint, and even publish it (thus giving the authority of print to

11 Porché, *Verlaine tel qu'il fut*, 133 *sqq.*

what was only being whispered), other people were saying much worse. During a visit to Mathilde shortly afterwards, he explained that he had written the squib to teach Verlaine and Rimbaud a lesson. It was a lamentably weak excuse. He had been Paul's school chum; there was nothing to prevent him from discussing the matter privately. But he was offended by Verlaine's neglect, and Rimbaud had insulted him as provocatively as he insulted everybody else, calling him a "pisseur de copie" because he wrote for the papers. Whatever its justification, however, the article was a nasty stroke. It has a catty, underhand quality surprising in a man like Lepelletier. "S'il y a eu de mauvais propos tenus sur son ami," Mathilde notes very justly, "il a été le premier à attacher le grelot."[12] And once the talk began it could not be stopped. When Verlaine disappeared with Rimbaud eight months later, M. Mauté went looking for him in the cafés of the Latin Quarter and discovered that the relations between the pair were common gossip.

As this scandal ripened, home life in the rue Nicolet was becoming tumultuous. The sporadic domestic unpleasantness of 1870-71 turned into a permanent row which, had Verlaine not finally deserted his wife, might very well have ended in murder. How far was Rimbaud responsible? Lepelletier has no doubts: he accuses him of turning Verlaine into a drunk and disrupting his home, thus agreeing with Mathilde: "Quelles furent les causes de mon malheur? ... Rimbaud! L'absinthe!"[13] They both imply that, had Rimbaud not appeared, the marriage would somehow have survived. But according to Lepelletier's own testimony, Verlaine had had a long experience of alcohol by the time he met Rimbaud,

---

12 Mathilde, *Mémoires*, 185-86. Lepelletier's attitude toward Verlaine's homosexuality was never quite clear. He denies the charge in his biography of the poet, but he seems to have nourished a few doubts. "Entre nous," he asked some of Verlaine's friends one evening in the late eighties, "savez-vous si Verlaine l'est réellement?" –"Vous devez être édifié à ce sujet mieux que personne," was the answer. "N'avez vous pas été au collège avec lui?" The conversation ended in a burst of laughter. F. A. Cazals and Gustave Le Rouge, *Les Derniers iours de Paul Verlaine*, 182. – Verlaine introduced Rimbaud into some very eccentric circles. The musician Cabaner, with whom he lodged him, is mentioned in a police report dated August 18, 1878, which is now in the Verlaine file at the Préfecture, as a well-known homosexual. When Delahaye came to Paris looking for his friend, he found him stupefied with hashish. E. Delahaye, *Souvenirs familiers à propos de Rimbaud, de Verlaine et Germain Nouveau*, 162.

13 Mathilde, *Mémoires*, 98.

and the marriage was headed for the rocks months before the young poet got off the train at the Gare de l'Est; on that point Mathilde herself is sufficiently explicit. There is not much doubt, however, that Rimbaud did everything he could to hasten the catastrophe. He disliked Mathilde: partly because he knew that she disliked him, looked on him as a boor and a peasant, partly because she represented everything he hated – home, family, all the middle-class platitudes he had left behind in Charleville. Every thing too which had turned Verlaine from the poet of *Fêtes galantes* into the gushy rhymster of *La Bonne Chanson*. It is uncertain just when Rimbaud saw a copy of that volume,[14] but whenever he did he must have thought it disgusting – treason to the ideal of the seer – just the sort of drivel to expect from a man who wanted to marry and settle down. Added to these sources of irritation was his demonic pride. We can rule out jealousy. It is unlikely that he felt any genuine affection for Verlaine; his early admiration soon cooled into amused contempt. But he could not bear the idea that Paul should acknowledge any influence but his, and with that gratuitous sadism which is often part of the adolescent mind, he took a perverse joy in destruction. There was another motive also, an ignoble one, but of great weight. He was penniless, and here was a man willing to support him. On his first visit to Paris, a year before, he had nearly died of starvation, living out of garbage tins and sleeping in doorways. It was much more comfortable to have a devoted friend who got rooms, provided meals, picked up the checks in bars and cafés. Between September and November 1871, the pair went through 2000 francs together. Behind this pleasant life loomed Mathilde, a potential menace; Rimbaud's keen intelligence would soon have detected Paul's restlessness and discontent, even if the older man had not confided in him, and it is difficult to believe that there was anything Paul did not confide. Mathilde had to be got rid of; the time was ripe, and from the moment Arthur reached Paris a duel began between them for the possession of Verlaine.

14 In a letter from Charleville, August 25, 1870, he asked Georges Izambard to buy a copy of *La Bonne Chanson*, adding that he had not yet read it. Verlaine, Pléiade, 259.

The few epistolary fragments which survive leave small doubt about this. We can almost hear Rimbaud's sarcasms on marriage and the family, his ironic gibes whenever Verlaine had to go home from some night spot. The man of twenty-seven began parroting the boy of seventeen: at a dinner-party Elisa gave in hopes of getting him reinstated at the Hôtel de Ville (she had invited a high-ranking official as guest of honour) he arrived drunk and kept declaring that women and children were disgusting creatures and marriage a stupid farce of which he, personally, had had enough. The party broke up in disorder. It is clear that, as in 1869, he was wound up to a dangerous pitch, where the least incident would produce an explosion; and throughout, one factor never changed: his violence was less sadistic than infantile. He was not trying to sharpen sexual desire by inflicting pain. The matter was less complicated: Mathilde was an obstacle to his freedom, which meant life with Rimbaud, and he reacted to an obstacle the way a child does, with a fit of temper.

One evening (it was about six weeks after Rimbaud's arrival), as he and Mathilde got ready for bed, he told her how the boy used to steal volumes from bookshops. When she remarked off-handedly that such conduct was hardly decent, Verlaine dragged her out of bed and dashed her to the floor. She was on the brink of confinement; it is miraculous that there were no serious consequences.[15] Georges Verlaine was born shortly afterward, on October 30, 1871. For a few days Verlaine's behaviour improved: he had perhaps frightened even himself. But the lull was brief. The child, after all, was another chain upon him. In less than a fortnight his behaviour was worse than ever. He used to curse Mathilde in low tones and hit her when she maintained a tight-lipped, white-faced silence. The peasant streak in his nature emerged at moments like these, a heritage from his great-grandfather the wagoner and brawling Henry-Joseph, men who no doubt held with many others of their kind that a whack or two never did *la bourgeoise* any harm. What especially infuriated him was Mathilde's genteel self-control; she received his abuse in contemptuous silence which

15 Mathilde, *Mémoires*, 195–96.

he did everything he could to break, putting lighted matches to her hair, threatening to kill her and the baby as well. On the night of Coppée's play he was so brutal that the nurse in charge of the still convalescent mother had to drive him off with a pair of red-hot tongs. Mathilde did her best to conceal these outrages. When he left traces like a cut lip or scratches she could not hide, she told her parents that she had had a fall. "J'étais si honteuse, si humiliée d'avoir épousé un ivrogne, que je préférais tout supporter sans me plaindre plutôt que d'avouer la vérité."[16]

But at last a scene occurred which could not be hidden. Verlaine had arrived late for dinner (January 13, 1872). Mathilde was unwell in her room, but her parents prepared a cold supper for him and sat up with him while he ate it. When he came to his wife she was in front of the fire with her child. "Tes parents m'ont fait servir de café froid; donne-moi la clef du tiroir, que je prenne de l'argent pour aller en prendre une tasse au café." – "Il n'est pas nécessaire de chercher un prétexte pour sortir," she replied quietly. "Tous les jours tu me laisses de plus en plus seule, et aujourd'hui je ne t'ai pas vu de la journée." He seized the baby and threw it against the wall. Fortunately his aim was bad and it fell to the bed without injury. Mathilde's calm deserted her. She screamed. By the time her parents got upstairs, Verlaine had her on the bed, one knee on her chest, trying to strangle her. M. Mauté pulled him off and he rushed out of the house. He headed for a sordid little attic in the rue Campagne-Première where Rimbaud was lodging, and stayed there four days.

The Mautés must have long suspected the truth, and Mathilde now had to tell them everything. Her father was naturally outraged. Next day she was feverish and could hardly speak. A doctor was called. He drew up a statement about the bruises on her throat. Then Mauté told her to pack and took her and the baby away to Périgueux. Verlaine, using this trip as a pretext, later pretended that Mauté had broken up his marriage. The statement scarcely needs refutation. Like most fathers, Mauté thought his daughter much too good for her husband, just as Elisa Verlaine

16 *Ibid.*, 195.

thought Paul much too good for Mathilde. But there is no evidence that he ever tried to come between them. The trip to Périgueux was perfectly justified; he was protecting his daughter from a drunk. And there is no reason to question the account Mathilde gives of Verlaine's behaviour. It reads like Victoire Bertrand's letters, not to mention a good deal of other testimony. Indeed the whole crisis of 1871–72 is a repetition of the alcoholic violence of two years before, and for the same reason: a deep-rooted sexual conflict. It is significant that one of the worst scenes (when Verlaine threatened to *kill* his wife) occurred the night of *L'Abandonnée*, just after he had made such a public spectacle of his affection for Rimbaud. "La voilà, l'abandonnée!" he exclaimed as he entered the room and pointed at her. To his drunkard's imagination she symbolized womanhood itself, the homosexual's eternal rival. The theme was to reappear later, at the time of his relations with Lucien Létinois.

When he came to the rue Nicolet four days afterward, his mother-in-law told him that Mathilde had gone away (she did not say where). During the next few weeks he wrote several affectionate letters to the Mauté house, expressing repentance. They were forwarded to Mathilde, who read them with mixed feelings. She was ready to come back: "Je l'aimais encore et j'étais attristée de vivre loin de lui." But she made conditions: he must drop Rimbaud, "cause, à mon avis, de tous nos malheurs, puisque les dissensions de notre ménage dataient de son arrivée." This was to be her thesis until the end. "Rimbaud, qui ne valait rien, tous nos amis l'avaient constaté, avait une mauvaise influence sur le caractère faible de Verlaine ... il l'entraînait à boire de l'absinthe, ce qui lui faisait perdre la raison et donnait lieu à des accès d'alcoolisme et à des violences aussi pénibles qu'inexplicables."[17] Despite her entreaties, Verlaine resisted; he said he could not prevent Rimbaud from living in Paris. She replied that if he stopped giving the boy money, he would have to return to Charleville. To her astonishment, Verlaine continued to refuse.

It was certainly an incredible situation. Five months after the

17 *Ibid.*, 201.

arrival of an unknown youth, the wife had had to fly the house; and she refused to come back until the intruder left, not just the house, where he no longer was, but Paris itself. And to crown all, her husband, supposedly repentant, refused to meet her wishes. Did father and daughter never ask themselves, during those quiet days at Périgueux, just what the explanation was? Even though pederasty (unlike Lesbianism) had not figured much in art or literature, it was a well-known phenomenon and on occasion a much discussed one. The gossip about Verlaine and Rimbaud in Paris proves this, as does the talk aroused at Coulommes when the poet lived there with Létinois ten years later. And Coulommes was a rustic township, not the sophisticated capital. Mathilde, of course, well bred as she was, knew nothing of sexual inversion, but her father was a man of the world. It is strange that, confronted with an anomaly of which he must at least have heard, he could not recognize it for what it was.

Far from seeking to prolong the breach or dissolve the marriage, he was anxious to arrange matters. Living away from home in a provincial hotel was expensive and inconvenient. Since his son-in-law was deaf to persuasion, he decided to put a little pressure on him. He sent the doctor's certificate to his lawyer, with instructions to start proceedings for a legal separation, and Verlaine received a summons charging him with brutality to his wife. This brought him up short. A normal man guilty of such misconduct would scarcely have expected anything else, would even have welcomed separation as a convenient solution. But when his emotions were involved, Verlaine was incorrigibly immature, and nowhere more obviously so than in his dealings with Mathilde. He really did not remember, once he was sober, how outrageous he had been in his cups. He was willing to repent and ask forgiveness, and that, he thought, should wipe the slate clean. Repentance was part of the child pattern, another form of emotional self-indulgence, like the spree which preceded it. Now for the first time he had to face the consequences of his actions. He could injure his mother with impunity. She always forgave; it was her vocation. But Mathilde was a wife, and a wife supported by a justly incensed father. M. Mauté's will blocked the usual exit – lachrymose contrition – like a granite boulder. Paul had to choose between two things he craved, Rimbaud and Mathilde. A hard choice since he wanted them both.

Rimbaud fascinated him: before he met the boy his experiments in drink and sex had been half clandestine, plagued by a sense of guilt. Arthur made him see debauchery not as an end in itself, but as a means to complete freedom, a sloughing off of all lies and hypocrisy. "Le Poëte se fait *voyant* par un long, immense et raisonné *dérèglement* de *tous les sens*. Toutes les formes d'amour, de souffrance, de folie ..." Already the sterility in which Verlaine had lived since *La Bonne Chanson* was thawing; he was writing again. The first of *Romances sans paroles* date from precisely these frantic opening months of 1872. Yet, despite Rimbaud, he still wanted Mathilde. He had never thought for a moment of losing her, as is made quite clear by the letters and poems he wrote her *after* their final separation. His feeling for her, like his feeling for Rimbaud, was not purely erotic. Mathilde symbolized the hearth, the home, the lighted lamps, the warmth, and the refuge, things that were part of his earliest memories and which obsessed him until his death. He always wanted a home, tried to make one with Lucien Létinois, and even with Philomène and Eugénie. Only one side of his nature was vagabond; the other (as Rimbaud noted contemptuously) was profoundly bourgeois. Faced now with Mathilde's ultimatum he could not reach a decision. And like the child he was he tried to keep both his wife and his friend.

As far as he had a plan, it consisted of yielding to the Mautés until the marriage was "patched up again" (his own words), and then persuading Mathilde that he and she could live quite well together – with Rimbaud as a third! A few months later, after he had left Paris with Arthur, he proposed this solution in a letter, going so far as to assure her that *Rimbaud had no objection*. "Rimbaud sera très heureux de t'avoir avec nous."[18] Only Verlaine, perhaps, could have put forward such an idea seriously. For the time being, however, he had to give in. Mathilde and her father showed no signs of weakening and they had the law behind them.

18 *Ibid.*, 221.

The combination was too much for Verlaine. He wrote that Rimbaud was going back to Charleville, and a few days later (early in March 1872) Mathilde came home.

Outwardly she had won, but it was a fatal victory. All Verlaine's promises were lies. Rimbaud was not in Paris, but an elaborate method of correspondence had been arranged. Verlaine was to write him in care of Charles Bretagne; Arthur's replies concerning his "martyrdom" (as Verlaine called his exile from the capital) were to go to Elisa Verlaine's apartment. Any replies about his future return would be received by the designer Forain, who had a studio in the Ile Saint-Louis and with whom the two poets were on friendly terms. It was understood from the beginning that the separation was only temporary. Mathilde was no longer fighting a character like Lucien Viotti, who effaced himself as a gentleman should. Rimbaud was furious. He had escaped his mother's penny-pinching and the killing dullness of Charleville, had tasted the chaotic delights of the Parisian Bohemia, and now he was back where he had started from six months before. And all because of a snobbish little bourgeoise, unable to tell good verse from bad, a woman Verlaine should never have married in the first place. He was stranded; but he still had his pen and his hold over Paul, and he proceeded to use both. His savage, adolescent pride burst forth in a series of violent letters. When later on Mathilde read them, she thought the writer must be insane. He accused Verlaine of sacrificing him to "a caprice"; and the suggestion Elisa had put forward – that he find work and stop living at her son's expense – aroused all his fury: "Le travail plus loin de moi que mon ongle l'est de mon œil. Merde pour moi! ... Quand vous me verrez manger positivement de la merde, alors seulement vous ne trouverez plus que je coûte trop cher à nourrir!..."[19]

Verlaine cringed before the storm in a delicious agony. His replies show his willing and infantile submission to a stronger personality. "Merci pour ta bonne lettre! Le *petit garçon* accepte la juste fessée ... et n'ayant jamais abandonné ton martyre, y pense, si possible, avec plus de *ferveur* et de joie encore ..." And then the

19 Rimbaud, Pléiade, 283; Mathilde, *Mémoires*, 212.

full, ecstatic confession, the most self-revelatory he ever wrote: "Aime-moi, protège et donne confiance. Etant très faible, j'ai très besoin de bontés." A month later, when Rimbaud's return was imminent: "Ecris-moi et me renseigne sur mes devoirs, la vie que tu entends que nous menions, les joies, affres, hypocrisies, cynismes, qu'il va falloir! Moi, tout tien, tout toi ... Dernière recommandation: dès ton retour, m'empoigner de suite, de façon à ce qu'aucun secouïsme, – et tu le pourras si bien!"[20]

Vain as the reconciliation with Mathilde therefore was, she nevertheless found her husband changed for the better, at least during the first weeks after her return. He was not drinking, and his mother had found him a job with the Belgian Lloyd. He went to the office every day; it was rather like the early months of their marriage all over again. The only bad sign (and Mathilde did not recognize it as such) was Verlaine's new friendship with Forain: "Un gentil garçon," she calls the artist, who was then twenty, "nullement intempérant; de là la sobriété relative de Verlaine, et je lui suis reconnaissante de cette courte accalmie dans mon existence." She did not suspect that Forain too was playing her false by receiving Rimbaud's letters. "Quand je vais avec la petite chatte brune je suis bon," Verlaine told her one day (Forain was dark), "parce que la petite chatte brune est très douce; quand je vais avec la petite chatte blonde, je suis mauvais, parce que la petite chatte blonde est féroce." Mathilde did not immediately understand who the *chattes* were. She soon learned.[21]

As far as we can fix the dates, Rimbaud was back in Paris by the middle of May, after an absence of something over two months. He brought some new poems, even better than the earlier ones. Meanwhile the first two of Verlaine's *Romances sans paroles* were about to appear.[22] For, by one of those fascinating contradictions of the human mind, this appalling pair were poets of genius; it even seems that the more outrageous their behaviour the better their verse.

20 Rimbaud, Pléiade, 281-82, 284-85.
21 Mathilde, *Mémoires*, 204.
22 "C'est l'extase langoureuse" and "Le piano que baise," in *La Renaissance littéraire et artistique*, May 18 and June 29, 1872.

The gossip about them before Rimbaud's exile may possibly have been exaggerated, but this was hardly the case after his return. As often happens, separation broke down what little reticence still existed; they met in a state of exasperated desire which culminated in something like pure algolagnia. "Mais quand diable commencerons-nous ce *chemin de croix?*" Verlaine had asked in his letter of April 2. Hints of what he meant have come down to us. Charles Cros told Mathilde that he was sitting with the two poets in a café shortly after Rimbaud's return. The boy asked his companions to put their hands on the table, he was going to show them an experiment. When they obeyed, thinking that it was a joke, Rimbaud whipped an open knife from his pocket. Cros was able to withdraw his hands in time, but Verlaine received several cuts on the wrist, and as they left the place, two or three jabs in the thighs. A police report (dated, it is true, a year later, and chiefly concerned with their stay in Belgium, but the details are too similar to be ignored) states that the two men "se battaient et se déchiraient comme des bêtes féroces, pour avoir le plaisir de *se raccommoder.*"[23] For if Verlaine tolerated such treatment the reason is obvious: he liked it. Besides satisfying his old desire for atonement, it relieved him of the responsibility of the male role he had to assume with Mathilde. The extraordinary sonnet, "Le Bon Disciple," which sums up as far as possible in fourteen lines just what his relations with Arthur Rimbaud meant to him dates from this moment, May 1872:

> Je suis élu, je suis damné!
> Un grand souffle inconnu m'entoure.
> O terreur! *Parce, Domine!*
>
> Quel Ange dur ainsi me bourre
> Entre les épaules tandis
> Que je m'envole aux Paradis?
>
> Fièvre adorablement maligne,
> Bon délire, benoît effroi,
> Je suis martyr et je suis roi,
> Faucon je plane et je meurs cygne!

23 The spy underlined the word himself. Auguste Martin, "Verlaine et Rimbaud."

> Toi le Jaloux qui m'as fait signe,
> Or me voici, voici tout moi!
> Vers toi je rampe encore indigne!
> – Monte sur mes reins, et trépigne!

It is one of Verlaine's best poems, and we need merely compare it with *La Bonne Chanson* to see how Rimbaud, with his genius, his beauty, and his sadism had reached depths in Paul's nature which Mathilde could not touch, which she did not even know existed: all the festering masochism, the stifled fascination for the abysses of sensation and desire. And since, obscurely, this imbalance was linked to his poetic faculty, to all that was best as well as worst in his unstable personality, Rimbaud's mastery was bound to be absolute.

Knives began to play an unpleasant role in the story generally. Sometime in the late spring of 1872, Elisa invited Paul and Mathilde to dinner. The poet was drunk. Each time his mother left the room he drew a blade from his pocket (Mathilde recognized it as one Rimbaud had stolen from her father's hunting equipment) and threatened her. With her usual well-bred calm she pretended to pay no attention, but secretly she was terrified; she knew what he was capable of. The evening ended with friends, the Burtys; and since Verlaine's muttered threats continued she told her hosts what was going on. They got her off by the back stairs, accompanied by Mme Burty's maid. Once home she had Georges' crib rushed downstairs, and when Verlaine got in Mme Mauté told him that Mathilde was unwell and would spend the night in a room next to her own. Verlaine began to draw his sword cane. But M. Mauté was still a vigorous man; he tore the weapon from his son-in-law's hands and told him sharply to go to bed. Did Verlaine hear, through the alcoholic smog that clogged his brain, some echo of the past, some accent of his father's voice imposing a discipline no one else could enforce? At any rate the order produced its effect; he went upstairs without another word.

Next day, as usual, he appeared ashamed, and the family agreed to say nothing for fear of renewing the scene. But when Mathilde went that afternoon to thank Mme Burty, she learned that Rimbaud was back in town; mutual friends had seen him several times. From then on the turmoil began again. The Mautés scarcely dared sleep, waiting in nervous tension for the drunkard's return, fearing murder for their daughter and grandson. Sometimes Verlaine would weep and swear to drink no more, but his remorse never lasted. "Il a toujours été l'homme des repentirs périodiques," says Mathilde, "la moitié de sa vie s'est passée à faire le mal et l'autre à se repentir ... Il avait une nature double, et, dans l'ivresse, la mauvaise reparaissait toujours."[24]

Things dragged on in this way until July 7, 1872. Mathilde awoke that morning with a slight fever. There had been no quarrel the night before. Verlaine even appeared in an affectionate mood; as he left for the Belgian Lloyd office he promised to send a doctor, and kissed his wife good-bye. No doctor came, nor did Verlaine return that evening. When next day he was still absent, M. Mauté set out to find him. He went first to Elisa's, who declared that she had not seen her son, then to the Belgian Lloyd, where he learned that Verlaine had dropped his job over a week before. He tried the police stations, even the morgue; all to no avail. At last he looked through the Latin Quarter cafés, where some of the habitués gave him a full account of what was being said about Verlaine and Rimbaud. For the time being he kept this information to himself, but it stayed in his mind. Verlaine's whereabouts remained unknown for a week, then Mathilde received a note from Brussels: "Ma pauvre Mathilde, n'aie pas de chagrin, ne pleur pas; je fais un mauvais rêve, je reviendrai un jour."[25]

Exactly what had happened is still uncertain. According to Verlaine's tale (which is usually accepted) he was walking away from the Mauté house to call a doctor when he met Rimbaud. The boy was tired of Paris and had come to tell him that he was leaving. "Why don't you come with me?" They hung about the city for the rest of the day, then got tickets for the north. Early next morning, in a café near Arras, they could not resist the temptation ot

24 Mathilde, *Mémoires*, 208. Rimbaud's comment on this point is interesting: "C'est un enfant charmant, violent et dangereux quand il a bu." Cazals and Le Rouge, *Les Derniers jours*, 134.
25 Mathilde, *Mémoires*, 210.

scandalize the other patrons with a whispered conversation, loud enough to be overheard, hinting at mysterious crimes. Public opinion was still touchy; the war and the Commune were vivid memories. Somebody notified the police and the two friends found themselves haled before a judge. Their papers were in order, and Verlaine had plenty of money; there was no reason to hold them. Nevertheless, the magistrate ordered them sent back to Paris. They reached the capital next day, less than twenty-four hours after their initial departure, went directly from the Gare du Nord to the Gare de l'Est, and entrained for Charleville. They made no effort to see Rimbaud's mother, but stopped with Charles Bretagne. After an evening of drink and talk, he hunted up a wagoner he knew, and they were driven over the frontier during the night of July 9-10. Next day they walked to Brussels.

This is the kind of story Verlaine liked to tell over his absinth during the last years of his life. It fitted his legend: the Bohemian genius who walked out on his wife without notice. Certain facts suggest that the departure was not quite so off-handed. His meeting with Rimbaud could hardly have been accidental; they had been spending every evening of the last two months together, and every day as well since Verlaine dropped his job with the Belgian Lloyd at the end of June. He was lying when he told Mathilde he was going to his office; he had had no office to go to for over a week. And Lepelletier writes that for some time Rimbaud had been demanding a complete rupture with Mathilde more and more imperiously.[26] He had never forgiven her for her brief victory in March; who knew when she might intervene again? And there is the matter of the money in Verlaine's wallet at the time of the Arras arrest; this alone shows that the escapade was planned in advance. Only one person could have supplied it – Elisa Verlaine – which means that she financed Paul's desertion of his wife. Her motives are not so obscure that we cannot guess at them. It may be true (as Mathilde herself states) that she had joined the Mautés in getting Rimbaud out of Paris in March, that she had found her son the job at the Belgian Lloyd, and done what she could to patch up his home. But she had never much liked the marriage.

26 Lepelletier, *Paul Verlaine*, 271.

Mathilde – the fact emerges everywhere in her memoirs – always considered her mother-in-law a very ordinary person: very provincial, almost half-peasant. Relations between them were "good," which seems to mean that they never actually came to blows, but Elisa must often have noticed a shade of amused tolerance, a hint of condescension, things impossible to forgive. The Mautés, too, had carried through the marriage negotiations with a high hand, almost suggesting that Verlaine was trying to marry above him. And what had been the result of their pretensions? Paul had signed a contract which loaded the girl on him without a dowry. Elisa considered that her son had been swindled.[27] But she connived at the final disaster for an even simpler and more elemental reason: maternal jealousy. She never wanted her son to marry at all. If the thing had to be done, then let it be for reasons of moral therapy, to some woman he did not love, like the Amazonian cousin from the provinces; a kind of glorified housekeeper who would bring up his children, provide a measure of domestic discipline, and leave Elisa in possession of his heart. Not to some charming, flighty baggage who would take him away from his mother. When she saw that Verlaine wanted a new plaything in the shape of Mathilde, when he began to stamp and scream, she did her best to get it for him. But she was biding her time. She must have felt a good deal of satisfaction when she discovered that things were going badly. She never scrupled to receive Rimbaud's letters to her son, and when Paul asked for money she knew would enable him to leave Paris, she handed it over without protest and lied to M. Mauté when he came looking for Verlaine next day. Her son wanted another toy, Rimbaud; she could satisfy him and appease her own jealousy at the same time. Till the end of her life she blamed Mathilde for the catastrophe. On the very few visits she paid the Mautés after Verlaine's departure, she suggested (with what sugary acrimony!) that had her son married his cousin all would

27 *Ibid.*, 272: "Mme Verlaine mère, trop indulgente pour les écarts de son fils ... consentit au départ de son fils. Elle lui fournit même des subsides. C'était un encouragement fâcheux, cet argent." Mathilde's opinion of Elisa was little more favourable than Elisa's of her; it pierces several times through the well-bred texture of the *Mémoires*: "Vieille paysanne intéressée et rancunière" (122); "les questions d'intérêt étaient les seules qui la touchassent véritablement" (190). She also mentions her "parcimonie ordinaire" (192).

have been well. M. Mauté was driven to outbursts of tragi-comic exasperation: "Mme Verlaine ne tarit pas en éloges sur Mlle X ... elle a eu la naïveté de me faire entendre que si son fils avait épousé cette personne, il n'aurait pas fait de sottises, il aurait évité ses malheurs ... Ah! combien je voudrais, moi aussi, qu'il eût épousé Mlle X ... Car cela était beaucoup mieux, en effet ... pour ma fille!"[28]

Whether Elisa understood the true nature of her son's relations with Arthur Rimbaud cannot be known. But if so, would she have behaved any differently? She would probably have concluded that, though his new passion might be monstrous, it had nothing of the legalized permanence of marriage. It destroyed all his resources and made her necessary to him again. Henceforth she was to be the only woman in his life, the one he turned to in time of need, the confidant of his struggles and his sufferings. She had won out against Mathilde; she dropped the Mautés completely and made no effort to see her grandchild. Paul alone interested her; with brief interruptions they were to be together until she died, and that was all she asked.

Verlaine and Rimbaud reached Brussels on July 10. What scraps of information we have of their life together are both illuminating and contradictory, as is usually the case where Verlaine is concerned. Now that he had Rimbaud he began to regret Mathilde. The situation was just the opposite of what it had been in March and April. "Ecris-moi toujours en deux parties séparées," he said in a letter to his mother, "l'une montrable à Rimbaud, l'autre relative à mon pauvre ménage."[29] It was now his friend he had to deceive, not his wife; he thought of her more and more as the days passed. His first letter to her was dated less than a week after he reached Belgium, and a few days later he wrote again, enclosing his Brussels address, the Hôtel Liégeois. He said that he had met some Communard exiles, and that he intended to write a book about them and about the excesses of the Versailles army. Since this would require time, he asked her to send him

28 Delahaye, *Verlaine*, 90.
29 Mathilde (*Mémoires*, 214) quotes this letter and says that Elisa showed it to her. One wonders why.

clothes and also some papers that were in an unlocked drawer in his desk. All this was merely an excuse for writing. He was putting her on his track. Subconsciously, he wanted her to be able to reach him.

As she went through the papers, Mathilde came on Rimbaud's letters to her husband. They enlightened her on a number of unpleasant facts, particularly as to the young man's departure for Charleville in March. Verlaine had sworn that it was a definite break, and she now learned that it had been nothing but a trick to get her back. She also discovered the savage grudge Rimbaud bore her; she discovered a good many other things which she did not understand, things so shocking that even in 1907, when she wrote her memoirs, she could not repeat them. And the tone of the letters, their violent abuse and sadistic invective, appalled her: "Ces lettres étaient tellement étranges," she says, "que je les crus écrites par un fou et fus très effrayée de voir Verlaine parti avec un pareil compagnon."[30] She was still reading when her father came in. He took the letters away from her, carried them off to his room, and locked them up.

During the next few days she thought the matter over and decided that she must try to save her husband. She could see no other solution than a trip to Brussels. She proposed it to her mother and father and they consented. Mme Mauté had always felt a certain amount of affection for her son-in-law, but how Mauté can have agreed to such a scheme is difficult to understand. He had seen Verlaine's brutality, and even more he had heard the stories that were current about Rimbaud. Although he had not acted on them at the time, they so impressed him that he stopped his daughter from reading Arthur's letters, and presumably he read them himself after taking them away from her. (His conduct even suggests prior knowledge; it is hard to see why he should confiscate the papers unless he already knew what they contained.) Perhaps he had had no suspicions when he took Mathilde to Périgueux, or stifled them if they occurred. But bland ignorance of this sort was now impossible. The letters proved that the gossip he had heard

30 *Ibid.*, 211-12.

was true, and that his son-in-law was not merely a dangerous alcoholic, but a homosexual as well, two things which, to a right-
minded bourgeois like M. Mauté, were the very depths of infamy.
Yet he let Mathilde go to Brussels for the sole purpose of persuading such a man to live with her again. The explanation doubtless lies in the nineteenth century's conception of marriage. It was
a tie not to be lightly broken. Divorce did not yet exist in France,
was not to exist until 1885. Separation alone was possible, and
since marriage was a respectable woman's only career, this meant
that she had to return to her parents if she left her husband.
Mathilde's union with Verlaine had been satisfactory as far as
money went; she had been settled with no financial hardship to
her father. And now he found her back on his hands, with a child
to boot. This was more than he had bargained for. He seems to
have been an easy-going man, and he was no miser. But he would
have welcomed any means of setting the marriage right. His behaviour at this moment shows once more how groundless were
Verlaine's subsequent accusations that his father-in-law came between husband and wife. If anything, Mauté closed his eyes to too
much.

Mathilde wrote Verlaine that she was coming to Brussels, and
left Paris on July 21, 1872, accompanied by her mother. In the
train she mulled over in her mind what she would say. The trip,
she declares, "fut un acte de pur dévouement" – "Depuis un an,
je n'avais pas cessé de souffrir ... tremblant pour la vie de mon enfant qui était aussi menacée que la mienne. En outre, je venais
d'avoir la preuve que les lettres affectueuses que mon mari m'avait
écrites pendant mon séjour dans le Midi n'étaient que pièges et
mensonges pour me faire revenir. Tout cela m'avait fortement
détachée de lui ..."[31] She decided that it would be impossible for
them to take up life in the rue Nicolet again. (Did she realize,
somewhat late, what a strain the arrangement had been on Verlaine?) It might be better to leave Paris altogether, even to leave
France. Verlaine had quarrelled with all his old friends over Rimbaud; there was nothing to keep him at home. A long voyage was

31 *Ibid.*, 215.

necessary, a good long one, so long that Rimbaud wouldn't be able to find them again. Why not New Caledonia? Lots of the old Communards had been exiled there; if Verlaine wanted to write about them, he could find no better place.

These statements are sincere enough. She only juggles the truth a little when she says that her love for Verlaine had waned. In reality, it was nearly as strong as ever. She was only a girl (her nineteenth birthday took place on April 17, 1872) and Verlaine had been the first man in her life. She owed him her sexual awakening, and this is a form of emotional slavery which even the strongest cannot always shake off. Had she understood Rimbaud's letters they might have helped her free herself, but she was too innocent; their dreadful import escaped her. Verlaine had loved her once; she had seen his despair when their marriage was twice postponed. He had written *La Bonne Chanson* for her. As the train rattled on towards the Belgian frontier she repeated some of the lines to herself. She could not believe that such passion was totally extinct; it was her trump card and she intended to play it.

The two women reached Brussels at five in the morning. When they got to the Hôtel Liégeois, they were told that Monsieur Verlaine no longer lived there; he had left word that he would come round at eight. Mathilde had committed her first tactical error: in forewarning her husband – and Rimbaud – of her arrival. They were consequently forearmed. One can suppose, without too much difficulty, the excitement her letter caused: the hasty search for other quarters, the furious confabulations, the plans drawn up, Rimbaud's irritation ("Pourquoi lui avoir donné ton adresse? Merde!"), Verlaine's desperate attempts at reassurance. When he knocked on Mathilde's door three hours after her arrival, he had just left Rimbaud and he was fully primed how to handle the situation. He had sworn that he would not yield as he had yielded in March. There would not be a second "martyrdom."

And yet, there very nearly was. Mathilde's instinct had been quite right; his love for her was by no means dead. And now he found her, affectionate and imploring, in a cosy bedroom. Both have left accounts of what happened; with minor discrepancies, the stories agree. According to Verlaine (as he wrote out the incident a month or two later in "Birds in the Night," one of *Romances sans paroles*), Mathilde was lying naked on the bed:

> Je vous vois encor. J'entr'ouvris la porte.
> Vous étiez au lit comme fatiguée.
> Mais, ô corps léger que l'amour emporte,
> Vous bondîtes nue, éplorée et gaie.
>
> O quels baisers, quels enlacements fous!

Mathilde says: "J'étais si heureuse de le retrouver ... que je me blottis dans ses bras, riant et pleurant à la fois ... Je proteste seulement," she adds primly, "contre le mot *nue*. Très fatiguée après une nuit passée en chemin de fer, je m'étais étendue sur le lit tout habillée de ma robe 'blanche et jaune à fleurs de rideaux'."[32] She is probably telling the truth; Verlaine's description is a bit too literary, with its reminiscent image of Aphrodite springing from the foam. Mathilde, after all, was a very well brought up young woman, and the idea of sprawling naked on a bed to wait for a man – even when he was her husband – was not likely to occur to her. But given Verlaine's inflammable temperament and her own desire to get him back, the flowered dress was an irrelevancy. If she was wearing it when he came in, she soon took it off, and this was her second – and fatal – error. Had she teased the satyr, kept the comfit-box of sex just out of his reach, she might have got him back to Paris; he might have deserted Rimbaud just as he had deserted her two weeks before. But she began where she should have left off; she let him glut himself within minutes of their reunion. The excitement over, they had to get dressed, and by then the poet's ardour had noticeably cooled. He was no longer facing an ecstatic nymph, but a wife. The old marital platitudes looked out at him from beneath her veil; it was the rue Nicolet all over again. "Birds in the Night" continues:

> Mais vous n'aviez plus l'humide gaîté
> Du plus délirant de tous nos tantôts.

32 *Ibid.*, 217, 234.

La petite épouse et la fille aînée
Etait reparue avec la toilette
Et c'était déjà notre destinée
Qui me regardait sous votre voilette.

In this atmosphere of slaked passion Mathilde was foolish enough to return to the attack. "Je dis mon affreux chagrin de son absence et le priai de revenir avec moi. Je ne veux pas raconter ici ce qu'il me répondit: ce n'était pas bien clair, pour moi surtout ... Ce qui est certain, c'est qu'il commença par refuser, ne voulant pas quitter Rimbaud."[33]

Verlaine was trying to explain his feeling for the younger poet, and we can well believe that what he said was not very clear. He could scarcely go into details; he had to be content with hints and half statements, and they were naturally incomprehensible to Mathilde who (as she says herself) had never even heard of such a thing as homosexual love. The police report to which I have already referred gives an account of this interview in which Verlaine is represented as telling Mathilde that Rimbaud possessed him to such a point that he was no longer his own master: "Je ne m'appartiens plus." – "La vie du ménage m'est odieuse," he added; "nous avons des amours de tigres!" He then showed her his chest, tattooed and scarred from knife-wounds Rimbaud had made.[34] This tale is hard to accept. We know that the two men fought with knives, but had Verlaine really shown his wife such evidence of their combats, it is strange that she does not mention it in her memoirs. It was a detail so shocking that she was unlikely to forget it, the more so as she well remembered the knife-play Charles Cros had told her about. And it is difficult to see how a police spy could come by such information. Mathilde and Verlaine were alone in their room, in an age before microphones and tape-recorders. There was nobody to overhear them unless some chambermaid were listening at the door; and this is unlikely if only because Mme Mauté was hovering in the background (she had

33 *Ibid.*, 217.
34 Martin, "Verlaine et Rimbaud."

effaced herself discreetly as soon as Verlaine appeared), and doubtless keeping an eye on her daughter's room. At all events, the conversation reached a stalemate, and it was then that Mathilde proposed her New Caledonian scheme. To her joy, Verlaine seemed
interested; he finally agreed to return to Paris with her. They
made an appointment to meet in a public garden at four that afternoon; the train was at five. He then left. And when Mme Mauté
came in, Mathilde told her that she had won him back.

In reality, she had finally lost him. The interview must have
been over by noon; how can she have been so heedless as to turn
her husband loose for four or five hours in a town where Arthur
Rimbaud was lurking? It was her third mistake, although by now
she had played her hand so badly that a few more scarcely made
much difference. Verlaine had no intention of going to Paris or
New Caledonia with her, or anywhere else. After the brief sexual
interlude, she had so badgered him (just like his relatives at Mme
Grandjean's funeral) that agreement was the only way of getting
away from her. He had wanted her back, yes; but only when she
was not there. Once he had her again, his need of Rimbaud reas-
serted itself; he returned to the young man, told him that he had
refused all Mathilde's propositions, and that he was going to escort
the two women to the train at four o'clock.

He was once more in the situation a weak man fears most: he
had to make up his mind. He had lied to Mathilde and Rimbaud
both; committed himself in two opposite directions at the same
time. When he came to the public garden he had been drinking,
and he probably did not yet know what he was going to do. He
let the ladies manoeuvre him onto the train, first buying himself a
cold chicken at the station buffet. He devoured the bird with his
hands, then dozed until the frontier. Everybody got out for the
customs examination, and when Mathilde and her mother reached
their seats again, Verlaine had disappeared. The train was just pull-
ing out when they saw him on the platform. "Montez vite!"
cried Madame Mauté. "Non, je reste!" And he drove his hat down
over his eyes with a blow of his fist. The platform glided by, lamp

standards, the station house. There was a bend in the line. He van-
ished from their sight and Mathilde never saw him again.

It was the end of the marriage. Nothing remained but to start
proceedings for a separation (and this time it was no bluff) which
M. Mauté did as soon as his daughter reached Paris. Exit Mathilde:
it was three years, almost day for day, since she had gone into her
brother's room and been introduced to Paul Verlaine. She does
not leave the scene without honour. It is easy to laugh at her, the
mediocre little bourgeoise, with her snobbery and her pretensions,
caught up in the frantic destiny of a great poet. But according to
her lights she acted throughout with courage and devotion. Looking back, it is difficult to see even one reprehensible action that can
be laid to her charge. True, she was no wife for Verlaine. But the
marriage was as much his doing as hers, and in any case, who
would have been a wife for Verlaine? Some foul-mouthed, brawling trollop with twenty years of the sidewalk behind her – a
Philomène Boudin or Eugénie Krantz, giving blow for blow,
curse for curse, tippling at the brandy bottle and liable to sudden
attacks of nostalgia for her old trade? It is hardly to Mathilde's
discredit that she was different. She had her faults: her memoirs
are not always veracious (but whose are?); she arranges matters a
little, tells fibs or glosses over inconvenient details. She does not
say that after divorcing Verlaine in 1885 and remarrying a year
later (the man was a building contractor, Delporte) she was again
divorced in 1905; it was hardly a fit conclusion to her role as mar-
tyred wife. And she was a snob to the end. She ran a boarding-
house at Nice during the last years of her life, until she died in
1914, yet she always craved distinction. Did she finally realize that
her frenzied marriage with Paul Verlaine was the nearest she ever
came to it? There is reason to suppose so. She was very much
flattered when some of his admirers invited her to attend the in-
auguration of a monument to him near Marseilles in 1908; there
he was in marble, as good as a President of the Republic. As the
years passed, she must often have noticed a gleam of curiosity in
the eyes of people she met, have overheard quickly smothered

murmurs when she entered a room: "You know who she was, don't you?" Perhaps she even came to expect it. But, such trifles aside, she did her best to tell the truth; her book is neither acrimonious nor unjust. She had married Verlaine because she loved him and admired his talent. She put up with treatment so shocking that it came very close to murder, and even tried to get him back afterwards. Few wives have less to reproach themselves with. If things ended badly, she could say with perfect truth that it was not her fault.

5/Rimbaud/
Romances sans paroles/
The Brussels drama

THE TRAIN HAD SCARCELY disappeared down the track when Verlaine scribbled off an obscene note of rupture. It reached Paris next morning. All the pent-up irritation of that long day burst forth, a torrent of insult and childish spite: "Misérable fée carotte, princesse souris, punaise qu'attendent les deux doigts et le pot, vous m'avez fait tout, vous avez peut-être tué le cœur de mon ami; je rejoins Rimbaud, s'il veut encore de moi après cette trahison que vous m'avez fait faire."[1] Which proves that Rimbaud had been waiting somewhere in Brussels ever since four that afternoon. It would be interesting to know just how Verlaine explained his long absence.

He was now launched on his destiny, although, in his heedlessness, he may not have realized the fact. He had left Paris with Rimbaud on July 7, 1872; they were to separate catastrophically in Brussels a year later – July 10, 1873. The episode has left its mark on literary history; during the course of it Verlaine wrote *Romances sans paroles*, and Rimbaud composed (or conceived) *Les Illuminations* and *Une Saison en Enfer*.[2] With its setting of cheap hotels and rooming houses, misty sunlight in Belgium and massive gloom in London, plunging Channel crossings on Victorian steam-packets, curses, tears, raging letters, sudden ruptures, and ecstatic reunions, the story is one of the strangest on record. Other escapades of the

1 Mathilde, *Mémoires*, 219.
2 On the dates of composition see the excellent notes in Rimbaud, Pléiade.

same kind – George Sand's flight to Venice with Alfred de Musset
– pale into insignificance by comparison. Elisa, now hovering in
the background, now directly involved, the innocent bystander
of that delirious saraband, provided the cash. She later said that
the twelve-month spree cost her 30,000 francs – a colossal sum in
those days, perhaps an exaggeration; but even if we reduce it by
half the total is still impressive.[3] Captain Verlaine's little fortune
was well on the way to extinction, and the sordid rooms in the
Hôtel du Midi, half hotel, half brothel of the Cour Saint-François,
were awaiting their tenants like a heavy stage-set, ready in the
wings for the appropriate cue. At any time during the next few
years, as she went down the rue de Lyon, Elisa could turn beneath
the massive arches of the elevated railroad and contemplate the
last scene of her life.

The first six weeks were spent in Belgium, in the kind of Bohemian vagabondage Verlaine loved. "Laeti et errabundi" he called it in *Parallèlement* – "happy and wandering." It recalled his
adolescent debauches in much the same district ten years before.
Promenades in Brussels, Malines, Bruges, and other towns, visits
to country fairs, long stations at café tables, and always the evasion
from reality that comes through absorption in another personality. The pair made no secret of their relationship: "A Bruxelles,
on a vu les deux amants pratiquer ouvertement leurs amours."[4]
They behaved even more flagrantly than in Paris; and to an impartial observer, it must have looked as though they were enjoy-
ing themselves thoroughly. But as their intimacy deepened, so did
certain fundamental differences of temperament and intention
which were to widen into a chasm nothing could bridge.

To Verlaine, the whole adventure was instinctive and sensuous,
an abdication of responsibility: "Je nous voyais comme deux bons
enfants," are the words Rimbaud puts into his mouth in *Une Saison en Enfer*, "libres de se promener dans le Paradis de tristesse."
Childhood, freedom, Paradise: the three terms give us the essentials. Even the sexual factor played a secondary role by compari-

---

3 Mathilde, *Mémoires*, 222. Elisa told her this at the time of the separation demand.
4 Martin, "Verlaine et Rimbaud."

son. Emotionally trapped in memories of his first years, Verlaine was forever seeking to combine them with the brutal facts of adulthood. It was an obstinate tropism towards a security he never found. To think that he had found it in Rimbaud was of course illusory, but the victims of this sentimental entropy pay no heed to the lessons of experience and the evidence of the senses. Each new adventure is the ultimate one, resolving all contradictions; his affection for Rimbaud poured forth in a cloying flood, unastringed by judgment or restraint. He used to rise at night to watch his sleeping companion, and murmur with incoherent tenderness over the miracle of their life together:

> Ce soir, je m'étais penché sur ton sommeil ...
> Qu'on vive, ô quelle délicate merveille,
> Tant notre appareil est une fleur qui plie![5]

This sort of thing was hardly to Rimbaud's taste. He was eighteen, an age when deep emotion is usually embarrassing, and his nature was intellectual: he viewed the break-up of Verlaine's marriage and the flight from Paris as part of his programme of *raisonné dérèglement de tous les sens*, not as a search for yet another sentimental Eden. Talk of "wilting flowers" and "delicate marvels" struck him as ridiculous; his contempt for Verlaine, embryonic ever since they first met, began to turn precise and savage. The sketches he has left of him border on the grotesque: "Pitoyable frère!" he says of these bedside scenes. "Que d'atroces veillées je lui dus! ... 'Je m'étais joué de son infirmité. Par ma faute nous retournerions en exil, en esclavage.' ... Presque chaque nuit, aussitôt endormi, le pauvre frère se levait ... et me tirait dans la salle en hurlant son songe de chagrin idiot. J'avais en effet, en toute sincérité d'esprit, pris l'engagement de le rendre à son état primitif de fils du soleil."[6] The ambition, he discovered, was impossible; Verlaine was a weak instrument that broke in the hand. The *chagrin idiot* refers to Mathilde, and this point was a further source of

---

5 Finally published twelve years later in *La Revue critique*, 28 mars 1884, and then in *Jadis et Naguère* as "Vers pour être calomnié," Verlaine, Pléiade, 330, 1151.
6 *Les Illuminations*, XVIII, "Vagabonds," Rimbaud, Pléiade, 190.

discord. Even after the fiasco at the Hôtel Liégeois, Verlaine kept writing his wife in hopes of a reconciliation, and Rimbaud must have been aware of the fact. In *Une Saison en Enfer* he dubs Verlaine "the Foolish Virgin" (and himself "the Infernal Bridegroom": the very titles tell us a good deal about the nature of their relations), depicts him wallowing in self-pity, and notes his growing religious tendencies. The passage is remarkable, foretelling as it does Verlaine's subsequent conversion: "O divin Époux, mon Seigneur, ne refusez pas la confession de la plus triste de vos servantes," the Foolish Virgin implores Christ. "Je suis perdue. Je suis soûle. Je suis impure. Quelle vie! ... Que de larmes! et que de larmes encore plus tard, j'espère! Plus tard, je connaîtrai le divin Époux! Je suis née soumise à Lui. – L'autre peut me battre maintenant! ... Ah! je souffre, je crie. Je souffre vraiment. ... Je suis esclave de l'Époux infernal, celui qui a perdu les vierges folles ... Lui était presque un enfant ... Ses délicatesses mystérieuses m'avaient séduite. J'ai oublié tout mon devoir humain pour le suivre ... C'est un Démon, vous savez, *ce n'est pas un homme*. Il dit: 'Je n'aime pas les femmes. L'amour est à réinventer ...' Je l'écoute faisant de l'infamie une gloire, de la cruauté un charme ... A côté de son cher corps endormi, que d'heures des nuits j'ai veillé, cherchant pourquoi il voulait tant s'évader de la réalité."

It was the tragic situation between love and indifference, where the partner who loves most is always the victim. *Une Saison en Enfer* is one of the few cases in literature where the indifferent one has undertaken to express the victim's agonies: "Je lui dis quelquefois: 'Je te comprends.' Il haussait les épaules ... J'avais de plus en plus faim de sa bonté. Avec ses baisers et ses étreintes amies, c'était bien un ciel, un sombre ciel où j'entrais, et où j'aurais voulu être laissée, pauvre, sourde, muette, aveugle ... Je nous voyais comme deux bons enfants, libres de se promener dans le Paradis de tristesse."[7]

Just as in his relations with Mathilde, the childhood fixation dominated every crisis of Verlaine's dealings with Rimbaud, and it is all the more striking when we recall that he was ten years

7 *Une Saison en Enfer, ibid.*, 228, *sqq.*

older than his friend. The two children image sounds as though
he had told Arthur about his hours of play on the Esplanade at
Metz, which is very probable. He used the same image himself in
the fourth *Ariette oubliée* of *Romances sans paroles*, composed about
this time: "Soyons deux enfants, soyons deux jeunes filles." The
memory of that Edenic calm still obsessed him; like all those in
love he asked for permanence, while Rimbaud, given his age and
temperament, craved perpetual change, and made no secret of the
fact that, as far as he was concerned, their relationship was purely
transitory – always the worst threat to which love is exposed. To
quote the Foolish Virgin again: "Après une pénétrante caresse, il
disait: 'Comme ça te paraîtra drôle, quand je n'y serai plus, ce par
quoi tu as passé. Quand tu n'auras plus mes bras sous ton cou, ni
mon cœur pour t'y reposer, ni cette bouche sur tes yeux. Parce
qu'il faudra que je m'en aille, très loin, un jour ...' Tout de suite
je me pressentais, lui parti, en proie au vertige, précipitée dans
l'ombre la plus affreuse: la mort. Je lui faisais promettre qu'il ne
me lâcherait pas. Il l'a faite vingt fois, cette promesse d'amant.
C'était aussi frivole que moi lui disant: 'Je te comprends.'"[8] The
older man was reduced to the emotional prying and desperate
supplications which defeat their own end by driving the loved one
to exasperation. Like so many others in the same position, Rimbaud felt no pity for these sentimental tempests. He considered
them further proofs of Verlaine's inability to follow the path of
the seer: "Drôle de ménage!" he concludes his sketch of their life
together: he already foresaw the end.

It was perhaps this antinomy between them, and the sense of
ultimate disaster they both shared, that led them to embark for
London on September 7, 1872. Faced with Rimbaud's bouts of
boredom and impatience, forced to realize that his own company
was not enough to keep the boy amused, Verlaine may have
thought that a change of scene, new experiences shared in common, would strengthen the bonds between them. And there was
also the money problem. As Delahaye (one of Rimbaud's school
chums) tells the story, finances had run low and the two poets

8 *Ibid.*, 231.

hoped to make a living for themselves in England. Both were totally unrealistic in such matters, Rimbaud as much as Verlaine. They thought that as French teachers they would find a better market for their talents in London than in Brussels, where everybody spoke the language. Besides which England had its attractions; they were both interested in English literature, and Verlaine knew in advance that he would not be among total strangers: a number of his old Communard friends were living in exile in London. It was one of them, the designer Régamey, who found him rooms (34-35 Howland Street, Fitzroy Square), and the next few weeks were spent exploring the metropolis. Régamey describes Verlaine as gay, cheerful, and apparently without worries of any sort: "Il est beau à sa manière, et quoique fort peu pourvu de linge, il n'a nullement l'air d'être terrassé par le sort. Nous passons des heures charmantes. Mais il n'est pas seul. Un camarade muet l'accompagne, qui ne brille pas non plus par l'élégance. C'est Rimbaud."[9] The same outward cheerfulness appears in Verlaine's letters to Lepelletier. They give a vivid picture of late-Victorian London: the gloomy evangelical Sundays, the piled up energy and squalor of the great city, its strange mixture of vice and prudery, all set down in bright, vivacious terms such as only a Frenchman (and a Frenchman like Verlaine) could have found.

"Plate comme une punaise qui serait noire, London! Petites maisons noirousses, ou grands bahuts 'gothiques' et 'vénitiens'; quatre ou cinq cafés potables, et encore! ... Tout le reste c'est des dining rooms, où l'on ne boit pas, ou des coffee-houses, d'où l'Esprit (spirits) est soigneusement écarté. 'Nous ne tenons pas d' 'esprit', m'a répondu une 'maid' à qui je posais cette question insidieuse: 'One absinth, if you please, Mademoisell!, [sic] Une nuée de boys rouges frotte vos bottes du soir au matin, pour un penny. Quand ils ont obtenu, grâce à leur mélange sirupeux, ce vernis ... ils lèchent positivement votre soulier, et repartent de plus belle, la brosse molle d'une pince et de l'autre la brosse dure! et la botte reluit, sacrebleu! ... Et les théâtres! L'odeur des pieds montait! ... Dans les cafés-concert, Alhambra, Grecian Theatre,

9 Quoted by Underwood, *Verlaine et l'Angleterre*, 57.

etc., on y danse la gigue, entre deux *God save* ... La Tamise est
superbe! Figure-toi un immense tourbillon de boue: quelque chose
comme un gigantesque goguenot débordant. Ponts véritablement
babyloniens, avec des centaines de piles en fonte ... et peintes en
rouge-sang ... Grâce à l'inouïe circulation de voitures, cabs, om-
nibus, infects par parenthèse, tramways, chemins de fer incessants
sur des ponts de fonte splendides de grandeur lourde, passants in-
croyablement brutaux, criards ... l'aspect des rues est sinon parisien ... du moins très distrayant ... Au résumé, très inattendu, tout
ça, et cent fois plus amusant que les Italie, Espagne et autres bords
du Rhin." – "Les établissements de consommation anglais propre-
ment dits méritent une description ... La devanture est en bois
couleur d'acajou, mais avec de gros ornements de cuivre. A hau-
teur d'homme, le vitrage est en verre dépoli, avec des fleurs,
oiseaux, etc. ... Tout petit l'intérieur: au comptoir d'acajou une
tablette en zinc, le long duquel, soit debout, soit perchés sur de
très hauts tabourets ... boivent, fument et nasillent messieurs bien
mis, pauvres hideux, portefaix tout en blanc, cochers bouffis ...
Derrière le comptoir, des garçons en bras de chemise retroussés,
ou des jeunes femmes généralement jolies, toutes ébouriffées, élé-
gamment mises avec mauvais goût, et qu'on pelotte de la main,
de la canne ou du parapluie, avec de gros rires, et apparemment de
gros mots, qui sont loin de les effaroucher ... Aujourd'hui diman-
che: aoh! very dull! Tout fermé. Nul commerce. Les boîtes aux
lettres fermées aussi. Pas de décrotteurs ... Trop vantés les 'lieux à
l'anglaise'. L'eau envahit tellement la cuvette que le 'visiteur' se
voit et se sent éclaboussé ... Les lieux dans les cafés s'appellent
lavatory, parce qu'il y a des robinets, cuvettes, savons dans l'endroit
même. Quand vous sortez, vous tombez ès-mains de jeunes garçons, qui, pour deux sous, vous brossent des pieds à la tête:
j'ignore ce que, pour un peu plus, ils doivent faire aux bien in-
formés, mais ils ont l'air formidablement suspect, avec leur petit
costume collant, et leurs figures généralement charmantes." – "Vu
Macbeth. L'orchestre prélude par l'ouverture de *la Dame Blanche*,
et, dans les entractes, joue des quadrilles d'Olivier Métra. D'ailleurs, d'assez beaux décors. Ceci à Princess Théâtre." – "C'est très

bien cette incroyable ville, noire comme les corbeaux et bruyante
comme les canards; prude avec *tous les vices se proposant*; saoûle
sempiternellement ... immense ... sans monuments aucuns, sauf
ses interminables docks (qui suffisent d'ailleurs à ma poétique de
plus en plus moderniste). C'est très bien, au fond!"[10]

This carefree existence (although with *Une Saison en Enfer* before us we can see that it was only superficially carefree) was suddenly interrupted by a broadside from the rue Nicolet. Mathilde
filed a request for permanent separation on October 2, 1872, and
on the 13th was granted custody of Georges and authorized to
take up residence with her parents. She had described her husband's brutality, told of his flight with Rimbaud, and even worse,
produced Rimbaud's letters as evidence. The accusation of homosexuality was now official and was soon widely known in Parisian
literary circles, where it was taken as confirming previous gossip.
When the news reached Verlaine he was sincerely dismayed.
However strange the fact may seem, he had never (as I have
pointed out more than once) visualized a complete break with his
wife. He might insult her grossly, as in the letter he sent her after
their Brussels meeting, but that was only an infantile paroxysm;
he probably did not even remember it. And the accusation of abnormal relations with Rimbaud was something he refused to admit until his last years – and even then only when he was drunk.
To meet his wife's charges he decided to separate from Rimbaud
once again, so that we can allow Mathilde one last victory over
the boy, although by now she cared nothing either way. Rimbaud
returned to Charleville in November 1872; Verlaine remained in
London, writing letters to his Paris friends in a tone of outraged
virtue: "Quant à l'immonde accusation, je la pulvérise ... et en
rejette tout le dégoûtant opprobre sur ces misérables ... Toute
cette affaire de cul ... est une simple intimidation (*sive* chantage), à
l'effet d'une pension plus grosse."[11] He even visited the French
Embassy and told one of the attachés there (for what reason we
can only guess) that his wife's charges were false.

10 Lepelletier, *Paul Verlaine*, chap. IX, *passim*.
11 Letter to Lepelletier of 8 novembre 1872, *Correspondance*, I, 55.

False or not, they had disturbed him seriously, and Rimbaud also – as we see from a curious episode. Shortly before quitting London, Arthur wrote his mother and asked her to go to Paris, see the Mautés, and persuade them to drop the separation demand. The scene between the grim matron and elegant little Mathilde must have been interesting; it is a pity that Mathilde refers to it so briefly. "La bonne dame venait tout simplement me demander de renoncer à la séparation, parce que, disait-elle, cela pourrait nuire à son fils. Je la reçus poliment, mais je n'ai pas besoin de dire que sa démarche n'eut pas de succès."[12] After the failure of her mission, Mme Rimbaud wrote her son that the only way to disprove the wife's allegations was to leave Verlaine; she therefore knew what grounds Mathilde was pleading.

At first glance, it seems surprising that the two poets, with their professed scorn for convention, should have yielded to such pressure. Verlaine, indeed, as Rimbaud's portrait of him in *Une Saison en Enfer* proves, was always haunted by a feeling of sin, and never gave up hope of reconstructing his home. But what of his haughty young friend? Considering his intransigent ideas, one would have supposed him indifferent to any accusation, however degrading. The truth is that he was heedless, cynical, violent, and overbearing; but only when he could be so with impunity. Faced with genuine authority, all his truculence oozed away, as when, eight months later in front of the Brussels magistrates, he denied any perverted relations with Verlaine, even though he had been parading them for over a year. He also had an eye to the future, which was his reason for sending his mother to see Mathilde; he had no desire to be cited as co-respondent in a separation demand. There was a hard peasant sense of realities in him; he was already thinking of another career (in teaching, in trading) and he quite understood that a scandal might be harmful later on. And fear of Mathilde was not his only reason for leaving Verlaine – at least for a time.

12 Mathilde, *Mémoires*, 223. Verlaine mentions, not this visit, but its possibility in a letter to Lepelletier of 14 novembre 1872. "Rimbaud a récemment écrit à sa mère pour l'avertir de tout ce que l'on disait et faisait contre nous, et je suis à présent en correspondance réglée avec elle. Je lui ai donné ton adresse et celle des Mauté." *Correspondance*, I, 71.

He was growing more and more tired of his friend's obstreperous affection, particularly in London in an atmosphere of ebbing finance.

Abandoned in England and alone, Verlaine fell sick. By the end of December 1872, he had written both Mathilde and Elisa, begging them to come to him. Characteristically (he was always Verlaine) he asked Elisa to send Rimbaud money so that he could make the trip also. Mathilde left the missive unopened, but Elisa was in London by the first week in January. She brought one of Verlaine's Dehée cousins with her (perhaps the same girl she had tried to get him to marry four years before) and a family tradition represents her as doing her best to bring about a sick-bed repentance – preaching a return to Mathilde and to respectability. It is probably a tradition and nothing more. Elisa disapproved of her son's chaotic life (it was ruining her) but after the way she had behaved to the Mautés it is hard to imagine her trying to re-establish the marriage, nor can she have brought the cousin with her for matrimonial reasons, since divorce was not yet possible by French law. And if she wanted Verlaine to go back to Mathilde – or to interest himself in another woman – why did she act on his request and send money to Rimbaud for the trip to England? He reached London two days after her. This is another of those extraordinary facts that are forever cropping up in the story of Verlaine's relations with his mother. However we consider her behaviour, it is inconsistent with any desire to mollify Mathilde or to find another wife.

She stayed a month, then returned to France early in February, leaving Rimbaud once more in possession of the field. That he remained with Verlaine we know from his reader's card at the British Museum, dated March 25, 1873, which he obtained by declaring brazenly that he was over twenty-one, when in fact he was not yet nineteen. From now until they finally separated, they led a life of quarrels and reconciliations – explained partly by the fact that they were incompatible, partly by Verlaine's increasing regret for his ruined home. On April 4, they left England suddenly for Belgium. The trip seems to have been another effort on Verlaine's part to appease Mathilde. Rimbaud went to his mother's farm at Roche, not far from Charleville, and continued working at *Une Saison en Enfer*; Verlaine settled at Jehonville with his aunt Julie Evrard. He was once more in touch with priests, including his old friend the Abbé Delogne. They had not lost sight of him; they pressed him to regularize his life and return to the Church, and he promised to do so. He also asked them to intervene in his favour with Mathilde. He may have been serious, although what he expected to do about Rimbaud is a question. In any case, Mathilde had had enough – even when told that her husband was seriously ill from "a cerebral attack" (whatever that may mean). She not only refused to see him again, but wrote a brief note requesting him to stop bothering her with his letters.[13]

During the six weeks at Mme Evrard's house, Verlaine completed *Romances sans paroles* and sent the manuscript to Lepelletier on May 19. It was dedicated to Rimbaud. "Je tiens beaucoup à la dédicace à Rimbaud," Verlaine wrote. "D'abord *comme protestation*, puis parce que ces vers ont été faits, lui étant là et m'ayant poussé beaucoup à les faire."[14] The book owed its genesis to their life together from the winter of 1871-72 to the early months of 1873. We are therefore surprised, reading it, to discover that it contains a good deal more of Mathilde than of Arthur. Out of a total of twenty-three poems, five are in her honour – either by allusion or direct address – and one of them, "Birds in the Night," is the longest of all, eighty-four lines. Rimbaud only appears under camouflage; Verlaine had not yet reached the stage of complete avowal as in *Parallèlement* seventeen years later, although several of the *Parallèlement* themes (the identification of Rimbaud with movement and innovation) can be detected.

There are three sections, *Ariettes oubliées*, *Paysages belges* and *Aquarelles*; ("Birds in the Night" stands by itself). The first of the *Ariettes* dates from the spring of 1872. Given the circumstances of Verlaine's life at that moment, it is hard to see to whom the poem could be addressed if not to Rimbaud. It is a delicate, ecstatic

13 Mathilde, *ibid.*
14 *CML*, I, 1039. Lepelletier apparently persuaded him to drop this dedication.

treatment of fresh love, rather in the style of the best of *La Bonne Chanson*.[15] The poet was celebrating his new passion in the same terms he had employed for the old (forest wind, twilight, bird-song); as yet he had no others at his command:

> C'est l'extase langoureuse,
> C'est la fatigue amoureuse,
> C'est tous les frissons des bois
> Parmi l'étreinte des brises,
> C'est, vers les ramures grises,
> Le chœur des petites voix.

The second piece alludes to the old problem of sexual dualism which, with Rimbaud's advent, had assumed a new urgency:

> Je devine, à travers un murmure,
> Le contour subtil des voix anciennes ...
>
> Et mon âme et mon cœur en délires
> Ne sont plus qu'une espèce d'œil double
> Où tremblote à travers un jour trouble
> L'ariette, hélas! de toutes lyres!
>
> Ô mourir de cette mort seulette
> Que s'en vont, – cher amour qui t'épeures, –
> Balançant jeunes et vieilles heures!
> Ô mourir de cette escarpolette!

This poem first appeared (in *La Renaissance artistique et littéraire*, 22 septembre 1872) as "L'Escarpolette," and *escarpolette* is certainly the key word. The swing, the oscillation between sensuous extremes: at one end of the parabola Mathilde ("le contour subtil des voix anciennes"), at the other Rimbaud ("l'ariette, hélas! de toutes lyres!"). Drawn in contradictory directions, each point of the trajectory equidistant from a fixed sexual obsession, the poet's nature is fatally divided, becomes "une espèce d'œil double," anxious for the new yet regretting the old – the "jeunes et vieilles heures." The fourth poem (also of 1872) subtitled "De la douceur, de la douceur, de la douceur," sounds like a plea for reconciliation with Rimbaud after one of their numerous quarrels. The feminine

15 See Mathilde's ironic comment on these poems, *Mémoires*, 233-35.

adjectives ("heureuses," "pleureuses") surprise at first glance until we come to their justification, the "âmes sœurs" of the second stanza:

> Il faut, voyez-vous, nous pardonner les choses:
> De cette façon nous serons bien heureuses
> Et si notre vie a des instants moroses,
> Du moins nous serons, n'est-ce pas? deux pleureuses.
>
> O que nous mêlions, âmes sœurs que nous sommes,
> À nos yeux confus la douceur puérile
> De cheminer loin des femmes et des hommes,
> Dans le frais oubli de ce qui nous exile!
>
> Soyons deux enfants, soyons deux jeunes filles ...
> Qui s'en vont pâlir sous les chastes charmilles ...

Is there here (as I have already suggested) some far off, perhaps unconscious memory of the Esplanade at Metz, a theme which may also lie behind a phrase in *Une Saison en Enfer*? At any rate the lines are very characteristic of this side of Verlaine: a desire for escape ("frais oubli") from the problems of adulthood into the heedless world of "deux enfants, deux jeunes filles." Nowhere is the antinomy between illusion and reality more obvious. The "deux enfants" in question were a sentimental lecher and a brutal young iconoclast who can hardly have relished hearing himself described as a *pleureuse* and a *jeune fille*, and who certainly had no intention of going off to *pâlir sous les chastes charmilles*.

Poems five and seven of this section belong to Mathilde. The first, "Le piano que baise une main frêle," probably refers to one of their evenings together when Mme Mauté sat at the piano. The second is an exquisite example of what Rimbaud called *chagrin idiot*. Even though the poet had deserted his wife he still longed for her.

> Ô triste, triste était mon âme
> A cause, à cause d'une femme ...
>
> Je ne me suis pas consolé,
> Bien que mon cœur s'en soit allé.

Other poems to Mathilde are equally fine, notably "Green" and "Spleen" of the last part, *Aquarelles*.[16] Reading these delicate lines ("Green" is one of the most beautiful of all love-songs) with Mathilde's account of Verlaine in mind, it is hard to believe that the same man is in question. Of course, she was no longer with him when he wrote; he began the poems about the time of her flight to Périgueux and continued writing in Belgium and London. Had they been living together she would doubtless have inspired nothing but a row.

Romances sans paroles, indeed, is one of the best examples in literature of how poetic imagination and sensibility can transform the sordid and the banal into symbols of enduring beauty. The personal element, the tragi-comic disaster of marriage, the insane flight with a teen-age youth, are beside the point by comparison with the verse they occasioned. This is particularly true of *Ariettes oubliées*: poetry of like quality exists nowhere else in French. It is the successful expression of what Verlaine had been groping for in his first collections, and had only partly achieved ("En sourdine," "La lune blanche"): an attenuation of meaning, a harmony trembling on the verge of silence. The title of the volume suggests what he was trying to do (he borrowed it from Mendelssohn, *Songs without Words*) and he had had it in mind since at least the "À Clymène" of *Fêtes galantes*:

> Mystiques barcarolles,
> Romances sans paroles ...

He achieves his effects partly by a syllabification in odd numbers (five out of the nine *Ariettes* are written this way; a year later, in "Art poétique," he was to make the technique one of the rules of composition), partly by an unparalleled skill in managing vowel sounds and alliteration. The most evanescent impressions are captured, felt rather than heard, murmurs of a summer night, music in the dusk, the mysterious rustle of city rain:

> Ô le frêle et frais murmure!

16 If "Spleen" really refers to Mathilde and not to Rimbaud. See Eléonore M. Zimmermann, *Magies de Verlaine*, 60, note 13 for a full discussion of the problem.

> Cela gazouille et susurre,
> Cela ressemble au cri doux
> Que l'herbe agitée expire ...
>
> ...
>
> Ô bruit doux de la pluie
> Par terre et sur les toits!
> Pour un cœur qui s'ennuie
> Ô le chant de la pluie!

All the poems inspired by Mathilde are not equally good. Some are downright bad, particularly "Birds in the Night" and "Child Wife." Both belong to the rhymed anecdote category, for which Verlaine had a weakness and where he was not at his best, but their main defect is even graver. They give his version of the rupture with Mathilde, and, considering the truth behind that catastrophe, they are shamelessly mendacious, written in a tone of pompous sorrow and noble self-deception which sets the reader's teeth on edge. Verlaine was not only lying; he believed his own lies.

> Vous n'avez pas eu toute patience ...
> Vous n'avez pas eu toute la douceur ...
> Aussi, me voici plein de pardons chastes,
> Non, certes! joyeux, mais très calme en somme
> Bien que je déplore en ces mois néfastes
> D'être, grâce à vous, le moins heureux homme.

This from the husband who had deserted her for Rimbaud, and who was still living with Rimbaud when he wrote.

> Vous n'avez rien compris à ma simplicité,
>   Rien, ô mon pauvre enfant! ...
> Et vous n'aurez pas su la lumière et l'honneur
>   D'un amour brave et fort,
> Joyeux dans le malheur, grave dans le bonheur,
>   Jeune jusqu'à la mort![17]

All faults, in short, are laid at Mathilde's door. For the rest of his

17 "Child Wife."

life Verlaine maintained this version with childish obstinacy, growing more and more acrimonious and insulting as his complaints went unanswered. He was even capable of accusing Mathilde of leaving *him*: "C'est moi le quitté," he wrote Victor Hugo on October 4, 1872. We like him better when, in a moment of cynical honesty, he admitted that "c'est moi qui ait fait ma femme c..., et encore d'une drôle de façon!"[18] But such lucidity was rare; his general tone is one of whining self-pity, and the whole episode is the most discreditable in his career.

Yet, if nothing can excuse the smugness of "Birds in the Night" and "Child Wife," nor the sullen peevishness of the other verse and prose he subsequently emptied over Mathilde's head, we cannot deny that, from the point of view of poetry, his escape from the trammels of marriage was sheer necessity. I have attempted to do Mathilde justice; perhaps the time has come, apropos of *Romances sans paroles*, to render her husband the same service. Verlaine was not just another debauchee, with odd sexual cravings and a taste for alcohol and wife-beating. He was also a poet; and, without subscribing to the Romantic notion that sets genius above all moral laws, we have to admit that this fact outweighs everything else. Seduced by a passing fancy, he had uttered the fatal "Verweile doch, du bist so schön"; and the Mephistopheles who ruled his destiny had seized, not his soul, but something more precious: his poetic genius. During the two years he lived with Mathilde he wrote nothing. This is one of those unpleasant truths which can neither be denied nor argued away. It means that Mathilde could no longer provide the sort of stimulation he needed. For this reason alone he was justified in acting as he did. Let us suppose that Rimbaud had never appeared, that the marriage had jogged on with its ups and downs as so many incompatible unions have done before and since. Verlaine's life would have been a failure in the sense that he would never have written his best poetry; we should have neither *Romances sans paroles*, nor *Sagesse*, nor *Jadis et Naguère*, nor *Parallèlement*. Little effort is needed to imagine

18 Quoted by J. H. Bornecque, "Les Dessous des Mémoires d'un veuf," *Revue des Sciences humaines*, avril-juin 1952.

his existence under such circumstances: a job of some kind, an outward respectability, with periodic bouts of clandestine debauchery and a growing reputation as an alcoholic; from time to time a book of verse, never going beyond the first volumes and therefore showing an obvious decline. Literary history is full of such abortive careers; one of Verlaine's friends, Albert Mérat, ended in just this way.

Rimbaud seems to have understood the danger. He saw that his friend's genius, as it appeared in the first collections, was passive and involuntary, liable to weak caprice and disconcerting lapses. He encouraged Verlaine to compose *Romances sans paroles* as a rediscovery of a poetic vein that had been almost entirely lost. It is worth noting that the first title Verlaine thought of was *La Mauvaise Chanson*, hardly relevant to the content, but a clear indication that the book was intended as a reaction against the facile outpourings to his fiancée. When Rimbaud spoke of liberty in his letters – "Avec moi seul tu peux être libre" – he meant liberty to create new poetry, to expand further the verbal and harmonic frontiers.

Romances sans paroles justifies him completely. Verlaine not only developed to the utmost the lyric and suggestive sides of his talent (*Ariettes oubliées* alone contains some of the world's purest lyric verse), he also made a number of technical experiments of great interest. In the sections entitled *Paysages belges* and *Aquarelles* he attempted light, quick sketches of the towns and landscapes seen during his travels in Belgium and England. The poems owe something to Baudelaire's example (the "modernism" Verlaine admired in *Les Fleurs du mal*), but they resemble even more closely – as far as one art can resemble another – the canvases of the great Impressionist painters, who were just beginning their work. Verlaine had long been in touch with the art circles of Paris. He met Edouard Manet (who had also been Baudelaire's friend) at Nina de Callias's in 1869; and it was in January 1872, that, with Rimbaud, he sat for Fantin-Latour's famous canvas, "Le Coin de Table," now in the Louvre. In a way, of course, all his poetry is "impressionism," bathed from first to last in a sensuous reverie which is recorded without question, and which nobody ever expressed as intensely as he. The poems of *Paysages belges*, however, are less lyrical, more impersonal – like Monet's haystacks or Cézanne's apples:

> La fuite est verdâtre et rose
> Des collines et des rampes
> Dans un demi-jour de lampes
> Qui vient brouiller toute chose.

Not the object, but the light reflected from it; an interesting technique. Not that the lyrical Verlaine is entirely absent. Indeed he is everywhere present, and the piece ends with the same themes and at least two of the rhymes of "Chanson d'automne":

> Triste à peine tant s'effacent
> Ces apparences d'automne,
> Toutes mes langueurs rêvassent,
> Que berce l'air monotone.

"Je caresse l'idée de faire ... un livre de poèmes (dans le sens *suivi* du mot) ... d'où l'*homme* sera complètement banni," he wrote Lepelletier on May 16, 1873, three days before sending him the manuscript of *Romances sans paroles*.[19] The project crops up in his letters for some years, but as far as we know *Aquarelles* and *Paysages belges* are the nearest he came to realizing it. The results cannot be classed among his greatest achievements, but they are charming none the less; and at least one of them, "Chevaux de bois," a delightful evocation of a merry-go-round seen at a street fair in Saint-Gilles in August 1872, is very successful; written with all the naïve sophistication and rueful humour of which he was capable.

Meanwhile, having completed the book, he was once again obsessed by memories of Rimbaud. Mathilde had refused to return to him, he could therefore consider himself free. (Even had she done so, could he have given up Arthur for the rue Nicolet or a trip to New Caledonia? Mathilde was well advised to mistrust

19 Verlaine, *Correspondance*, I, 98.

his protestations.) On May 18, he wrote Rimbaud to join him at Bouillon: "Je t'embrasse bien et compte sur une bien prochaine entrevue, dont tu me donnes l'espoir pour cette semaine. Dès que tu me feras signe, j'y serai."[20] Under the playful surface the letter is tense, its smothered passion breaking out in a sudden jet at the end, an obscene English phrase which later aroused the suspicions of the Belgian police.

Rimbaud was only too willing to leave Roche, whatever his reasons for going there in the first place. Life with Verlaine might be exasperating, but life in the provinces was abominably dull. "Quelle chierie! et quels monstres d'innocince [sic], ces paysans. Il faut, le soir, faire deux lieux, et plus pour boire un peu ... Je suis abominablement gêné. Pas un livre, pas un cabaret à portée de moi, pas un incident dans la rue. Quelle horreur que cette campagne française."[21] He met Verlaine at Bouillon on May 25, 1873, and on the 27th they were again in London – 8 Great College Street, Camden Town.

This time the arrangement scarcely lasted a month. The money problem was still acute. Rimbaud, as ever, refused to do any work, and the burden fell on Verlaine. At a cost of some effort, he managed to find a few pupils and give lessons, not, apparently, with much success.[22] Just why Elisa did not step in once more is not known. From time to time even she revolted against her son's extravagance, and she was terrified at what his latest escapade had already cost. Besides, he was no longer with her to enforce his demands; she found it possible to resist his letters. But even lack of money was not the decisive factor. Verlaine and Rimbaud, just like Verlaine and Mathilde two years earlier, had reached the point of all ill-assorted unions, whatever their nature, when disparities of character at first unnoticed in the excitement of sentimental discovery lead to constant friction.

Rimbaud's genius was developing with meteoric rapidity, becoming more and more intransigent with the passage of months,

20 Quoted in Rimbaud, Pléiade, 290.
21 *Ibid.*, 287-88.
22 Lepelletier, *Paul Verlaine*, 239.

even of weeks and days. His initial esteem for Verlaine (such as it was) had evaporated; he looked on him as a mere convenience, a source of money, and now money had become scarce. And he made one serious miscalculation about Paul's nature. Because Verlaine accepted indifference and brutality and came back for more, Rimbaud concluded that this was the best way of handling him. He misread Verlaine's demands for affection in this sense. It is the sort of reasoning a pimp uses in taming a skittish whore, and it succeeded for a while: the child's paradise involves a certain amount of masochism; discipline in one form or another is part of the child's world. But discipline implies a return in protection, reassurance, and love; and Rimbaud never took this into account. It is a mistake frequently made by those who think they have found the key to a personality like Paul Verlaine's: they fail to allow for the intolerance of restraint and the sudden starts of exasperation which characterize the emotionally immature. Verlaine found himself yoked to a companion who snarled when spoken to, shrugged off every demonstration of love as so much gush, and was perpetually ill tempered. The situation was as bad in its way as Mathilde's well-bred martyrdom had been, and the breaking point came abruptly on July 3, 1873.

Verlaine's story, as he told it twenty years afterward, fits so well into what we know and what we surmise that we are obliged to accept it as true. "À Londres, quand la dêche était pire, on mangeait à la maison. Ce jour-là, c'était à moi d'aller aux provisions. J'y vais. J'en reviens apportant d'une main un hareng, de l'autre une bouteille d'huile. Je les tenais comme il fallait, n'est-ce pas? ... enfin très bien. J'approche de la maison et je vois Rimbaud qui me guettait par la fenêtre ouverte. Il se met à ricaner. ... Je monte quand même, et j'entre. 'Ce que tu as l'air con, avec ta bouteille d'huile d'une main et ton hareng de l'autre!' me dit Rimbaud. – Moi, je riposte, parce que je vous assure que je n'avais pas du tout l'air con, avec ma bouteille d'huile et mon hareng, nom de Dieu!..." It was one of those tiny incidents, trifling on the surface, but detonating vast accumulations of resentment and frustration.

Verlaine threw the herring at his friend: "Eh bien! porte-le, toi! Moi, j'en ai assez, je m'en vais."[23]

This was something Rimbaud had never imagined – that the worm would turn. Astounded, he watched Verlaine throw clothes into a valise and rush downstairs to the street, heading for a wharf where the Belgian packet was under steam. He followed, protesting, his protests rapidly turning into supplications. But Verlaine was in a fury – wilful, unreasoning, careless of results. The weak are capable of these desperate resolutions. Unfortunately, the effort usually exhausts them and they fall back into a worse state of moral debility than what went before. Verlaine hurried up the gangplank. Rimbaud was penniless and could not follow. The vessel pulled out for Ostend, and as it disappeared down the Thames, he was still standing on the dock. The seer had become a frightened adolescent, alone and moneyless in a strange city. He went back to Great College Street and there wrote a desperate appeal, a heartbroken wail which far surpasses anything Verlaine himself ever put on paper:

"Reviens, reviens, cher ami, seul ami, reviens. Je te jure que je serai bon. Si j'étais maussade avec toi, c'est une plaisanterie où je me suis entêté, je m'en repens plus qu'on ne peut dire. Reviens, ce sera bien oublié ... Ah! je t'en supplie ... Quand je te faisais signe de quitter le bateau, pourquoi ne venais-tu pas? Nous avons vécu deux ans ensemble pour arriver à cette heure-là! ... Si tu ne veux pas revenir ici, veux-tu que j'aille te trouver où tu es? ... Oui, c'est moi qui ai eu tort. Oh! tu ne m'oublieras pas, dis? Non, tu ne peux pas m'oublier. Moi, je t'ai toujours là ... Est-ce que nous ne devons plus vivre ensemble? ... O reviens, à toutes les heures je repleure."[24]

And as the ship plunged on across the Channel, Verlaine was seized with remorse. He could not forget the image of Rimbaud lonely and forlorn on the wharf. Before reaching Ostend he scribbled off a note dated en "mer," July 3, 1873: "Tu dois, *au fond,*

---

23 Rimbaud, Pléiade, 821-22.
24 *Ibid.*, 291 *sqq.*

comprendre, *enfin*, qu'il me fallait absolument partir, que cette vie violente et toute de *scènes* sans motif que ta fantaisie ne pouvait m'aller foutre plus!" A frank statement of the sort of existence they had been leading together, and a confirmation of all the other evidence. "Seulement, comme je t'aimais immensément (Honni soit qui mal y pense!) je tiens aussi à te confirmer que, si d'ici à trois jours, je ne suis pas r' [sic] avec ma femme, dans des conditions parfaites, je me brûle la gueule. Trois jours d'hôtel, un *rivolvita*, ça coûte: de là, ma '*pingrerie*' de tantôt. Tu devrais me pardonner ..."[25]

The letter is the same devil's brew of contradictions and cross-purposes he had been stewing in for the past eighteen months: his love for Rimbaud, his need of Mathilde, the obsession with death and suicide. He was like a savage dancing in monotonous ritual before some monstrous Trinity – now prostrate, now erect, feet shuffling, stamping to the ceaseless tom-tom of frustration and desire. "Ma dernière pensée sera pour toi, pour toi qui m'appelais du *pier* tantôt, et que je n'ai pas voulu rejoindre, *parce qu'il fallait que je claquasse*, – *enfin*! Veux-tu que je t'embrasse en crevant?" And, with yet another shift of purpose (giving Rimbaud his address just as he had given it to Mathilde on another occasion): "Nous ne nous reverrons plus en tout cas. Si ma femme vient, tu auras mon adresse, et j'espère que tu m'écriras. En attendant, d'ici à trois jours, *pas plus, pas moins*, Bruxelles poste restante, à mon nom."[26]

He was in the same emotional turmoil when he got to Brussels next day, July 4. As soon as he had found a room (at the Hôtel Liégeois) he settled down to an orgy of letter-writing. We do not know in what order the missives were composed, but they were all mailed the same day. He asked Mathilde to meet him at once, and threatened to kill himself if she did not. The address on the envelope, Hôtel Liégeois, must have awakened unpleasant memories in her mind. Nothing could have persuaded her to rejoin him, but in any case she left the letter unopened for five years when (as she notes) its menace of suicide sounded rather flat, since Verlaine was still very much alive.[27]

25 *Ibid.*, 290-291.   26 *Ibid.*   27 Mathilde, *Mémoires*, 222.

The second letter (and how characteristic of Verlaine to write it!) was to Mme Rimbaud. It was the next best thing to writing Arthur. Verlaine had never met the stern lady, yet here he was telling her that he intended to commit suicide, and that her son's conduct was the reason! Vitalie Rimbaud was the last person to go to with a story like that; her reply is a fine piece of common-sense stoicism which, had it been addressed to anybody else, might have had some point. To Verlaine, considering the state he was in, it had none whatever: "J'espère que le calme et la réflexion sont revenus dans votre esprit ... Se tuer, quand on est accablé par le malheur, est une *lâcheté* ... J'ignore quelles sont vos disgrâces avec Arthur; mais j'ai toujours prévu que le dénouement de votre liaison ne devait pas être heureux. Pourquoi? ... Parce que ce qui n'est pas autorisé, approuvé par de bons et honnêtes parents, ne doit pas être heureux pour les enfants."[28] In a sense she did him too much honour by taking him at his word. He was in no danger of suicide. The very deluge of letters was itself a form of childish exhibitionism: "Look! I'm going to hurt myself. Then you'll be sorry!" There was none of the true despair that usually precedes self-destruction.

His last letter was to Elisa, and, as usual, she was the only one who believed him. She arrived in Brussels next day, the 5th. By then the suicide fever had considerably fallen. "Ma femme refusant de venir après ma menace de suicide," Verlaine wrote the same day to a Communard friend in London, Matuszewicz, "je commence à trouver trop connard de me tuer comme ça et préfère – car je suis malheureux, là vraiment! – m'engager dans les volontaires républicains espagnols." He could not end without asking about Rimbaud: "Enfin parlez-moi de Rimbaud. Vous a-t-il vu après mon départ? Ecrivez-moi là-dessus. Ça m'intéresse tant."[29]

Rimbaud, in fact, had regained all his old mastery. One can imagine his sarcastic smile as he read the latter dated "en mer," his

---

28 Rimbaud, Pléiade, 295–96.
29 Rimbaud, Pléiade, 294. Verlaine later repeated this story almost word for word to Kessler, who quotes it in "Besuch bei Verlaine."

contemptuous shrug: "The idiot's come round!" He answered at once, in a very different style from that of the day before: "Londres, 5 juillet 1873. J'ai ta lettre datée 'En mer'. Tu as tort, cette fois, et très tort ... Ta femme ne viendra pas ... Quant à claquer, je te connais. Tu vas donc ... te démener, errer, ennuyer des gens ... Crois-tu que ta vie sera plus agréable avec d'autres que moi? Réfléchis-y! – Ah! certes non! Avec moi seul tu peux être libre, et, puisque je te jure d'être très gentil à l'avenir, que je déplore toute ma part de torts, que j'ai enfin l'esprit net, que je t'aime bien, si tu ne veux pas revenir, ou que je te rejoigne, tu fais un crime, et *tu t'en repentiras* ... Resonge à ce que tu étais avant de me connaître." He had even recovered sufficient arrogance to make a threat or two of his own, to hint at the possibility of a definite separation: "Je ne rentre pas chez ma mère. Je vais à Paris. Je tâcherai d'être parti lundi soir. Tu m'auras forcé à vendre tous tes habits, je ne puis faire autrement. ... Certes, si ta femme revient, je ne te compromettrai pas en t'écrivant – je n'écrirai jamais. Le seul vrai mot, c'est: reviens. Je veux être avec toi, je t'aime. Si tu écoutes cela, tu montreras du courage et un esprit sincère. Autrement, je te plains."[30]

Before receiving this letter, Verlaine had again been in touch with him indirectly, by writing Mrs. Smith, the landlady in Great College Street, asking her to forward his belongings to Paris. He apparently told her that he would soon be back in England, although since only a rough draft of his note survives (written in curious English), in which he does not mention the project, we cannot know what he said. But she showed the scrawl to Rimbaud (as Verlaine knew would be the case), who wrote again on the 7th. His tone is cooler than ever, and the possibility of Verlaine's return to London is the first point he mentions. In direct contrast with his two earlier appeals, he does his best to discourage it. We can only conclude that, the first shock of desertion over, his attitude had begun to harden. He was thinking matters over and making plans for the future. As subsequently transpired, they did not include life with Verlaine, either in London or elsewhere. Into

30 *Ibid.*, 293-94.

the bargain, he had sold most of Verlaine's clothes, and was once
again in funds. "J'ai vu la lettre que tu as envoyée à Mme
Smith ... Tu veux revenir à Londres! Tu ne sais pas comme tout le
monde t'y recevrait! Et la mine que me feraient Andrieu et autres,
s'ils me revoyaient avec toi!" Andrieu, like Régamey, was another
ex-Communard, and to hear Rimbaud expressing apprehension of
"what people might say" is indeed a delicious inconsistency. Had
his relations with Verlaine aroused gossip amongst the London
exiles, gossip confirmed by Paul's sudden departure? And had
somebody hinted as much after Verlaine left? Most of the ex-
Communards were in touch with Paris; they may have heard
some of the rumours that were afloat there. "Néanmoins, je serai
très courageux. Dis-moi ton idée bien sincère. Veux-tu retourner
à Londres pour moi? ... Il n'y a plus rien dans la chambre. Tout
est vendu, sauf un paletot. J'ai eu deux livres dix." The letter is a
tissue of contradictions; it gives an ambiguous impression, unusual with Rimbaud, who most often said what he thought re-
gardless of consequences. He was hiding his true feelings, which
boiled down to the fact that he had had enough of Paul Verlaine,
but did not want to break with him entirely if only because the
man could still be useful – financially if no other way. For after
this chilly opening, in which he does his best to discourage Verlaine's return, he concludes: "Mais pourquoi ne m'écris-tu pas, à
moi? Oui, cher petit, je vais rester une semaine encore. Et tu vien-
dras, n'est-ce pas? ... Sois sûr de moi, j'aurais très bon caractère."[31]

Was it the indifference he sensed beneath the lines that sent
Verlaine rushing next day to a telegraph office as soon as it opened?
"Bruxelles, 8 juillet 1873 – 8 h.38 matin. Volontaire Espagne.
Viens ici, Hôtel Liégeois. Blanchisseuse, manuscrits, si possible."[32]
The statement about volunteering was premature. He presented
himself at the Spanish Embassy that very morning and learned
that as a French citizen he was not eligible. Rimbaud left London
at once, and met Verlaine in Brussels the same evening, with Elisa
as a third. Other lodgings had to be found; it was just possible

31 *Ibid.*, 296-97.
32 *Ibid.*, 297.

that Mathilde might turn up, and it would never do for her to find them all at the Liégeois. They went a short distance off to the Hôtel de Courtrai; the two poets shared a double bed in a room communicating with Elisa's, and the stage was set for the last act of the drama.

Rimbaud made clear his intentions immediately. Despite his hysterical appeal of five days before and the protests of affection in his letters of July 4, 5, and even the 7th, he now declared that he was going to Paris, and going alone. He was fed up with the "Foolish Virgin's" nerve-storms and sentimental crises, and the desertion of July 3 had been the last straw. The heartbroken letter immediately after the event had been dictated by fright more than affection; and its desperate phrases concealed a core of resentment. Verlaine had exposed him to dereliction, had then written incoherently about committing suicide or returning to Mathilde (the *chagrin idiot* all over again); he was flighty and unstable, could not be counted on, one never knew when he would fly off on another crazy tangent; and his gushy love-making now filled Rimbaud with disgust. Arthur's mind was made up: the affair was over. If he came to Brussels at all, it was only to get money for a ticket to Paris.

This new development threw Verlaine into an agony of despair. For over a year he had been subjected to a corrosive emotional trauma, a life alternating between violence and voluptuous frustration; "scenes," as he said, "which had no other cause" than Rimbaud's whims. He had thrown away his marriage and whatever position he held in the literary world, squandered a small fortune, and all for the boy who was now slipping from his grasp. They spent all of July 9 drinking and arguing, Elisa hovering about them in powerless anguish. What were her thoughts? Or did she have any? Any beyond the realization that Paul was desperate? Rimbaud's attitude was exasperating; he kept asking for money in a contemptuous monotone, as though he were arguing with an imbecile.

At nine o'clock next morning, the 10th, Verlaine went out as soon as the shops opened and bought a seven-chamber revolver.

He then stopped at a bar and by the time he got back to the hotel at noon he was thoroughly drunk. "Qu'est-ce que tu comptes faire de cela?" Rimbaud asked when he saw the gun. "C'est pour vous, pour moi, pour tout le monde!" They lunched together and were back in their room by two. Elisa joined them and Rimbaud asked *her* for the twenty francs to buy a train ticket. She would certainly have given him the money had she not been afraid of infuriating her son. From time to time as the dispute went on Verlaine slipped out for more drinks, and finally, discovering that Rimbaud was still adamant, he locked the outer door (Elisa had retired to her own room), threw a chair against it and sat down. Rimbaud was leaning against the wall in languid sarcasm, repeating his demand for money. Verlaine never forgot the scene: "Je nous revois à Bruxelles, dans cet hôtel borgne de la rue Pachéco où nous étions descendus," he told Adolphe Retté many years afterwards.[33] "J'étais assis sur le pied du lit. Lui debout, près de la porte, croisait les bras et me défiait par toute son attitude. Ah! la méchanceté, la flamme cruelle de ses yeux d'archange damné! Je lui avais tout dit pour qu'il restât avec moi. Mais il voulait partir et je sentais que rien ne le ferait revenir sur sa décision ... Je haletais, je voyais rouge: il me semblait qu'il emportait ma cervelle et mon cœur." Suddenly he raised the gun: "Tiens! je t'apprendrai à vouloir partir!"

The moment was decisive. For years he had flirted with the idea of murder and suicide, had threatened Lepelletier, threatened his mother, threatened Mathilde and M. Mauté, and others, perhaps, of whom we have no record. Always at the last second, something or somebody intervened to save him from the irreparable gesture: Lepelletier escaped through the trees of the Bois, Victoire Bertrand dragged him away from Elisa, M. Mauté tore the sword-cane from his hands. Now he was alone with his victim, and suddenly the essential sham of all these episodes became evident. They were tantrums, efforts to recover his plaything, have his own way. He

---

33 Adolphe Retté's account of a conversation with Verlaine in hospital, sometime after Rimbaud's death (1891), quoted by J. H. Bornecque, *Verlaine par lui-même* (Aux éditions du Seuil), 86-87.

had never been intent on murder, much less suicide, and he was not intent on murder or suicide now. He fired twice. Rimbaud was not more than nine or ten feet away. Had Verlaine really wanted to kill, nothing could have been easier. But the aim was suddenly deflected, subconsciously, obeying a deeper impulse than he understood himself. The first bullet struck Arthur in the wrist, inflicting nothing more than a flesh wound; the second embedded itself in the wall. As Rimbaud later testified – and the detail is important – the muzzle was no longer pointing at him when the second shot was fired. The echoes had hardly died away than Verlaine thrust the gun into his friend's hands: "Brûle-moi la cervelle!" Then, when Elisa rushed in, he entered her room and collapsed in tears on the bed.

Thus far the whole incident might have been hushed up. By a singular piece of luck, the hotel was nearly empty at that hour, and nobody but the actors in the drama had heard the shooting. And when Elisa and Verlaine took Rimbaud to a hospital shortly afterwards, and he told the surgeon in charge that he had had an accident, his wound was dressed without question. (The bullet had lodged in the wrist; it was not extracted until July 17, but there were no complications of any sort.) Unfortunately, however, Verlaine was still in a condition of drunken exasperation, and Rimbaud still obdurate. The gunplay had not budged him one inch. He was going to Paris and going alone. Back at the hotel, the scared Elisa took matters into her own hands and gave him the twenty francs he needed. The train was due to leave at 7:00 PM; a little before that hour Rimbaud left to catch it. Verlaine followed, still beseeching him not to go, and Elisa followed her son. The extraordinary trio had nearly reached the station when Rimbaud suddenly broke away from his companions and took to his heels. A policeman was standing nearby on the sidewalk. And the seer, the poet who despised all laws human and divine, took refuge with the very symbol of bourgeois authority. He was terrified; he poured out his story in a rush of words, showed his bandaged wrist: Verlaine had wounded him at two o'clock that after-

noon and was still pursuing him with the same gun.[34] The officer
had no choice but to arrest Paul at once. He marched him off to
the nearest police station, with Rimbaud following as the plaintiff
and Elisa as a material witness.

By eight o'clock they had all made statements in front of a
deputy commissioner. Rimbaud said that for a year he had been
staying with Verlaine in London, where they made a living by
writing newspaper articles and giving French lessons (two patent
exaggerations). "Sa société était devenue impossible, et j'avais
manifesté le désir de retourner à Paris. Il y a quatre jours, il m'a
quitté pour venir à Bruxelles et m'a envoyé un télégramme pour
venir le rejoindre." No mention, of course, of his letters begging
Verlaine to see him again; he had reached Brussels at his friend's
desire, not his own. He then tells of his arrival, his disputes with
Paul, the shooting at the hotel, the walk to the railroad station:
"Verlaine m'a devancé de quelques pas, puis il est revenu vers moi:
je l'ai vu mettre sa main en poche pour saisir son revolver; j'ai fait
demi-tour et ... j'ai rencontré l'agent de police." He concludes: "Si
Verlaine m'avait laissé partir librement, je n'aurais pas porté plainte
à sa charge pour la blessure qu'il ma faite."

Elisa's testimony was naturally as favourable to her son as she
could make it: "Depuis deux ans environ, le sieur Rimbaud vit
aux dépens de mon fils, lequel a à se plaindre de son caractère
acariâtre et méchant ... Mon fils est venu à Bruxelles il y a quatre
jours ... Rimbaud est venu loger avec nous depuis deux jours. Ce
matin, mon fils, qui a l'intention de voyager, a fait l'achat d'un
revolver ... Une discussion s'est élevée entre eux. Mon fils a saisi
son revolver et en a tiré deux coups sur son ami Rimbaud: le premier l'a blessé au bras gauche, le second n'a pas été tiré sur lui ...
Après avoir été pansé à l'Hôpital Saint-Jean, Rimbaud témoignant
le désir de retourner à Paris, je lui ai donné vingt francs ... Puis,
nous sommes allés pour le reconduire à la gare ... lorsqu'il s'est
adressé à l'agent de police pour faire arrêter mon fils, qui n'avait

34 The police officer's report to the commissioner of police, July 11, 1873, Rimbaud, Pléiade, 824.

pas de rancune contre lui et avait agi dans un moment d'égare-
ment".

As for Verlaine, he was a dangerous witness in his own defence.
He talked too much; he committed the astounding folly of drag-
ging Mathilde into the affair, of mentioning her allegations (which
Rimbaud and Elisa had left in the dark), and of thus arousing
suspicions which, given the facts of the case, the police were only
too ready to entertain. Was it because he thought that the details
of his separation would eventually be known, and he hoped to
minimize his wife's charges by being the first to mention them?
Or was he driven by a sort of confession complex, plagued as he
was by a feeling of guilt, incapable of hiding what was uppermost
in his mind – his eternal sexual conflict? "Je suis arrivé à Bruxelles
depuis quatre jours, malheureux et désespéré. Je connais Rimbaud
depuis plus d'une année. J'ai vécu avec lui à Londres, que j'ai
quitté depuis quatre jours pour venir habiter Bruxelles, afin d'être
plus près de mes affaires, plaidant en séparation avec ma femme
habitant Paris, laquelle prétend que j'ai des relations immorales
avec Rimbaud. J'ai écrit à ma femme que si elle ne venait pas me
rejoindre dans les trois jours je me brûlerais la cervelle; et c'est
dans ce but que j'ai acheté le revolver ce matin ... Depuis mon
arrivée à Bruxelles, j'ai reçu une lettre de Rimbaud qui me de-
mandait de venir me rejoindre ... il est arrivé il y a deux jours.
Aujourd'hui, me voyant malheureux, il a voulu me quitter. J'ai
cédé à un moment de folie et j'ai tiré sur lui. Il n'a pas porté
plainte à ce moment ... Ma mère lui a donné vingt francs pour
son voyage; et c'est en le conduisant à la gare qu'il a prétendu que
je voulais le tuer."[35]

All three statements differed on a crucial point: the course of
events during the walk to the station. Rimbaud declared that Verlaine threatened to shoot him again; Verlaine and Elisa maintained
that this was not so. We have no way of deciding which version
is correct. It would seem, however, that there must have been
some new menace on Verlaine's part. He was quite capable of it,
drunk as he was, and it is hard to understand why Rimbaud, who

35 All these declarations are reproduced *ibid.*, 297 *sqq.*

had shown commendable fortitude after the earlier attack, should suddenly panic and rush up to a constable without fresh cause.[36] But, whatever the exact truth, one lurid fact emerged from each story: a man of twenty-nine had fired two shots at a boy of eighteen because the latter wanted to leave him; and he was a man whose wife, as he admitted himself, had just obtained legal separation charging him with homosexual relations with the same boy. The case bore all the earmarks of a depraved *crime passionnel*, and even the strange presence of the accused's mother on the scene was hardly a mitigation. There was enough material to warrant serious investigation, the more so as Rimbaud was, after all, a minor. Within an hour Verlaine was locked in a cell, "prévenu de blessures, au moyen d'un revolver, sur le nommé RIMBAUD Arthur."[37] The cogs of justice had got their teeth into the matter, and Verlaine was drawn into one of those appalling legal snarls where a man ends by being tried for everything except the crime of which he is accused.

Leaving him incarcerated, Rimbaud and Elisa returned to the hotel to await next day's hearing. The fact appears strange (although in the tale of Verlaine's life nothing should any longer astound us): after her son's arrest, his mother and the youth he was accused of shooting returned together to the rooms they had been sharing. What, one wonders, can they possibly have had to say to one another, especially after Elisa had just described Rimbaud as "acariâtre et méchant"? The fact that he had no other place to stay hardly seems a sufficient explanation. It is more likely that neither he nor Elisa had any idea how badly matters were going to turn out.

36 Verlaine told Retté a somewhat telescoped version of the story: he followed Rimbaud downstairs and shot him (for the first and last time) in the street. Bornecque, *Verlaine par lui-même*, 87.

37 The police commissioner's phrase, Rimbaud, Pléiade, 824.

6/ Prison/
The religious crisis/
Cellulairement

MATTERS BEGAN TURNING BADLY the very next day, July 11. Interrogated before an examining magistrate, Verlaine repeated his first statement. He continued to insist on his intoxication at the time of the shooting, on his despair when Mathilde did not come, and on his even greater despair when Rimbaud decided to leave. The authorities viewed this combination of Rimbaud and Mathilde with a sceptical eye. They could not understand that it was quite sincere, and had obsessed Verlaine for the past two years. They saw only that he had shot Rimbaud because Rimbaud wanted to leave him; and they took the story about wanting his wife in Brussels as a red herring, designed to throw them off the scent. What normal man would have fallen into such frenzy because a friend decided to go away? The magistrate's questions showed what direction the inquiry was taking: "Je ne comprends pas que le départ d'un ami ait pu vous jeter dans le désespoir. N'existe-t-il pas entre vous et Rimbaud d'autres relations que celles de l'amitié?" It was useless for Verlaine to protest: "Non; c'est une calomnie qui a été inventée par ma femme et sa famille pour me nuire; on m'accuse de cela dans la requête présentée au tribunal par ma femme à l'appui de sa demande de séparation."[1]

The more the Belgian officials looked into the business, the more they were convinced that their first suppositions were well founded. And when, on July 12, all papers the two poets had with them

1 Rimbaud, Pléiade, 301.

were seized by court order, the results were everything the most
ardent inquisitor could desire: Verlaine's two letters to Rimbaud
of April, 1872, two more in May of the same year, the note from
Jehonville fixing a meeting at Bouillon, the frantic scribble dated
"En mer," the telegram of July 8. There was also Rimbaud's
"come back" letter of July 4, 1873, and his subsequent missives
of July 5, 6, and 7 – not to mention the sonnet, "Le Bon disciple,"
of May 1872, which he had been carrying about pinned in his
wallet.[2] It was a damning collection, and on Rimbaud's appearance to testify the same day, he was inevitably asked whether his
intimacy with Verlaine was not one of Mathilde's reasons for fil-
ing a separation demand. Since the court already knew that it was
(through Verlaine himself), the question was something of a trap,
but Rimbaud did not fall into it. "Oui," he answered, "elle nous
accuse même de relations immorales; mais je ne veux pas me donner la peine de démentir de pareilles calomnies." Rimbaud seems
to have realized almost at once what the police were looking for,
and he was even more anxious than Verlaine to side-track them.
Just as the previous winter, when he had listened to his mother
and left Verlaine, he had no desire to be involved in a scandal. In
denouncing his friend he had started the processes of the law rolling; he was now willing to stop them as far as lay in his power.
During the course of his interrogation he made as light of the
shooting in the hotel as possible ("le médecin m'a dit que dans
trois ou quatre jours ma blessure serait guérie"), noted Verlaine's
immediate remorse, his drunken state which made him quite irresponsible, and added that when the second shot was fired the gun
was pointing at the floor, thus confirming what Elisa had said.
And finally, on July 19, in an effort to bring matters to an end, he
voluntarily withdrew his charges. "Au moment où M. Paul Ver-
leine ... a tiré sur moi ... il était dans un tel état d'ivresse qu'il
n'avait point conscience de son action ... Je suis intimement per-
suadé qu'en achetant cette arme, M. Verlaine n'avait aucune intention hostile contre moi, et qu'il n'y avait point de préméditation
criminelle dans l'acte de fermer la porte à clef sur nous ... La cause

2 See the notes to this poem in Verlaine, Pléiade, 1108.

de l'ivresse de M. Verlaine tenait simplement à l'idée de ses contrariétés avec Madame Verlaine, sa femme."[3]

This moderate attitude, joined to the boy's resolute denial of homosexual practices, had at least one good result: Verlaine was not tried for corrupting a minor, an added horror which carried a stiff penalty. But the accusation of *coups et blessures ayant entraîné une incapacité de travail* is provided for in the Belgian legal code. It was quite certain that Verlaine had wounded Rimbaud, and despite the latter's withdrawal a trial must still be held. If Verlaine could not be sentenced for sexual perversion, he could at least be condemned for *something*, and Justice was determined to do the best with what she had. Besides, on July 15, some new and (so it appeared) decisive evidence was produced: Verlaine underwent a physical examination to determine whether or not he showed any traces of abnormal sexual practices. Medical science now admits that data of this sort prove nothing; people thought differently in those days, and the two doctors who looked him over declared that he had been guilty of both active and passive pederasty.[4] When he appeared in court on August 8, his case was already lost. The judge considered the circumstances of the affair so unsavory that he handed down the maximum sentence: two years in prison and 200 francs fine. There was only one hope left – an appeal. Verlaine tried it, but the court wrote the Paris police for information on him, and the reply (dated August 21) was enough to seal his fate. It mentioned his association with the Commune (a further aggravation; the Belgian authorities liked ex-Communards as little as the French did), and noted his "passion honteuse pour le nommé Rimbaud."[5] The Belgian magistrates must have felt that their worst suspicions were more than confirmed; they probably regretted that they could not make the sentence even heavier. His appeal was denied on August 27, and on October 25, having spent

---

3 Rimbaud, Pléiade, 301, 305, 306.
4 This report is what Mathilde calls "l'horrible pièce" in her *Mémoires*, 228. Besides enabling her to obtain a separation and a divorce, it later ruined Verlaine's chances of reintegration in the civil service. See Porché's comment, *Verlaine tel qu'il fut*, 324, on the inconclusive nature of such evidence.
5 Porché, *Verlaine tel qu'il fut*, 325.

a little more than three months in the Petits Carmes prison in Brussels, he was transferred to the penitentiary at Mons. During the following year, Elisa and the faithful Lepelletier did what they could to have his sentence reduced, but in vain; he was not liberated until January 16, 1875, benefiting by a clause in the Regulations which allowed him 175 days off for good behaviour.

This period of eighteen months is one of the richest in his career as a poet, and goes far towards proving the contention that art, like divine grace, is a vocation demanding the renunciation of all else. In the eyes of the world, he was a ruined man. When the news of his trial and sentence reached Paris, he lost what little consideration he still possessed: the most scabrous rumours of the past two years were now accepted as certainties, and only a few of his friends, like Lepelletier, Blémont, and Delahaye continued to write him. Elisa, of course, never forsook her son. She found quarters near the Belgian frontier, and during the whole course of his imprisonment she was always at Mons on visiting days. Fate had created her for this *via dolorosa*, and perhaps she is less to be pitied than might be thought. Maternal love like hers is a powerful drug; the anaesthetized victim can pass through any disaster, protected by a sort of sublime inconsistency. Elisa never accepted the Belgian drama for what it was, even though she had been an eyewitness. Paul was involved, and Paul could do no wrong. And there were certain things about her son's jail months she found almost pleasant; as long as he was locked up, she always knew where to find him and where to find him alone. She shared him with no one else. Would those brief interviews at the penitentiary have been so thrilling had Mathilde (for example) been present?

In prison, Verlaine was thrown back on himself, with no resources but what he could find in his own heart and mind. It was one of those situations which tries a man to the utmost. If he has not got the root of salvation in him, he dies or peters out in a prolonged sterility. A comparison with Oscar Wilde has some point. Both writers were condemned to two years' penal servitude for offences which branded them with infamy; both lost all but a few devoted friends and both turned for comfort to the Roman

Church. But the parallel goes no further. Wilde's talent was slight compared with Verlaine's, and he used it to make himself the jester of the British aristocracy. Snobbery was the basis of his existence, and when he was no longer socially presentable his life was over; prison inspired him with nothing better than the cantankerous prose of *De Profundis* and the rather over-rated *Ballad of Reading Gaol*, which is only good alongside the verse he had written earlier. He had none of Verlaine's verbal genius, nor any of the passion which transmutes reality, however deplorable, into the eternal symbolism of poetry. Verlaine's productivity under prison conditions was amazing, and it began within twenty-four hours of his initial arrest.

During the first three days at the Petits Carmes he wrote a poem a day, and sixteen others followed (some of them among his very best) while he was awaiting transfer to Mons in October. The record at Mons is even more impressive, including as it does such splendid verse as "Art poétique," "Ah, vraiment c'est triste," and the ten sonnets of "Mon Dieu m'a dit," that tremendous dialogue between the poet and Christ which is the summit of his work and one of the greatest mystic outpourings in literature. He wrote thirty-two poems while in jail (or forty-one, since "Mon Dieu m'a dit" consists of ten sonnets). Both in quantity and in quality this output is so important that it merits detailed examination, the more so when we recall under what circumstances it was composed and the problems to which it gives rise.

His first intention (conceived shortly after his liberation in January 1875) was to publish the prison verse as a single volume, *Cellulairement*. He eventually abandoned this idea and issued the poems in one or other of his subsequent collections during the next twenty years. Seven appeared in *Sagesse* (1880), twelve in *Jadis et Naguère* (1885), eight in *Parallèlement* (1889), three in *Invectives* (1896), and two ("Vieux Coppées") were not printed until after his death. In other words, the Verlaine of 1880-96 is often the Verlaine of 1873-74; and when we discuss the volumes he wrote after and including *Sagesse* we are no longer dealing with collections like *Fêtes galantes* or *La Bonne Chanson*, composed and printed at a definite moment, but with complex works, altered and added to over long periods of time. The pattern of composition is far from clear and was further muddled by his incorrigible habit of self-dramatization. During his last years, when the very squalor of his life gave the story added piquancy, he used to say that he had produced *Sagesse* in jail: "De cette époque date à peu près tout *Sagesse*."[6] The story was another part of his legend, like his desertion of Mathilde, his fracas with Rimbaud, his mania for absinth; and the fact that it contained a grain of truth adds to the confusion: "Mon Dieu m'a dit" was unquestionably written at Mons immediately after the poet's conversion in April 1874; and "Mon Dieu m'a dit" is the best verse of *Sagesse*. Yet the book, after all, includes fifty-seven items, and the seven prison poems, despite their value, are not much by comparison with that.

A second problem arises when we examine the quality of *Cellulairement*. It is prodigiously uneven, including some of Verlaine's greatest poetry and also some of his worst. He was completely disoriented during his first months in a cell. He had just finished *Romances sans paroles*, and its pure music still echoed in his brain; his passion for Rimbaud had led him through abysses of despair and wrecked his life; he was thinking of Mathilde again, had never stopped thinking of her during his catastrophic year with Arthur; and he was on the brink of a mystic experience which had been ripening ever since childhood and which was to change the pattern of his inspiration. In the poems and letters of his first weeks of confinement, we see him groping, trying first one issue, then another in search of a way out of this moral chaos. Inevitably, what he produced is unequal and contradictory, now reaching the highest levels, now sinking to the depths of bathos.

The pieces in the manner of *Romances sans paroles* are beautiful – "Dame souris trotte," "Je ne sais pourquoi," "Un grand sommeil noir," and the unforgettable "Le ciel est, par-dessus le toit," which with the passage of time has become almost his signature. "Pardessus le mur de devant de ma fenêtre ... je voyais, c'était en août, se balancer la cime, aux feuilles voluptueusement frémissantes, de

6 Quoted by Louis Morice, *Sagesse, édition critique commentée*, 12.

quelque haut peuplier d'un square ou d'un boulevard voisin. En
même temps m'arrivaient des rumeurs lointaines, adoucies, de
fête ... Et je fis, à ce propos, ces vers qui se trouvent dans *Sagesse*:
'Le ciel est, par-dessus le toit'."[7] During these prison months he
even put his ideas on harmony into a kind of poetic theory. In the
spring of 1874, Blémont reviewed *Romances sans paroles*, concluding with the remark: "C'est encore de la musique"; and when
Lepelletier sent Verlaine the article he caught up the phrase as the
starting point of "Art poétique":

> De la musique avant toute chose,
> Et pour cela préfère l'Impair
> Plus vague et plus soluble dans l'air ...
>
> De la musique encore et toujours!
> Que ton vers soit la chose envolée
> Qu'on sent qui fuit d'une âme en allée
> Vers d'autres cieux à d'autres amours.

As things turned out, it was almost his farewell to this type of verse;
a poet's theories, however, are sometimes most potent after he has
given them up: "Art poétique" was not published until 1882,
when Verlaine had long since turned to another style and another
content, but it aroused such enthusiasm amongst the Symbolists
that they haled him as a master.

Not surprisingly, however, his memories of Rimbaud preoccupied him more than anything else. They were a mixture of resentment and fascination, a searing emotional experience which
he turned over, analysed and wrote down in five long poems –
récits diaboliques as he called them. The first four were composed in
July and August 1873, while he was still at the Petits Carmes:
"Crimen Amoris," "La Grâce," "L'Impénitence finale," "Don
Juan pipé"; the last, "Amoureuse du Diable," a year later at Mons;
and together they total nearly seven hundred lines, more than
double his other work at this time. Aside from "Crimen Amoris"
they are all deplorably bad; rhymed anecdotes in the style of Musset's *Rolla* – except that they are worse than the worst of *Rolla*.
They are probably the poorest verse Verlaine ever turned out. His

7 Verlaine, Pléiade, 1131.

genius was lyric, sensuous, instinctive, and he forgot this fact at his peril. He was no psychologist, he had no critical sense, and, despite his good-natured parodies of Heredia and Coppée, not much sense of the ridiculous either. How otherwise could he have written such trash at the same moment as "Le ciel est, par-dessus le toit" and "Mon Dieu m'a dit"? The lines unravel like badly knit stockings, and the content is even more distressing than the style.

But if this Rimbaud cycle has small poetic value, it is a revealing document. Verlaine was rebelling against his friend's ideas which, after all, had landed him in jail – particularly his theories on love ("L'amour est à réinventer") and his conception of man as a rival of God. The boy's sexual and ideological intransigence comes out in the hero of "Don Juan pipé":

> Mais, s'étant découvert meilleur que Dieu
> Il résolut de se mettre en son lieu.[8]

Don Juan preaches the moral and physical emancipation of man, and is suitably punished by an outraged divinity. It is a well-worn theme: Milton, Molière, Mozart, and, of course, Baudelaire. The poem resembles one of those marine animals, squid or octopus, whose mass conceals a tiny skeleton – in this case Baudelaire's "Châtiment de l'orgueil" – which we can detect here and there beneath the gelatinous tissue of the verse. "La Grâce" is a mediaeval legend: an adulterous countess has murdered her husband and now expiates her crime in a cell with his skull for company. Since he was in a state of mortal sin when she killed him, he is in Hell and his ghost invites her to join him there. Again the accent is Rimbaud's:

> Je te dis que je suis damné! Tu t'extasies
> En terreurs vaines, ô ma Reine. Je te dis
> Qu'il te faut rebrousser chemin du Paradis,
> Vain séjour du bonheur banal et solitaire,
> Pour l'amour avec moi! ...
> Et c'est l'éternité que je t'offre: prends-la!
> Au milieu des tourments nous serons dans la joie ...

8 *Ibid.*, 390.

In "Amoureuse du Diable" another countess elopes with a black-haired Italian gigolo, who squanders her fortune and then deserts her. His unending demands for cash are probably the way Verlaine remembered the scenes with Rimbaud in London and Brussels. An important detail about all these poems is that Verlaine identifies himself each time with the woman – the victim of a hard-hearted and unscrupulous lover.

Resentment, in short, is the main note; but fascination takes its place in "Crimen Amoris." In a palace of silk and gold, at Ecbatana, a group of beautiful adolescent Satans is holding a feast in honour of the Seven Deadly Sins. The handsomest of them all (we recognize Rimbaud at once: sixteen years old) remains sombre, untouched by the revelry: he is the same sulky beauty over whom the "Foolish Virgin" shed such floods of tears in *Une Saison en Enfer*. He quits the orgy and mounts a tower from which he preaches a kind of sermon. The sentiments are much the same as Don Juan's; the two poems were written within a month of each other:

> Je serai celui-là qui créera Dieu.
>
> Ô les Pécheurs, ô les Saints ouvriers tristes ...
>
> Vous le saviez, qu'il n'est point de différence
> Entre ce que vous dénommez Bien et Mal ...
> Je veux briser ce Pacte trop anormal.
>
> Il ne faut plus de ce schisme abominable!
> Il ne faut plus d'enfer et de paradis!
> Il faut l'Amour! meure Dieu! meure le Diable ...
>
> Par Moi, l'Enfer ...
> Se sacrifie à l'Amour universel ...[9]

He then drops a lighted torch onto the building and perishes in the flames. But God punishes the sacrilege in a crash of thunder. Rimbaud's ambition was nothing but overweening pride, "un vain rêve évanoui." Peace returns to the earth, the peace of "le Dieu clément qui nous sauvera du mal."

9 *Ibid.*, 378 *sqq.* I quote the first version of the poem, Verlaine, Pléiade, 1161-63.

This poem has aroused much discussion. Writers as diverse as André Gide and Charles Maurras admired it highly; Enid Starkie calls it Verlaine's finest poem; Octave Nadal has written some acute pages on its versification. Verlaine chose to compose in lines of eleven syllables (instead of the more usual ten or twelve) thus obeying the rule set forth in "Art poétique"; and this is a point of great interest to French critics.[10]

François Porché, on the other hand, finds the piece over-adorned, and compares it to Gustave Moreau's paintings. The tone is certainly very *fin-de-siècle*, in the manner of the eighties and nineties, the poems and novels of Mendès, Péladan, Milosz, Samain, who all had a passion for Sin in exotic settings. Rimbaud is rigged out in Persian costume: necklaces, fringes, a jewelled tiara. The whole Persian setting is rather unfortunate, and grotesquely out of keeping with the Miltonic context. Various sources have been proposed, such as Baudelaire's prose-poem "Les Tentations"; but none of them account for this flea-market orientalism. Perhaps Verlaine got the initial idea from Dryden's "Alexander's Feast," which he may have read in an anthology or heard sung to Handel's music while in London. Both poem and oratorio have always been popular. It is true that the palace Alexander burned was at Persepolis, not Ecbatana, but Ecbatana provides a better rhyme.

The true importance of the *récits diaboliques*, however, is less a matter of style than of theme. They are dramas, or melodramas, of sin and redemption: inadequate both in language and situation; hackneyed, exaggerated, false, but none the less written from a metaphysical point of view. Sexual sin and the sin of Pride come to a bad end; there is always a Jealous God noting man's transgressions. The poems continue the "Foolish Virgin's" laments as Rimbaud noted them in *Une Saison en Enfer*, and show that Verlaine's conversion, at least in its preliminary stages, began some months before he wrote "Mon Dieu m'a dit"; began within the first weeks of his confinement at the Petits Carmes.

The precise moment – the sudden burst of light all mystics

10 For Octave Nadal's remarks, see his preface in *CML*, II. Enid Starkie's judgement is in her *Arthur Rimbaud*, 175; Porché's in *Verlaine tel qu'il fut*, 324.

know, when doubt vanishes, and God suddenly manifests Himself – took place during the seventh or eighth month of incarcera-
tion, and can be very nearly pin-pointed. Verlaine's arrest had not
put an end to his efforts for a reconciliation with Mathilde; Mathilde for her part had proceeded steadily with her separation demand. The court decision of the previous October had given her
the first round; on April 24, 1874, the separation was declared
official. She received custody of Georges and 1200 francs a year
alimony. Her lawyer had procured a transcript of the Brussels
trial to support her case: "Attendu qu'il résulte de la correspondance de Verlaine qu'il a abandonné le domicile conjugal pour aller
habiter à Bruxelles, où il s'est livré en toute liberté à ses habitudes
d'ivrognerie; que cette correspondance établit en outre que Verlaine avait des relations infâmes avec un jeune homme; qu'il a été
condamné le huit août mil huit cent soixante-treize par le Tribunal
correctionnel de Bruxelles à deux ans de prison et à deux cents
francs d'amende pour coups et blessures envers cette personne,
violences qu'il aurait exercées dans un accès de jalousie ..."[11] With
proofs of this kind on her side, the wife's victory was a foregone
conclusion: it would have been surprising had she lost. When the
official notification reached Mons at the beginning of May, the
warden took it to Verlaine's cell: "Mon pauvre ami, je vous ap-
porte un mauvais message. Du courage! Lisez!"[12] The prisoner
burst into tears and shortly afterwards sent for the chaplain and
asked for a catechism.

The chaplain was the Abbé Eugène Descamps, and he may very
well have been waiting for just such a summons. He knew the
Abbé Delogne, Verlaine's old mentor. The devout little conspiracy to save Paul which Mme Grandjean had set afoot five years
before had never entirely lapsed. When news of the Brussels sentence reached Delogne, he wrote the chaplain asking him to keep
an eye on Verlaine. From the beginning, the prisoner was surrounded by a gentle mesh of pious hopes.

Descamps gave him Monseigneur Gaume's *Catéchisme de persé-*

---

11 The court's judgement (dated April 24, 1874) is reproduced in *CML*, I, 1417-18.
12 Verlaine, *Mes Prisons, CML*, II, 768.

vérence. There are eight substantial volumes; for fear of wearying his penitent with such a deluge, the Abbé recommended that he concentrate on the sections dealing with the Eucharist. For the next five or six weeks they discussed various points of dogma together. "Je ne sais si ces pages constituent un chef-d'œuvre," Verlaine wrote of Gaume's book in *Mes Prisons*. "J'en doute même. Mais, dans la situation d'esprit où je me trouvais, l'ennui profond où je plongeais ... et le désespoir de n'être pas libre et comme, aussi, de la honte de me trouver là, dèterminèrent ... après quelle nuit douce-amère passée à méditer sur la Présence réelle – tout cela, dis-je, détermina en moi un extraordinaire révolution ... Je ne sais quoi ou Qui me souleva soudain, me jeta hors de mon lit, ... et me prosterna en larmes, en sanglots, aux pieds du Crucifix ... Deux heures au moins peut-être après ce véritable petit (ou grand?) miracle moral ... je vaquai, selon le règlement, aux soins de mon ménage ... lorsque le gardien de jour entra qui m'adressa la phrase traditionnelle: 'Tout va bien?' Je luis répondis aussitôt: 'Dites à monsieur l'Aumônier de venir'."[13]

Like most prison chaplains, the Abbé Descamps was a wise man. He had seen conversions before, and he insisted on at least a month's probation before taking the prisoner's declarations seriously. It was not until August 1874 that he admitted Verlaine to confession and communion. But the mystic leaven had been working meanwhile, and early in September the ten sonnets of "Mon Dieu m'a dit" were finished and sent to Lepelletier in a letter dated September 8. "Et c'est absolument *senti*, je t'assure. Il faut avoir passé par tout ce que j'ai vu et souffert depuis 3 ans, humiliations, dégoûts ... pour sentir tout ce qu'à d'admirablement consolant, raisonnable et logique cette religion si terrible et si douce ... Je ne parle pas des *preuves* historiques, scientifiques et autres qui sont AVEUGLANTES ..."[14]

Obviously such a seismic change was not caused solely by Mathilde's refusal to forgive. It had been prepared long before, as I have been at pains to show throughout the foregoing pages. There

13 *Ibid.*, 770.
14 *CML*, I, 1090.

was Verlaine's first communion, a half-forgotten experience, perhaps, but through its very circumstances linked to his memories of
father, mother, and the paradise of infancy. Even during his school
years, when he adopted the agnostic pose common to most French
intellectuals during the middle years of the nineteenth century, he
was never out of touch with the Church. Lefebve de Vivy suggests that during his summer holidays with the Grandjeans he fulfilled his religious duties, and the Abbé Delogne's letter to Mme
Grandjean implies the same thing. The priest mentions no loss of
faith – rather the contrary; and this impression is strengthened by
Delahaye's account of the religious crisis of 1869 (the most likely
moment for it) when Verlaine had decided to propose to Mathilde.
Even in the spring of 1873, during the height of his passion for
Rimbaud, he consulted Delogne about a reconciliation with his
wife and promised to reform. For a period of over twenty years
his life shows the same pattern: a return to the Church in difficult
moments.

Yet no one of these elements, however interesting in itself, was
really decisive. He was an *anima naturaliter christiana*, but a very
weak one. His religious sentiments in adolescence and young man-
hood were at best latent. To give them dynamism, to shake him
from his torpor, something more crucial was necessary than talks
with elderly priests or the persuasions of dying aunts; and here
again Rimbaud, the source of so much else, was the determining
factor. It was Rimbaud, the demon, the seer, the evil genius, who
turned the Verlaine of 1871, graceful Parnassian that he was, into
the great mystic poet of 1874.

To see how this was so we need only compare the boy's ideas
with those of Verlaine's friends like Lepelletier. The Parnassians
were neo-pagans and unbelievers to a man: "Par nos lectures, par
nos réflexions, nous étions persuadés de l'inexistence du surnaturel,
de l'impossibilité d'une providence tutélaire, et nous ne pouvions
croire à l'existence d'un autre monde, pas plus qu'à la suprématie
d'une puissance extérieure, indémontrable, qui domine l'humanité, la gouverne, se mêle de ses actes, les juge, les récompense, les
punit ... Verlaine était donc, à vingt ans, absolument incroyant,

par raisonnement, conviction, études ... Il avait l'athéisme rationnel et intelligent."[15] Here, as elsewhere in the *Vie*, Lepelletier did
not understand Verlaine as well as he thought. A man of *athéisme
rationnel et intelligent* would hardly have talked at such length with
the Abbé Delogne or thrown himself into a church in search of
confession and absolution. However, the passage does give us
some idea of the sort of atmosphere in which Verlaine was living
when he met Rimbaud. He was slipping into that state priests
learn to dread in their penitents: a kind of settled indifference. His
friends were not even particularly anti-clerical: "Dans nos réu-
nions parnassiennes, nous ne parlions jamais religion," Lepelletier
adds; they ignored such matters; they were not interested.

Rimbaud did not share this tepid scepticism. His mother had
raised him in the strictest devotion, allowing him no books but
the Bible, forcing the daily lesson on him, thrashing him when he
learned it badly[16]: God was one of the most vivid and unpleasant
memories of his childhood. He hated Him with a violence quite
foreign to the cool attitudes of scientific materialism. He did not
scribble "Dieu n'existe pas!" on the walls and park-benches of
Charleville, but "Merde à Dieu!" – which is something quite different. And he reached Paris in 1871 determined to take God's
place, to recreate the universe by the force of his own genius and
the power of his own verb.

In this way as in others he was carrying on the work of Baudelaire, and Verlaine must often have recognized, in the conversation of his young friend, echoes of the poet who had dominated
his adolescence. Not that Baudelaire – cynical, meditative, with
his profound sense of the moral nature of man and the contradictions of the universe – had any illusions about becoming God. But
reading Rimbaud after *Les Fleurs du mal* gives a sense of continuity.
The *tone* is the same: both poets knew the mystic virtues of blas-
phemy, and everywhere in their work is an impatience with mere
externals, a ceaseless probing into the realm of the spirit – always
with reference to two absolutes, God and Satan. Baudelaire and

15 Lepelletier, *Paul Verlaine*, 387-88.
16 The poem, "Les Poètes de sept ans," Rimbaud, Pléiade, 77.

Rimbaud, during the last half of the century, had more to do than anyone else with revolutionizing not merely poetry but literature itself. At the time, civilization was more blatantly materialistic than ever before. A thousand years of progress had masked the truths about man and his fate behind a mighty façade of platitude and convention, and the literature of the period showed a disconcerting tendency to accept this false front as something quite genuine, a realized ideal. Hence Victor Hugo's poems to democracy and flying-machines, Zola's conclusions in favour of socialism and applied science. Baudelaire and Rimbaud spent themselves in an effort to pierce this sham: their work gives an impression of self-immolation, as when Rimbaud drops his torch onto the palace of Ecbatana. Egocentric though they both were, self-revelation was not their main concern; and they were even less interested in the Parnassian formula of poetry as mere elegance, the equivalent of a marble bust or a Sèvres vase. It was an incantation, a sorcery – big magic, dissolving reality in an effort to discover the spiritual essentials – and its adepts engaged themselves, flesh and intellect, to the extreme limit:[17]

> Nous voulons, tant ce feu nous brûle le cerveau,
> Plonger au fond du gouffre, enfer ou ciel, qu'importe?
> Au fond de l'inconnu pour trouver du *nouveau*.
>
> ...
>
> Qui remuerait les tourbillons de feu furieux,
> Que nous et ceux que nous nous imaginons frères?
> A nous! Romanesques amis: ça va nous plaire.
> Jamais nous ne travaillerons, ô flot de feux!

Whatever else this may be, it is a refusal of the accepted, the conventional, the easy answer. The work of both poets (their best work) is essentially a sublimation of experience, a means to something else, something Baudelaire called *le nouveau* and Rimbaud *l'inconnu*. Such preoccupations were totally at variance not only with Parnassianism, but with most of the verse Verlaine had writ-

17 Baudelaire, "Le Voyage"; Rimbaud, "Vertige," Pléiade, 124.

ten before 1871 – particularly *La Bonne Chanson*: "Resonge à ce que tu étais avant de me connaître." Once joined to Rimbaud, Verlaine found himself in a disquieting world of infinite perspectives and ghastly depths, where the old Christian doctrines might be hostile, but where they were no longer so many exploded fables. Rimbaud gave him back a metaphysical view of the universe and his thought and style began to alter. Since he lacked his friend's will-power and probing, impatient intellect, he did not attempt a new set of symbols; he fell back on those he already knew in the doctrines of Catholic Christianity. There are no religious phrases or images in his early work; he did not use them until after he met the youth from Charleville. They then begin to crop us beneath his pen. He called his life with Rimbaud "a way of the Cross," and the imagery and language of "Le Bon Disciple" are so completely transcendental that the sonnet has been interpreted, not as a declaration of homosexual passion, but as a description of St. Michael overthrowing Satan.[18] There are also the passages in *Une Saison en Enfer* where Rimbaud shows him invoking Christ, and a couple of stanzas in "Birds in the Night" – almost a declaration of faith, the first of its kind in his published work:

> Par instants je meurs la mort du Pécheur
> Qui se sait damné s'il n'est confessé
> Et, perdant l'espoir de nul confesseur,
> Se tord dans l'Enfer, qu'il a devancé.
>
> Ô mais! par instants, j'ai l'extase rouge
> Du premier chrétien sous la dent rapace,
> Qui rit à Jésus témoin, sans que bouge
> Un poil de sa chair, un nerf de sa face![19]

He continued to use religious imagery during the rest of his life. We find it again, not merely in mystic works like *Sagesse*, but

18 A. Fontainas, *Verlaine-Rimbaud, ce qu'on présume de leurs relations ce qu'on en sait*, 58, refuses to see any obscene significance in the sonnet. See also Porché, *Verlaine tel qu'il fut*, 184, and Louis Morice, *Verlaine, le drame religieux*, 145.
19 Verlaine, Pléiade, 204.

even in his most obscene poetry – such as the "Balanide" from *Hombres*:

> Vêtu de violet,
> Fait beau le voir yssir ...
> Comme un évêque au chœur
> Il est plein d'onction ...[20]

Considering the context, this sustained metaphor is one of the oddest on record.

Rimbaud, of course, had no orthodox religious convictions of his own, nor any religious convictions at all: as far as we can know him from his letters and conversation he was a blasphemous scoffer, and he almost certainly lived through his adult life, including sixteen years of hardship and wandering, without seeking the spiritual consolations of the Church. His deathbed conversion in 1891, after months of suffering and an amputated leg, was no more and no less conclusive than such conversions usually are; those who, like Paul Claudel, attempt to turn him into a Christian poet are on dangerous ground. The canonization began with Isabelle Rimbaud's account of her brother's death agony. There is no reason to suppose that she misrepresented events; but she was an ardent Catholic, well satisfied to describe Rimbaud as dying in an odour of sanctity. Even Verlaine, convert though he was, thought that she exaggerated: "Elle tient à en faire un ange," he told Kessler in 1895, "ce qu'il n'était pas du tout."[21] However, from the theological standpoint, the pride that rivals God is the worst of sins, and this was Rimbaud's attitude, at least when Verlaine knew him. He did not throw off conventional belief because it interfered with his pleasures, but for intellectual and spiritual reasons: Church doctrine was a hindrance to achieving the *inventions d'inconnu* of which he dreamed. He was no easy-going voluptuary like the Verlaine of 1871, absorbed in a pleasant round of cafés, brothels, and literary discussions. This padded world was not to his taste; he thought it as false and limited as the world of or-

20 *Œuvres libres de Paul Verlaine, Les Amies, Femmes, Hombres*, 101.
21 Kessler, "Besuch bei Verlaine."

thodox piety. And when he tore Verlaine away from it, he destroyed his refuge, left him naked to despair, to his sense of unworthiness and desire for atonement, reawakened memories of the peace and spiritual security he had known as a believer. It was not at all what the boy intended. He had nothing but contempt for the converted Verlaine, especially when the convert tried to convert *him*. He dubbed him "Loyola," sufficient proof that he never meant his theory of *raisonné dérèglement de tous les sens* to end at the altars of the Roman Church. But it is a well known fact that one man's ideas may mean something quite different to another. Verlaine reached faith through Rimbaud and in reaction against him: the young poet's theories fell into his life like a cliff into a sluggish stream; the current was there, unseen and unheard until it began to foam against this sudden obstacle. Rimbaud gave him something to struggle with, threw him into a hell from which Christ (at least as far as Verlaine was concerned) was the only salvation. His early experiences, the whole bias of his nature, made conversion likely; association with Rimbaud made it inevitable.

In recent years, with the revival of interest in earlier mystics like John Donne, Jean de Sponde, St. John of the Cross, etc. there has been a tendency to undervalue Verlaine's religious poetry. He is too well known, and we like the thrill of discovery; and the man himself was so disreputable. During the rest of his life he never again turned atheist, but he did lapse into all his vices, both alcoholic and sexual, and wrote about them in horrifying detail. Anybody with religious convictions will always feel a bit uneasy about the poet who, though he composed *Sagesse*, also produced *Femmes* and *Hombres* – after *Sagesse* too, which is the unpardonable sin. A convert should be above such back-sliding. But a lily with its roots in the cesspool is none the less a lily, even though its festering may at times smell worse than weeds; and I will hazard the opinion that, as mystic poetry, Verlaine's sonnet-sequence "Mon Dieu m'a dit" has rarely been equalled and almost never surpassed. The style is not the pure music for which he is famous, which was inevitable. There can be nothing vague, subtle, suggestive, or escapist about a dialogue with Christ. To have written it in the style of *Fêtes galantes* or *Romances sans paroles* would have been ludicrous. But a good deal of the old Verlaine survives – the stammer, the calculated imprecision: in recording the supreme moment of his life he returned to the style he had used once before: the style of "Mon Rêve familier." The theme is nearly identical: the "femme inconnue" who loves and understands has become a God fulfilling the same function; the great sonnets are as murmurous and nostalgic as the earlier poem, and a similar technique is used – particularly *enjambement* at the caesura and from one line to the next:

> Mon Dieu m'a dit: Mon fils, il faut m'aimer. Tu vois
> Mon flanc percé, mon coeur qui rayonne et qui saigne,
> Et mes pieds offensés que Madeleine baigne
> De larmes, et mes bras douloureux sous le poids
>
> De tes péchés, et mes mains! Et tu vois la croix,
> Tu vois les clous, le fiel, l'éponge, et tout t'enseigne
> À n'aimer, en ce monde amer où la chair règne
> Que ma Chair et mon Sang, ma parole et ma voix.

But to quote these poems adequately would mean quoting them all. Verse of such quality is beyond criticism: we can point out its beauties, but what are its defects? It is also beyond mere dogma, even beyond religious faith itself, in the sense that religious faith is not necessary for its appreciation, any more than we have to be Greek pagans to understand Sappho's ode to Aphrodite. Verlaine did more than retell his own conversion. He expressed one of man's basic emotions: the need of consolation for the grotesque mishaps of existence. It is a fundamental longing, common to religion and agnosticism alike; as long as it haunts men they will find in these sonnets a supreme expression of their desire: a moment of light when one man – weak, vicious, self-contradictory though he was – spoke, however briefly, for the whole race.

7/ Obscure years/
Sagesse in progress

HIS MOTHER WAS WAITING for him at the gate of the prison, and together they were escorted over the frontier by the Belgian police (January 16, 1875), reaching Fampoux the same evening. Elisa had arranged a short visit with her brother, Julien Dehée. "Je suis ici depuis le 16 courant, en famille, chez d'excellents parents, avec maman," Verlaine wrote Lepelletier on the 25th. "Je ne puis trop préciser le jour, ni même la probabilité d'un prochain retour à Paris. On est si gentil ici pour nous, il est si bon de respirer l'air – même boréal – de la campagne, que la grande ville ne me tente que tout juste. Toutefois, je pense que nous ne tarderons plus guère à nous revoir ... De mes projets, nous causerons: tu me trouveras probablement bien changé, bien changé!"[1]

The Dehées' cordiality was only assumed. For many years there had been pursed lips and gravely shaken heads in the family over Paul's goings-on; his relations had long thought him a wastrel, spoiled by his mother ("Il a été habitué d'avoir toutce qu'il veut!"[2]); and, after the fashion of relatives, they felt a good deal of satisfaction when their worst predictions were verified. As far as the break-up of the marriage went, they sided with Mathilde. Verlaine, naïve as ever, suspected none of this hidden animosity. He took their welcome at face value; he had never been able to hide his feelings, and he talked of his wife without restraint: now re-

1 *CML*, I, 1097.
2 His aunt's remark to Victoire Bertrand, Lefebve de Vivy, *Les Verlaine*, 65.

pentant, now accusing her of every fault. This information was passed on to her at once: "Je t'engage à te méfier de Paul," one of the Dehée ladies wrote. "Il est venu ici à sa sortie de prison; nous l'avons reçu à cause de sa pauvre mère qui est bien à plaindre. Il nous a dit qu'il essaierait d'enlever son fils, non pas parce qu'il tient à l'avoir avec lui, mais pour se venger de ta demande en séparation."[3]

Thanks to these warnings, Mathilde was ready when he came to Paris a month later. She was quite determined never to take him back, and now she refused even to see him, and told her lawyer to do the same. It was a blind alley, and as far as the world of letters went, things were not much better. The scandal of his prison sentence had estranged nearly all his old friends; there was no point in remaining in Paris. Indeed, now that he had been converted, he found the city dangerous. Cafés and sidewalks swarmed with temptations he could not resist, particularly after two years' forced abstinence in jail: "Paris était séjour périlleux ... Il doutait de sa force de résistance dans ce mileu de facile perdition," writes Lepelletier, with whom he talked over the situation.[4] He only stayed a few days, but the experience was enough to send him back to the Church in panic-stricken flight, and to the Church in its most austere form: he went to Belgium (even though residence there was forbidden him by the 1873 sentence) and applied for entry to the Trappist monastery at Chimay. The abbot allowed him a week, then told him firmly that he had no vocation, a truth that even Verlaine had to admit.

Refuge with Mathilde and with the Trappists having failed (refuge was what he sought), there remained a third door on which he had not yet knocked – Rimbaud. Sooner or later Verlaine would have tried to find him again; it is impossible to believe otherwise. Rimbaud had changed considerably since their dramatic parting in Brussels two years before. He was at the end of his literary career. He had finished *Une Saison en Enfer* late in 1873, and had it printed in Brussels; most of the following year was

3 Mathilde, *Mémoires*, 237.
4 Lepelletier, *Paul Verlaine*, 402–3.

spent in London (during part of the time he was accompanied by a young artist-poet, Germain Nouveau), looking for a teaching position in Scotland or England.[5] Sometime during this period he completed *Les Illuminations,* usually considered his finest work. In March 1875, he was tutoring in a family at Stuttgart and studying German. He was less interested in a permanent job than in learning as many languages as possible to prepare himself for the life of travel he intended to begin. This may have been one of the reasons for his going to London with Verlaine in 1872, as a passage in *Une Saison en Enfer* suggests.[6] They were both corresponding with Ernest Delahaye, who served as intermediary. He had been Rimbaud's school chum at Charleville, just as Lepelletier had been Verlaine's, and took up teaching when he graduated. He seems to have realized the good luck which had put him on intimate terms with two great poets, and remained in close touch with both of them – later publishing reminiscences and critical studies of considerable value. Verlaine wrote Rimbaud a long letter and asked Delahaye to forward it: "Aimons-nous en Jesus!" Remembering what Verlaine had been, Rimbaud found the sentiment mildly disgusting. However, he told Delahaye to put Paul in touch with him. "Ça m'est égal. Si tu veux, oui, donne mon adresse à Loyola."[7] Three days later, Verlaine was at Stuttgart.

The only authentic account of their meeting is contained in a short letter Rimbaud sent Delahaye on March 5: "Verlaine est arrivé ici l'autre jour, un chapelet aux pinces ... Trois heures après on avait renié son dieu et fait saigner les 98 plaies de N. S. Il est resté deux jours et demi, fort raisonnable et sur ma remonstration s'en est retourné à Paris, pour de suite, aller finir d'étudier *là-bas dans l'île.*"[8] We can read a good deal between the lines. When he met Verlaine all Rimbaud's malice came to the surface. He thought Paul weak, sentimental, and (since his conversion) a hypocrite; it would be amusing to pour liquor into him and find out just how genuine his religion was. It was one of those appalling practical

5 See Vitalie Rimbaud's diary in Rimbaud, Pléiade, 517-83.
6 "Parce qu'il faudra que je m'en aille, très loin, un jour." *Ibid.,* 231.
7 Delahaye, *Verlaine,* 210-11.
8 Rimbaud, Pléiade, 307.

jokes Rimbaud loved, a rather obvious one, and of course it succeeded. But it is a question whether it succeeded quite as fully as
Delahaye later pretended. He relates (presumably on information
supplied by Arthur) that the pub-crawling led the two friends
outside the town onto the banks of the Nekar River, where a furious quarrel took place. Verlaine had been preaching conversion
from the moment of his arrival, and as alcohol overcame him his
arguments began taking an amorous turn. Rimbaud was no longer
the pretty boy of 1871, but a strong man of twenty; he knocked
Verlaine out and walked off. Some peasants found him unconscious on the river bank and carted him to their house, where he
stayed two days before he was sufficiently recovered to return to
Paris.

This lurid tale has fascinated biographers of Verlaine and Rimbaud ever since. The spectacle of two of the greatest modern poets
swinging at each other on the bank of an obscure German stream
has drama – all the more so when we recall that the manuscript of
Les Illuminations was in Verlaine's pocket. Rimbaud had given it
to him shortly after they met on the chance of getting it published.
And the scene fits the actors: Verlaine's weakness, his incurable
muddle of vice and faith, his never-quenched desire for Rimbaud
(it haunted him until he died); Rimbaud's intellectual sadism,
which made him quite capable of luring "Loyola" into making
an attempt on his virtue. For if this is really what happened, then
he was expecting it; it not only proved the shallowness of Verlaine's conversion, but was also a final step in denying God and a
further demonstration of his own power.

Yet, however alluring, the story is probably false – or greatly
exaggerated. It does not fit the rest of Rimbaud's account: "Il est
resté deux jours et demi, fort raisonnable ..." And it is hardly con-
sistent with the story about Les Illuminations. Where was the manuscript while the two men were trading blows? Supposing Rimbaud to have given it to Verlaine at all, it must have been before
the fight: did he then keep it with him during his two days' convalescence with the peasants, take it back to Paris and send it to

Germain Nouveau in March – as we are usually told?[9] It is perhaps easier to take Rimbaud's missive literally: he amused himself
by teasing Verlaine, getting him drunk, and thus proving to them
both that the new-found piety could be overturned by a few
glasses of brandy and the possibility of sex; then told him abruptly
that he had better go about his business, and that a teaching career
in England was no bad way of remaking his life. As for *Les Illuminations*, he was indifferent to literature. If it is true that he gave
the manuscript to Verlaine at this moment, then he was simply
liquidating the last scraps of his career as a poet. There was to be
an unpleasant little epilogue to their relations (as if what had gone
before were not unpleasant enough): as the months passed, he was
to remember Verlaine as a source of ready money. But they had
seen each other for the last time.

Verlaine reached London on March 20, 1875, took rooms a few
steps from his old lodgings in Howland Street, and applied for
work at a teachers' agency. "I wanted to be employed upon terms
of mutual exchange," he wrote later.[10] "That is to say, I would
teach French, drawing, and the dead languages in return for my
board, lodging, and laundry. I waited for about a week ... and at
the end of that time I received a notice from the agency in question, informing me that a schoolmaster in Lincolnshire had agreed
to engage me as a French and drawing master in a village called
Stickney, near Boston. The following day I packed up my traps
and started from King's Cross."

9 I have no desire to entangle myself in the problem of *Les Illuminations*, which
appears insoluble. According to Jacques Borel (in the chronology of the Verlaine Pléiade, xxviii), Rimbaud gave Verlaine the manuscript at Stuttgart and
Verlaine sent it to Germain Nouveau in March 1875. For a full discussion, see
Rimbaud, Pléiade, 779 *sqq.*, Starkie, *Arthur Rimbaud*, chap. VI *passim*, and Verlaine's letter to Delahaye, May 1, 1875, *CML*, I, 1102 ("Rimbaud m'ayant prié
d'envoyer pour être imprimés des 'poèmes en prose', siens, que j'avais" – if this
really refers to *Les Illuminations*). In a letter he wrote from Rethel on October
27, 1878 (*CML*, I, 1143), he says that the manuscript was for some time in
Charles de Sivry's possession. Verlaine and Nouveau met in London during the
summer of 1876. Underwood, *Verlaine et l'Angleterre*, 270 *sqq.*
10 "Notes on England, myself as a French Master," printed in English in the
Fortnightly Review, July 1894. *CML*, II, 1767-68.

Stickney was Victorian England at its best: a small town of 800 people, with a grammar-school under the direction of the local Anglican rector, George Coltman. Verlaine had come among heretics with a certain distrust, and he was astonished (and also, one feels, rather disappointed; he would have enjoyed a little martyrdom for his faith) to discover that Coltman, who spoke French fairly well, was not only friendly with the Catholic priest at Boston, eight miles away, but quite approved the new teacher's intention of going there every Saturday morning for Mass. As for the headmaster of the school, William Andrews, Verlaine boarded at his house and they were soon on good terms. Andrews needed Greek and Latin to obtain a higher diploma; in return for lessons he agreed to help Verlaine with his English. These were considerable advantages, and there was yet another: Mrs. Andrews was a good cook. Verlaine discovered traditional English food at her table. Anyone who has had the good luck to have an English mother or grandmother will sympathize with his enthusiasm for the stuffed chine, roast beef and boiled potatoes, lemon pudding and all the pastries, jams, preserves, and jellies with which generations of those admirable women kept the British Empire running – each meal washed down with cups of strong English tea. He soon had extra pupils, daughters of retired army men, of the local doctor: they were the gentry of the district and some of them invited him to dinner. It was an open-hearted society, honest and unpretending, anxious to make the foreigner welcome.

"Vie en famille," he summed it up in a letter to Lepelletier (April 9-10, 1875). "M. Andrews est un jeune homme qui *lit* le français, comme je lis l'anglais, mais qui ne le parle pas ... Du reste, charmant, cordial, très instruit. Mes 'élèves' sont des enfants très bien élevés et assidus, qui m'apprennent autant l'anglais que je leur apprends le français, et c'est ça que je cherche précisément."[11] The atmosphere was so pleasant that he even began to think of establishing himself definitely in England: "Combien de temps resterai-je ici? Trois ou six mois, selon que je saurai parler et *entendre*. Puis verrai à sérieusement gagner LA VIE, – en ce pays-ci, probable-

11 *CML*, I, 1098.

ment, où maman, j'espère, finirait par se presque fixer. [Elisa did in fact come over and stayed for some weeks; she was soon on the best of terms with Andrews and Coltman.] Je n'ai aucune distraction et n'en cherche pas. Lectures immenses, promenades ... à travers de magnifiques meadows pleins de moutons, etc. Depuis huit jours, c'est étonnant comme je me porte bien, moralement et physiquement." He was still of the same opinion a year later: "Il y a bien, c'est vrai, dans cette nouvelle façon de vivre, des heures fades et lourdes: du moins on n'y a pas d'occasion de se tromper; pas de fautes à commettre, partant pas de repentir à savourer après; *no drawbacks*, comme on dit ici ... Et la santé refaite! les économies réalisés, l'anglais acquis, le sérieux 'assumed', le latin resu, du temps suffisamment pour études *sérieuses* et même pour versifier aux heures de *revenez-y* ..."[12]

The old Verlaine was not dead – only under careful control. He quite understood that he must wear a mask; one can imagine the horror of those quiet people – the biblical disgust of Coltman, the white-faced indignation of William Andrews, had they known the details of the Brussels drama, or been able to listen to Victoire or Mathilde telling their stories about Verlaine drunk. He avoided the Stickney pubs; his only lapses occurred on Saturdays, when he drove over to Boston for Mass. The ceremony over, he had the rest of the day off, and he had discovered a few congenial spirits among the congregation of the Catholic chapel, such as Signor Cella, an Italian living in England. They piloted him through the bars and public-houses, and at least once a young medical student, Holmes, at that time living in Stickney, saw Verlaine come back from Boston "most gloriously tipt" as he described it.[13] But scenes of this kind were rare. The benign life, offering tranquillity and affection in return for certain disciplines, was easy for Verlaine to accept, and recalled his childhood: a child understands discipline when kindness goes with it. "His conduct was perfect," Mrs. Andrews wrote forty-two years afterward. "He never gave us any trouble." Looking back, an old woman now, and a widow

12 Letter to Emile Blémont, 8 février 1876, *CML*, I, 1123-25.
13 Underwood, *Verlaine et l'Angleterre*, 213.

(her husband died in 1893) she could marvel gently at the strange trick of destiny that had brought a Paul Verlaine into her house. "When he lived with us, I did not know that he was such a great poet. As soon as he had finished his classes he used to spend his time taking walks and writing in a note-book.[14]

The notebook was slowly filling with the last poems of *Sagesse*. Eight or ten of them are dated from Stickney, with notes like "Ecrit à Stickney en été 1875, sur l'herbe d'une prairie où paissaient des vaches," "Stickney, été 1875, à travers champs," "Stickney on a Sunday, 1875." Except for the prison months, his literary activity had never been greater. Intending to print *Cellulairement* as it stood, he sent Delahaye long extracts from May until October 1875, hoping to find a publisher in Charleville. The project, however, came to nothing, and meanwhile he had composed a quantity of new poems. He decided to group them (together with suitable extracts from the earlier collection) in two volumes, *Sagesse* and *Amour*. Besides the verse he actually wrote at Stickney, he had a number of ideas which proved abortive: a series of hymns in the manner of the Psalms ("avec mon triste *moi* dedans"), and a long sacred poem, *Le Rosaire*, on the Virgin Mary. "Depuis Adam et Eve jusqu'à présent. Toutes les civilisations, toutes les légendes ... le plan est tout théologique ..." Judging from this scenario, it is fortunate that the poem never got beyond the initial stage. Verlaine was not the man to rival Milton or Victor Hugo, and *Le Rosaire* would have been a disaster, another prolonged anecdote. He was also trying his hand at prose: "Mon livre patriotique sera court et simple ... J'ose croire que ce sera neuf, très doux, très touchant, et, autant que possible, très français et pas 'gaulois'. Très naïf, bien entendu, et je ferai tout mon possible pour être absurdement sincère."[15] The result was *Voyage en France par un Français*, completed five years later; it was another mistake, an effort at Catholic propaganda for which Verlaine had no talent.

This preoccupation with religious themes was not just the result of his conversion: it was part of his struggle with himself. He

14 Porché, *Verlaine tel qu'il fut*, 214.
15 Letter to Ernest Delahaye, 29 avril 1875, *CML*, I, 1099-1102.

clung to faith like a drowning man to a straw. He could not trust himself in Paris, and the brief interview with Rimbaud had shown him how fragile his piety was, ever at the mercy of a few drinks or a chance encounter. There were times when Rimbaud symbolized all the past, all the "old man" he had to vanquish: "Je ne me sens pas encore assez reconquis sur mes idiotismes passés, et c'est avec une espèce de férocité que je lutte à terrasser ce vieux Moi de Bruxelles et de Londres, 72–73 ... de Bruxelles, *Juillet 73*, aussi ... et surtout."[16] And the old nature proved hard to tame. Delahaye rather than Lepelletier (to whom his letters are relatively few) was his chosen correspondent during the years in England – and for a dangerous reason: he was Rimbaud's friend, and a means of keeping in touch with him. Rimbaud was still the flame round which Verlaine circled in mothy fascination. His name crops up in nearly every letter. September 3, 1875: "Quelle nouvelle de l'Œstre? Et s'est-il édulcoré?" – October 26: "Et quoi de l'Œstre?" – November 27: "Envoie nouvelles d'Homais ... Chez qui IL loge? ... Si quelquefois tu avais quelques vers (anciens) de l'être, envoie, je te prie, copie ... Je parle des vers d'avant son avatar et l'Homais actuel."[17] And during the summer of 1875, which he spent with his mother at Arras, an incident took place which shows how deep the old obsession was.

Delahaye was looking through the family album, where there was a picture of Mathilde, and as he turned the pages another photograph slid to the floor. "C'est M. Rimbaud," Elisa remarked naïvely. "En effet," Verlaine said. "C'est *mossieu* Rimbaud, mon fléau ... Donne un peu, veux-tu?" He took the album from Delahaye, removed the photograph of a relative facing Mathilde, and slipped Rimbaud into its place. Elisa turned pale: "Paul! je te le défends!" Verlaine slammed the album shut, crushing one portrait against the other. "Eh bien! quoi? ... Je réunis les deux êtres

---

16 *Ibid.*

17 *Ibid.*, 1105-19. I admit my inability to translate "L'Œstre." According to Larousse it is a parasitic fly. But was this Verlaine's meaning, or was he deliberately miswriting "l'être" or "l'autre"? He liked verbal tricks of this kind. "Homais," of course, is the obtuse rationalist in *Madame Bovary*; in choosing the name, Verlaine was replying to Rimbaud's "Loyola."

qui m'ont fait le plus souffrir ... Justice!"[18] Later on, Delahaye saw
Elisa slide Rimbaud back among the mere friends and acquaintances of the family. As ever, she is incomprehensible. Why did
she leave him there at all?

It is surprising that Verlaine left him there either, for ever since
the previous April Rimbaud had been writing him increasingly
nasty letters. He needed money, and Verlaine had always supplied
it: why not ask for more? Since the old friend was now living in
respectable circumstances, he was open to blackmail. Even Verlaine found this too much to bear. He refused to send anything
and asked Delahaye to conceal his address. "Tu peux lui dire que
toutes ses lettres, adressées *rue de Lyon*, ne me sont même pas en-
voyées ... Quant à la poste restante à London, inutile d'encombrer
cette institution de lettres qui ne seront jamais 'called for'. Le jour
où il sera sérieux, il connaît la voie (toi) pour me faire parvenir
sincérités."[19] – "Je lui expliquais en détail mes raisons arithméti-
ques de ne pas envoyer d'argent. Il a répondu: 1° des impertinen-
ces agrémentées d'annonces obscures de chantage; 2° par des comptes d'apothicaire, où il m'était démontré que c'était une bonne
affaire pour moi de lui prêter la somme en question. Sans compter
une missive absolument écrite en charabia d'homme soûl, où j'ai
cru démêler qu'il mettait à ses lettres futures cette condition que
je devais 'casquer', sinon, zut. En un mot, spéculation sur ma sottise ancienne, sur ma coupable folie d'il n'y a pas encore longtemps
de ne vouloir vivre que par lui et son souffle, plus la grossièreté à
la fois insupportable d'un enfant que j'ai trop gâté et qui me paie
(ô logique, ô justice des choses) de la plus stupide ingratitude. Car
n'a-t-il pas tué la poule aux œufs d'or vraiment?" Rimbaud, who
could be rather dense on occasion, had made another miscalculation – as he had done two years before in London, when his
savage taunts drove Verlaine across the Channel. At that time the
chain uniting them was still strong enough to bring Verlaine up in
a graceless sprawl once he got to the end of it, but now he could

18 Delahaye, *Verlaine*, 234-35.
19 Letter of 27 novembre 1875; *CML*, I, 1119. The friend in the rue de Lyon was
   called Istace; he had a café at no. 12.

measure the results of his weakness, and they were deplorable. It is a realization many men have to face on the brink of middle age. The old passion had reached the point of muddy liquidation when the victim asks himself what he got in return for so much expended. The mood did not last long (Rimbaud had stuck a dart in him which he was to carry forever, like Moby Dick), but while it did it left no room for illusion. "Après tout, il ne m'a pas fait grand bien, ce philomathe. Dix-huit mois de ce que tu sais, mon petit avoir fortement écorné, mon ménage détruit, mes conseils repoussés, la plus grossière impolitesse pour finir! ... Je commence enfin, et ce n'est pas sans mal, à saisir tout le côté profondément 'gâteux' de mon attitude de ces deux années passées à Bruxelles et à Londres, avec un qui, au fond, ... est positivement fermé, bouché par bien des côtés et que son féroce égoïsme *seul* déguise en individu plus intelligent qu'à son tour."[20]

On December 12, 1875, he attempted to set forth his reasons to Rimbaud himself: it is the last time they are known to have been in contact. He begins with a declaration of principles: "Je ne t'ai pas écrit ... parce que j'attendais ... lettre de toi enfin satisfaisante ... Aujourd'hui, je romps ce long silence pour te confirmer tout ce que je t'écrivais il y a environ deux mois. Le même toujours. Religieux strictement, parce que c'est la seule chose intelligente et bonne. Tout le reste est duperie, méchanceté, sottise ... Je m'étonne que tu ne voies pas ça, c'est frappant ... Et sept mois passés chez des protestants m'ont confirmé dans mon catholicisme, dans mon légitimisme, dans mon courage résigné ... Donc, le même toujours. La même affection (modifiée) pour toi. Je te voudrais tant éclairé, réfléchissant. Ce m'est un si grand chagrin de te voir en des voies idiotes, toi si intelligent, si *prêt* ... J'en appelle à ton dégoût lui-même de tout et de tous, à ta perpétuelle colère contre chaque chose ..." Then to the main point, the refusal of a loan: "Quant à la question d'argent, tu ne peux pas sérieusement ne pas reconnaître que je suis l'homme *généreux* en personne: c'est une de mes très rares qualités ... Mais, étant donné, et d'abord mon besoin de réparer un tant soit peu à force de petites économies les

20 Quoted by Porché, *Verlaine tel qu'il fut*, 217.

brèches énormes faites à mon menu avoir par *notre* vie absurde et honteuse d'il y a trois ans, – et la pensée de mon fils, et enfin mes nouvelles, mes fermes idées, tu dois comprendre à merveille que je ne puis t'entretenir. Où irait mon argent? A des filles, à des cabaretiers! Leçons de piano? Quelle *colle!*" Rimbaud had asked for money to study music, and oddly enough he was quite serious, though the reasons for this new craze are obscure.[21] "Tu m'as écrit, en avril, des lettres trop significatives de vils, de méchants desseins, pour que je me risque à te donner mon adresse, – bien qu'au fond toutes tentatives de me nuire soient ridicules et d'avance impuissantes, et qu'en outre il y serait, je t'en préviens, répliqué *légalement*, pièces en mains. – Mais j'écarte cette odieuse hypothèse. C'est, j'en suis sûr, quelque *caprice* fugitif de toi, quelque malheureux accident cérébral qu'un peu de réflexion aura dissipé. – Encore prudence est mère de la sûreté, et tu n'auras mon adresse que quand je serai sûr de toi."[22]

Rimbaud seems to have left this letter unanswered, and so their friendship petered out in bitterness and triviality. His attempt at blackmail was typical of the moral obtuseness and loutish disregard for others he often displayed, and from which Verlaine had suffered during their life together. "Inutile d'écrire ici *till called for*," he concluded. "Je pars demain pour de gros voyages, très loin ..." Verlaine was erecting barriers, and there is no better way of doing so than a change of address. He dated from London, not Stickney, making it even more difficult for Rimbaud to find where he was. Already during the summer holidays of 1875, when Delahaye saw the album, Rimbaud's conduct had inspired a poem of fifty lines which later appeared in *Sagesse*:[23]

> Malheureux! Tous les dons, la gloire du baptême,
> Ton enfance chrétienne, une mère qui t'aime ...
> Tu pilles tout ...
> La malédiction de n'être jamais las
> Suit tes pas sur le monde où l'horizon t'attire,

21 Enid Starkie discusses the point at some length, *Arthur Rimbaud*, 336-37.
22 *CML*, I, 1121-23.
23 Verlaine, Pléiade, 245.

L'Enfant prodigue avec des gestes de satyre! ...
– Dieu des humbles, sauvez cet enfant de colère!

Considering this background, it is not surprising that the verse of *Sagesse* – whether composed at Stickney or during holidays on the continent – should give an impression of struggle and torment. It might be said that this is also true of the sequence "Mon Dieu m'a dit"; and in fact Verlaine very rarely, almost never, describes the sustained ecstasy of his union with Christ. He tells us how he fought towards it and achieved it, but once the light has burst on him, he rings down the curtain:

J'ai l'extase et j'ai la terreur d'être choisi.

...

Et j'aspire en tremblant ...
– Pauvre âme, c'est cela!

The effect is magnificent, to be sure, but it is chiefly an effect, almost a literary device; he was always an artist, with an artist's eye for telling detail, and a poem should end when emotion is at its height. Nevertheless, there is a feeling of certitude, spiritual as well as aesthetic, about the great sonnets which we seek in vain in the other poems of *Sagesse*. It only occurs once or twice – in "Je ne veux plus aimer que ma mère Marie" and "O mon Dieu vous m'avez blessé d'amour"; and they may both belong to the period of *Cellulairement*. Verlaine sent them to Emile Blémont from Stickney in a letter of November 19, 1875, but later added the notation "Mons, Belgique, de la prison, 1874, 15 août."[24] The tone is much the same as that of "Mon Dieu m'a dit," and appears to reflect the mystic elan of the prison crisis; Verlaine may simply have copied them out for Blémont a year later, which explains why they are better than what he produced at Stickney. For, once the instant of illumination had passed, he found himself not so much a prey to doubt as in a state of waning ecstasy. And since he

24 *Ibid.*, notes to "O mon Dieu" and "Je ne veux plus aimer," 1124. The dates setting the time of composition in prison were added by Verlaine himself to Harry Graf Kessler's copy of *Sagesse*. Verlaine, Pléiade, 1116.

was Verlaine, living on his emotions, with little dogma to uphold him, he had to exist in perpetual conflict. The resulting poems are beautiful, and he usually resolves the battle on the side of the angels; but even when this is so (and it is not always so) a feeling of restlessness and tension remains. One sonnet, "Beauté des femmes," even bears a note, "Arras, 7bre ou 8bre (après quelle tentation!)"; another, "Les faux beaux jours ont lui," has "Paris, 8bre 1875 (sur le bord d'une rechute)"; and its successor, "La vie humble," "Paris, 8bre 1875 (après une sévère confession)." All of which corresponds with what Lepelletier tells us of his uneasiness in the metropolis. Nor was the present, with its moments of dullness and boredom, his only difficulty. At times memories of the past assailed him with diabolical precision – as when the flesh presented itself, not tricked out in a harlot's paint or Rimbaud's blasphemies, but in a pathos of sleep and tenderness which he found it almost impossible to resist:

> La tristesse, la langueur du corps humain
> M'attendrissent, me fléchissent, m'apitoient ...

The poem echoes the sonnet to Rimbaud, "Ce soir, je m'étais penché sur ton sommeil" (which, indeed, he originally intended to include in *Sagesse*[25]), and shows on what dangerous ground the book was constructed. Mrs. Andrews, as she watched him scribbling in his notebook, would have been astonished to learn what he was writing; they were strange poems for a Victorian schoolmaster.

He had been reasonably happy at Stickney, and from the point of view of poetry his year there (March 1875 – March 1876) was fruitful. But he thought that elsewhere he could do better financially; he now realized something of the enormous importance of money. At the time of his release from prison – as his letter to Rimbaud shows – he was sincerely remorseful for the way he had squandered his mother's fortune, and talked of earning a living with his pen. And now an incident occurred which showed him how illusory such hopes were.

25 Verlaine, Pléiade, 1151 (note to "Vers pour être calomnié").

A third number of *Le Parnasse contemporain* was to be published. Since he had contributed to the two first issues, he saw no reason why his verse should not appear in a third; he still had no idea of how the Brussels scandal has affected his reputation in literary circles. He sent Blémont some of the best pieces from *Sagesse* on July 7, and asked him to persuade the Parnassian committee (Banville, Coppée, and Anatole France) to accept them. Blémont did his best: he was, with Lepelletier, one of the few men who understood Verlaine's genius and had the courage to say so. But although none of the Parnassians were prudes they drew the line at a man who had spent two years in prison for attempted homosexual murder.[26] Banville and Coppée abstained from voting on Verlaine's offering, and Anatole France, left to himself, wrote that the author was personally ignoble, and his verse the worst the committee had received.[27] In other words, Verlaine was unsuitable both as a man and a poet.

He took the failure calmly. "Peu surpris du résultat annoncé. Peu désolé aussi," he wrote Blémont on October 27, 1875.[28] But a rejected manuscript is never a pleasure, and he realized that he would have to look for money elsewhere than in literature. He thought that at Boston he would earn more than in Stickney; the fact that there was a Catholic centre there was an added inducement. "Très probablement quitterai fin du mois. Quitte en très bons termes et emporterai testimonial magnifique. Me fixerai pour un temps en la ville où prêtre (Loyola!) m'aidera," he told Delahaye.[29] William Andrews was sorry to see him go and gave him the testimonial he wanted; he left for Boston in March 1876. Financially the move was an error. The priest in question was Father Sabela, who officiated at the Catholic chapel, and he did what he could, even sent his brother to take French lessons. But only three pupils could be found, and a few weeks later Verlaine

26 Edmond de Goncourt (*Journal*, 27 janvier 1895) refers to Verlaine as a "pédéraste assassin."
27 Mallarmé's *Après-midi d'un faune* was also rejected. Starkie, *Arthur Rimbaud* 151-52.
28 *CML*, I, 1111.
29 Underwood, *Verlaine et l'Angleterre*, 287, also 303, 304.

had to give up and return to London, where he once more put himself in touch with an agency.

Again he did not have to wait long. He was soon engaged as French and Latin master at St. Aloysius School, Bournemouth. The headmaster, Frederick Remington, was an Anglican parson who had gone over to Rome (without taking orders: his wife still lived with him); and the pupils were mostly Catholic. Board and tuition cost 100 guineas a year – expensive for the time. The school made a point of being "select," of providing instruction for children whose health was "not equal to the rigorous conditions of the Public Schools." It was, in fact, one of those establishments catering to rich families with lazy or mentally retarded sons, several of them on the brink of juvenile delinquency. "De vrais diables," Verlaine told Delahaye, particularly the Irish boys, one of whom knocked him out with a loaded snowball during the first winter. Discipline, indeed, was his main trouble, even though all his pupils were not equally bad nor equally stupid (a certain W. Clifford later made some important discoveries in radiography). Delahaye says that Verlaine was too familiar with the boys, and that when they tried to capitalize on it and he punished them they were resentful.

The Catholic atmosphere turned out to be much less congenial than the Anglicanism of Stickney; in any case Verlaine had been teaching for two years and was beginning to tire of the work and to miss Paris. On January 19, shortly after the snowball incident, he wrote Lepelletier that he would shortly return to the "Capital of the world." He intended to lead a strictly moral life – "vie plus monastique que jamais, avec, pour seule joie, le petit à voir de temps en temps" (January 19, 1877). He was thinking of Georges (and also of Mathilde) once more: was it at this moment that he attempted to put into effect his scheme for kidnapping the child? He was in Paris for a few days in June 1877, and Mathilde writes that he sent her a note from a café near the rue Nicolet, asking her to confide Georges to the bearer. With the Dehées' warning in mind, she refused to let the child leave the house.

His final return to Paris took place in mid-September. One of
the first people he saw was Delahaye, who had just resigned from
a Catholic school, the Institution Notre-Dame, at Rethel. Verlaine applied for the position, and thanks to his testimonials from
Andrews and Remington, was engaged at once. Notre-Dame was
run by the Church to provide the same programme as the state
lycées. Priests handled the Latin and Greek, lay professors the
other subjects. This was just the sort of environment Verlaine
wanted, or thought he wanted. "Je suis ici professeur de littérature,
histoire, géographie et anglais ... Régime excellent. Chambre à
part ... La plupart des professeurs ... sont ecclésiastiques et je suis
naturellement dans les meilleurs termes avec ces messieurs...J'ai la
paix, le calme et la liberté ... Appointements raisonnables."[30] Unfortunately there were certain disadvantages. As at Stickney he
had to conceal his past; in England that had been relatively easy –
he was a foreigner and certain eccentricities were allowed him –
and since he was dealing with heretics, he perhaps had fewer
scruples. But at Rethel he led a semi-monastic existence with young
priests of his own race and faith, and at times he felt like a perfect
fraud. Timidity led him to adopt an attitude of abnormal reserve
– to such a point that he rather frightened his colleagues. And behind this austere façade the struggle between past and present, the
old man and the new, which had dominated his life in the quiet
Lincolnshire village, continued as violently as ever. It was even
worse than before, simply because it had lasted longer. And, to
further complicate matters, life at Rethel included a potential
danger which had been absent at Stickney and Bournemouth –
alcohol.

Verlaine was a typical dipsomaniac, one of those drinkers who
cannot drink at all, who must choose between total abstinence or
complete surrender. For this reason England, with its unattractive
pubs and its relative sobriety, was a salutary experience. Not so
France. Even at Notre-Dame wine was served with meals, and in
the town there were the eternal cafés. In England a visit ended

30 Letter to Lepelletier, 14 novembre 1877, *CML*, I, 1135.

with tea; in France the host felt duty-bound to offer liqueurs and aperitifs. At Stickney it would have been scandalous for Monsieur Verlaine to keep a bottle in his room, but at Rethel it was the rule. All the good priests had a cordial or two in their cupboards, and Verlaine soon laid in a stock of his own. And as always, alcohol lowered the bars he had erected around his obsessive eroticism.[31] From the beginning of his installation at Rethel he was involved in an exhausting emotional combat, worse than anything he had known in England.

A number of incidents marked its course; they prove that he did not fall without a struggle. On leaving prison three years before, he had turned to the Church, to Mathilde and to Rimbaud; now the pattern repeated itself, although another figure soon took Rimbaud's place. At the end of the school year, in 1878, when the Cardinal-Archbishop of Rheims, Monseigneur Langénieux, paid a visit to Notre-Dame, Verlaine asked for an interview and made a full confession of his past life. It was less a need for absolution (which he had already received from the chaplain at Mons) than a desire to talk about his sins, to shift the burden of responsibility to other shoulders. The Archbishop's reaction was favourable: he gave the penitent his blessing and complimented him on his sincerity. Porché suggests that he decided then and there, however, that Verlaine was unsuitable as a teacher, and would have to be got rid of – which explains why his contract was not renewed for the following school year. But a man rarely becomes an archbishop and a cardinal of the Roman Church without a profound knowledge of men and things, and it is unlikely that Monseigneur behaved so narrowly. That he did not is proved by the fact that Verlaine's contract *was* renewed – for 1878-79. If Langénieux took any steps at all, it was probably to suggest to the school authorities that they keep a benign eye on Verlaine. Within a few months the teacher more than justified the caution, and without any further pressure from His Eminence.

His next effort was an overture to Mathilde. Projects for a reconciliation (including the rather dubious method of kidnapping

31 Delahaye, *Verlaine*, 283.

Georges) had preoccupied him during his months in England; he
even discussed them with Delahaye, who, in a letter of 1876, suggested various means of reaching her: "Le moyen décisif serait
peut-être de faire parvenir à la jeune personne *seule* – en évitant
soigneusement le contact du papa – quelques mots simples et
francs où tu lui proposais catégoriquement de venir te rejoindre
en England." [sic] – Delahaye had accepted Verlaine's story that
M. Mauté was the true source of the misunderstanding between
the couple. "Qui sait si ce petit coup d'état ne déchirerait bien des
toiles d'araignées?"[32] If the account Mathilde gives of her feelings
at this period is true, the "little stroke" would have had no effect
at all. But we do not know whether or not she ever received the
proposal.

There was another channel open between the couple: Verlaine
was still on friendly terms with Charles de Sivry. Through him he
sent Mathilde extracts from *Sagesse* as he composed them (she
eventually possessed almost the entire manuscript). In the spring
of 1878, at Rethel, he learned from Charles that Georges was seriously ill. He wrote Mme Mauté at once, asking to see his son, and
the request was granted. Mme Mauté received him near the child's
bed; Mathilde did not appear nor was she mentioned. He told his
mother-in-law of his life at Rethel, his good intentions, and his
sincere religious faith; and during a second visit a day or two later,
spoke of a possible reunion with his wife. Mme Mauté was touched.
She had always liked him, and although at bottom she did not
think that the marriage could or should be renewed, she did not
want to discourage him by a blunt refusal. "Vous êtes tous deux
si jeunes encore," she answered with a smile. "Plus tard on verra."[33]

These interviews inspired four poems in *Sagesse*: "Ecoutez la
chanson bien douce," "On n'offense que Dieu," "Les chères mains
qui furent miennes," and "Et j'ai revu l'enfant."[34] The first, written in the style of *Romances sans paroles*, is another example of the
"musical" Verlaine; one of his most successful efforts of this kind
and also one of the last. He was less and less interested in his earlier

32 Underwood, *Verlaine et l'Angleterre*, 318.
33 Mathilde, *Mémoires*, 238.   34 Verlaine, Pléiade, 1122.

manner; he even ridiculed the piece a little when he sent three stanzas of it to Charles de Sivry: "ça me semble ... d'un bête, d'un bête ... sans talent aucun, je le crains."[35] In reality, the poem is one of the most beautiful he ever wrote.

It is just possible that, had he persisted, he might have got his wife back. She and her parents, whatever he later declared, never prevented him from seeing Georges, and they even expected the 1878 visit to be followed by others. At first this appeared to be his intention. He wrote several letters to Mme Mauté from Rethel and sent the child a few gifts – illustrated albums, an English book. The family was therefore surprised when he suddenly fell silent. And in the autumn of the following year, 1879, they were even more surprised when not Verlaine, but Delahaye, arrived at the house, ostensibly to give them a photograph of the poet.

As Delahaye tells the story in his biography, Verlaine had commissioned him to make yet another appeal for a reconciliation; M. Mauté, every inch the stern father, refused point-blank: "Certaines choses," he declared pompously, "demeurent irréparables."[36] This cruel snub was the source of the heart-rending "O Jésus, vous voyez que la porte" in *Amour*; and the poet, frustrated in his paternal affection, proceeded to pour it out on one of his students, whom we now hear of for the first time, Lucien Létinois. In other words, the Mautés were responsible for all that followed.

None of this is true – as appears from one of Delahaye's own letters, written to Verlaine on November 6, 1879, immediately after his visit to the rue Nicolet. Astounded at not seeing his son-in-law, M. Mauté asked where he was: had he gone back to Bournemouth? Why had he left Rethel? Why had he not come to see Georges during the summer holidays? The last query proves that the family was expecting him and would not have refused to see him had he appeared. They were hard questions to answer, and Delahaye got out of the difficulty by some high-sounding verbiage about Verlaine's paternal love, his extreme piety, and about changes in the Rethel curriculum which made it impossible for him to remain there. He would not even give Paul's address;

35 Letter of 27 octobre 1878, *CML*, I, 1142.
36 Delahaye, *Verlaine*, 286.

he contented himself with saying "no" when M. Mauté asked if the poet was again at Bournemouth.[37]

All this secrecy was an elaborate game to throw Verlaine's in-laws off the scent. It was not for the first time. During his stay in England he referred to them as "leeches" and made a great parade of hiding his address, presumably because he was afraid they might sue him for Mathilde's alimony, none of which he ever paid.[38] His apprehensions were groundless; nothing suggests that the Mautés ever contemplated legal steps. Had they intended to gar-nishee his salary they could have done so when he wrote them from Rethel. He was always master of the situation, coy about his whereabouts when he chose; and if he now disappeared again it was because he had lost interest in the rue Nicolet and all its in-habitants. He was off on a new adventure – not through frustrated paternal love, but because Lucien Létinois interested him more than Georges and Mathilde put together.

As the truth slowly dawned, feelings in the rue Nicolet were naturally bitter. All the more so since a kind of semi-appeasement had been reached. The Mautés were left with a sense of dupery and vague insult. When Mathilde recalled the episode in her memoirs, it struck her as a final revelation of Verlaine's character: "de tout temps un enfant gâté, criant, trépignant, jusqu'à ce qu'il ait l'objet convoité, puis, son caprice satisfait, brisant le joujou désiré et le délaissant ... Il m'aime, m'épouse et me rend heureuse pendant un an; puis il m'abandonne pour vagabonder en com-pagnie d'Arthur Rimbaud ... Il vient voir son fils, fait part à ma mère de son rêve de réconciliation. Cela dure quelques mois; puis, brusquement, il cesse d'écrire, oublie de nouveau son fils et, pen-dant six ans, je n'entends plus parler de lui. C'est qu'il a quitté Rethel en compagnie de Lucien Létinois; et si, confiante dans ses promesses, je l'avais suivi à Rethel, rien ne me prouve qu'il ne m'aurait pas délaissée une deuxième fois pour partir avec ce nou-vel ami."[39] With the passage of time Mathilde had become cruelly lucid, and it would be difficult to maintain that she was wrong.

37 Underwood, *Verlaine et l'Angleterre*, 338-39.
38 Letters to Blémont and Lepelletier, 8 avril, 6 septembre 1875, 19 janvier 1877.
39 Mathilde, *Mémoires*, 246.

8/Lucien Letinois/
Sagesse completed/
Disorder and collapse

VERLAINE FIRST SAW Lucien Létinois in his English class during the autumn of 1878. The boy's father was a poor farmer at Coulommes, near Rethel, who had sent his only son to college in hopes that he would fit himself for a profession. Lepelletier disliked him: "Un grand garçon pâle, mince, maigriot, dégingandé, à l'air sournois et naïf; un rustre dégrossi, prétentieux légèrement et sentimental assez. Un berger d'opéra-comique. Colas à la ville."[1] He was convinced that Lucien and his parents exploited Verlaine's affection and ended by swindling him. Delahaye's portrait is more favourable: "Un jeune homme d'assez haute taille, d'allure très souple et très agile. Sa figure, aux traits réguliers mais non mièvres – légèrement hâlée par l'air des champs – aux yeux bruns et vifs, avait une expression de bonne foi, d'énergie. Le regard doux, candide et résolu ..."[2] On one point they both agree: Lucien was a substitute for Georges, kept from his father by the Mautés; Verlaine himself never fails to harp on this string. Lucien is "my son" throughout *Amour* and the *Voyage en France par un Français*:

> Je connus cet enfant, mon amère douceur,
> Dans un pieux collège où j'étais professeur.
> Ses dix-sept ans mutins et maigres, sa réelle

1 Lepelletier, *Paul Verlaine*, 416. The new passion probably exasperated him somewhat. The Rimbaud scandal was barely forgotten, and here was Verlaine starting again!
2 Delahaye, *Verlaine*, 312.

Intelligence, et la pureté vraiment belle
Que disaient et ses yeux et son geste et sa voix,
Captivèrent mon cœur et dictèrent mon choix
De lui pour fils, puisque, mon vrai fils, mes entrailles,
On me le cache en manière de représailles
Pour je ne sais quels torts charnels ...[3]

This was the initial ambiguity of the new passion, and it falsified Verlaine's relations with Lucien from the start. The poet was not kept from his son, he had dropped him; and in any case the child was seven and Lucien seventeen, a discrepancy which alone explodes the fable. The heart of the matter was very different. Lucien was not a substitute for Georges but for Rimbaud; he looked like Rimbaud, he had the same build, the same eyes, the same local intonation – he too came from the Ardennes. "Verlaine trouvait un peu partout des ressemblances avec Rimbaud," Cazals wrote later, presumably on information supplied by Verlaine. "Létinois le lui rappelait par la taille, l'accent et, je crois, les yeux."[4]

Whatever the similarities in appearance, however, Lucien did not resemble Rimbaud intellectually. His "réelle intelligence" was a lover's illusion. Far from being a genius, he was not even very bright. He had a commonplace mind and his class-work was mediocre. At the beginning, in a panicky movement of self-defence, Verlaine seized on these shortcomings as an excuse for penalties: sharp comments, extra work. But this very severity was itself a pleasure, a perverse sort of intimacy. It forced Lucien to come to his study after class. And there the open face, the eyes, the blurred accent did their work. Long talks and advice followed. The young peasant's very dullness, his admiration for the man whose knowledge and experience so far surpassed his own, was both soothing and reassuring. If he had none of Rimbaud's terrifying brilliance he was at least docile. Verlaine adapted himself to the lesser mind, and that too was a pleasure. Within a few weeks their intimacy was a settled thing.

3 Verlaine, Pléiade, 453.
4 Underwood, *Verlaine et l'Angleterre*, 326. But Rimbaud's eyes were blue and Lucien's brown. Perhaps Verlaine chose to forget this discrepancy.

It has been severely judged. Critics like Porché and Coulon have no doubts about its guilt, but M. Antoine Adam maintains the contrary.[5] His conclusions are now usually accepted, and I think rightly. Verlaine was still a devout man in the autumn of 1878; he never missed Mass and neither did Lucien, who had all a peasant's unquestioning faith. This mutual piety was one of the bonds between them, and religion occupied a large place in their conversations. There was also the father-son relationship. For a time Verlaine even talked of adopting the boy legally. It is hard to see, therefore, how he could have attempted anything in the nature of a seduction. He was the prisoner of his initial pose: he would have risked putting Lucien to flight by a sudden change of conduct. We can at least give him the benefit of the doubt. There was nothing "wrong" in their relations. But even admitting this to be so, the friendship was none the less deplorable. In some ways it leaves a worse impression on the mind than the frenzied escapade with Rimbaud.

That at least was frank, a sensuous and intellectual explosion which burst open the stifling atmosphere of the rue Nicolet and made Verlaine a great poet. The Létinois episode, on the other hand, was one of those horrible "sublimations" where nothing is what it seems. False, the religious prating – not a genuine love of God but a means of holding the youth – false too the gushy paternalism. The paternalism is the most objectionable element in the whole affair, concealing as it does an unpleasant interest in mere youth (youth was about all Lucien had to commend him), a form of sentimental degeneracy into which Verlaine lapsed with increasing frequency as the years passed. Dujardin and Viotti had been more or less his own age, but Rimbaud was ten years his junior and Lucien sixteen; it is clear that the boys celebrated in *Hombres* were younger still. He was becoming an aging libertine, the sort of person who makes a nuisance of himself in parks and steam baths. When religion is added to this mixture we get something very smelly indeed: there is a stench of hypocrisy about his

5 Porché, *Verlaine tel qu'il fut*, 229 *sqq.*; Marcel Coulon, *Verlaine, poète saturnien*, 151; Antoine Adam, *Le Vrai Verlaine, essai psychanalytique*, 54.

affection for Lucien from first to last. If he did not corrupt his pupil he would have liked to – though he never admitted the fact, not even to himself.

Or did he realize at times just how false the situation was? Throughout the autumn and winter of 1878, during the first flush of his passion, his drinking increased, always a sign of tension. Morning classes at Notre-Dame ended at 10:30, and Verlaine began slipping downtown to a little café, "Au Père Martin," where he drank so much absinth that he could scarcely walk back to college and was in no condition to teach in the afternoon.[6] Schedules had to be rearranged so that he had only morning classes, a most unsatisfactory situation. If Cardinal Langénieux had suggested that Verlaine be kept under discreet observation, what the school authorities saw must have disturbed them, and perhaps too there had been talk about the teacher's sudden intimacy with a student. At a small institution like Notre-Dame not much can be hidden. Several of the priests tried to warn him, but to no avail; then one night he came home completely drunk and in a bad humour. The Superior reprimanded him and Verlaine replied insultingly. He was therefore informed, in July 1879, that his services would not be required for the following academic year.[7]

This dismissal did not disturb him much. He would not have stayed even had he been asked – for the reason that Lucien had failed his examinations and was not coming back either. Gone were all thoughts of Mathilde; gone too all Verlaine's projects of an established position in an atmosphere of priests and sanctity. The past no longer counted: it was as though he had come to Rethel for the sole purpose of meeting Lucien. And now that they had met, nothing must come between them. Since they were both leaving, some way had to be found of staying together, and Verlaine thought of one immediately: Lucien should have his old position at Stickney. It did not matter that the boy was stupid, that he had failed his examinations, and that he knew nothing of

6 Coulon, *Verlaine*, 243.
7 Cazals and Le Rouge, Les Derniers jours, 131-32. Cazals was in a position to know the truth.

teaching. Verlaine wrote Andrews in glowing terms, and, since he had made an excellent impression himself, his recommendation was sufficient: there was a vacancy for September, and Lucien was engaged at once. Through a London agency Verlaine obtained a job for himself at the Solent Collegiate School, Lymington, near the Isle of Wight. Stickney and Lymington were at some distance from each other, but the main object had been achieved – isolation with Lucien in the charmed circle of a foreign country. Lucien's parents consented to the move without difficulty. A position teaching in England, under the guidance of a former master from Rethel, was a step up for their son; and in August Verlaine and his friend left France together.

They were in England for five months. Verlaine adapted himself well to his new surroundings: the whole experience was an adventure. He soon ingratiated himself with his headmaster, William Murdoch, and the days passed very much as at Stickney two years before – teaching, walks, outdoor sports, etc.; the little town, between the sea and the New Forest, was pretty and has left traces in Verlaine's poetry.[8] And always there were Lucien's letters, which he awaited with impatience and read over again and again.

All was not well with the young man. As one of his students (who had also known Paul) remembered later, "he was a great contrast with Verlaine"[9]: an awkward peasant with none of his master's charm. His pupils and colleagues found him dull, reserved, and not very well bred. And he could neither speak English, nor teach, nor keep order in his classes. Andrews soon decided that he would not do, and fired him at Christmas. As soon as Verlaine heard this he gave Murdoch notice. His mother's health, he said, forced him to return to France. This was nothing but an excuse for breaking his contract. The position at Lymington had had no other point than being in England with Lucien, and it was useless now that the boy could not remain. And there was another and even more potent reason for getting him back to France: in one of his last letters he had confessed that he was involved with a girl.

8 Underwood, *Verlaine et l'Angleterre*, 336.
9 *Ibid.*, 343.

If we knew just who she was and what she was we should be
better able to judge Verlaine's conduct at this juncture. Delahaye
calls her one of Lucien's pupils, and says that matters never went
beyond a mild flirtation; Verlaine, without entering into particu-
lars, maintains that his young friend sinned gravely.[10] He rushed
up to London, met Lucien there on Christmas day, 1879, and ex-
erted all his influence to break off the affair, talking about the boy's
immortal soul and sending him to a priest for confession. If the
girl was a common trollop he was justified, but, given the conditions of life at Stickney, Lucien cannot have met many trollops;
and supposing her to have been a student, then she was his social
equal (if not better) and a marriage would have been normal and
even suitable. In that case, however, she was even more dangerous
to Verlaine than if she had been a strumpet or a barmaid. His motives are almost too obvious: he behaved like a dog in the manger.
If he could not have Lucien himself he was not going to stand by
while some woman snapped him up. In the light of these ignoble
considerations, the famous eighth poem in *Amour*, describing the
Christmas interview in London, takes on a rather odious colouring:

> O l'odieuse obscurité
> Du jour le plus gai de l'année
> Dans la monstrueuse cité
> Où se fit notre destinée!
>
> Au lieu du bonheur attendu,
> Quel deuil profond, quelles ténèbres!
> J'en étais comme un mort, et tu
> Flottais en des pensers funèbres ...
> Un remords de péché mortel
> Serrait notre cœur solitaire ...
> Puis notre désespoir fut tel
> Que nous oubliâmes la terre,

---

10 Delahaye, *Verlaine*, 298; Verlaine, letter of 17 novembre 1883 (to an unnamed
  correspondent): "Lucien ... me confia sa faute (c'était grave, en effet) et sur mes
  vives instances ... alla se confesser ...", *CML*, I, 1177.

> Et que, pensant au seul Jésus
> Né rien que pour nous ce jour même
> Notre foi prenant le dessus
> Nous éclaira du jour suprême ...[11]

Until we know more about the girl (as things stand she is not even a name) Verlaine remains open to the suspicion of playing on his disciple's religious scruples to satisfy his own unavowed jealousy.

Back in France once more he had to find some other way of holding the boy. The Létinois were farmers: why not settle with them on the land? Their own property at Malval, near Coulommes, was too small. Verlaine therefore had Elisa buy a farm at Juniville, in the same neighbourhood; by the middle of March 1880, he had settled on it with the family. The property cost 30,000 francs, and Elisa was probably glad to pay it. Paul was realizing, spontaneously, Mme Grandjean's project of ten years before; and, just as he had brought his mother to Stickney (she was the necessary audience for each scene of his fate), so he invited her to Juniville during the summer of 1880. The tranquil atmosphere was restful to her, but did she never ask herself what had become of his teaching projects? And did she never reflect that his relations with Lucien were proving as expensive as his adventure with Rimbaud?[12]

Ever since Virgil wrote the *Bucolics*, farming has had a fatal attraction for poets.

> Tityre, tu patulae recubans sub tegmine fagi
> Silvestrem tenui Musam meditaris avena ...

The rolling aspects of sky, woods, and ploughed land – the ancient symbols, both pagan and Christian – Ceres and Bacchus, bread and wine – periodically seduce some rhymster from his desk into the fields, and the results are usually disastrous. Verlaine was a Parisian, a city-dweller; his idea of farming was to lie under a tree and watch the harmonious procession of the seasons. The labour of agriculture, the ploughing and reaping, were part of the com-

---

11 *Amour*, "Lucien Létinois", VIII, Pléiade, 448-49.
12 Apparently she did. Lepelletier, *Paul Verlaine*, 423, says that she did not like the idea of buying the farm in Père Létinois' name.

position, like figures in the foreground of a Claude: the hard work
they implied never occurred to him. On the few occasions when
he tried to help Lucien he was reduced to sweat and breathless-
ness, as ineffectual as Marie-Antoinette in the dairy at Trianon.
The aging Tityrus took to the shade again, with a bottle and a
glass, where he could write his sylvan lines and watch his young
friend – whose charm was doubled by the novel setting. Lucien
was no longer a student, an intellectual, but a shepherd in direct
descent from Alexis and Corydon, driving his team afield, watching the sky for clouds, consulting his elders on the best time for
seeding and harvest:

> Je te voyais herser, rouler, faucher parfois,
> Consultant les anciens, inquiet d'un nuage ...
> Je t'aidais, vite hors d'haleine et tout en nage.[13]

It was the most extraordinary of all Verlaine's evasions from reality – with two really "good" children this time; a safer insulation
from the world than anything he had thus far achieved. There was
not one jarring note, and he took care to see that there should be
none: he hid his address from all his friends: "*Je suis en Amérique*,"
he wrote Léon Valade.[14] Evenings passed at the dinner table (Mme
Létinois was an excellent cook) and on Sundays there was Mass in
the village church with the taproom of the inn afterwards or a
dance in the square.

During these idyllic months he corrected the proofs of *Sagesse*.
The manuscript had been ready for some time and in July 1880, he
went to Paris and found a Catholic publisher who agreed to print it
at the author's expense. The volume appeared in December, though
dated 1881.[15] It represents Verlaine's moral and spiritual evolution
during the seven years from prison at Mons to the first months in
Juniville (1873-80); it is his richest book, containing much of his
best verse, but it is a difficult one to judge. It lacks unity. At first
glance there seems no plan at all, and only on careful examination
do we perceive a kind of architecture. There are three divisions, of

13 Verlaine, Pléiade, 453.
14 Letter of May 30, 1880. The phrase is underlined. *CML*, I, 1144-45.
15 See the notes in Verlaine, Pléiade, 1108.

24, 12, and 21 poems respectively; with some effort they can be seen as three stages of a spiritual drama: Faith Desired, Faith Attained, Peace and Salvation – rather in the manner of the *Divina Commedia*, of which there are echoes.[16] The central point, the *clou* of the volume, is the "Mon Dieu m'a dit" cycle of the second part. The other poems are grouped around it as a setting. Had Verlaine been able to maintain the same high level throughout, *Sagesse* would be a very great work. But it was impossible to remain long on the ecstatic summit he had known in the spring and summer of 1874. The results, therefore, leave something to be desired.

The bulk of the first section was written in 1875-76, during the walks Mrs. Andrews saw him taking around Stickney, or the summer holidays he spent at Arras – "chez ma mère" he noted on the manuscripts. The dominant tone is restless, a constant effort to dominate the "old self." The style is occasionally flawed by allegory and an abuse of capital letters: "le Malheur," "l'Amour," "l'Orgueil," "la Faute," "la Chair," etc. And a few poems, like II, "J'avais peiné comme Sisyphe," in which Prayer, as a white-night-gowned female, descends to save him from temptation, smack of the pious art sold at St. Sulpice. For whenever faith is directly in question, a rather hackneyed symbolism takes over: the exquisite discrimination of "Mon Dieu m'a dit," where every epithet, rhythm, and sentiment is so completely right, did not last more than a year. The third poem is a good example of this failing; it begins splendidly, in cadences which recall Baudelaire's "Voyage":

> Qu'en dis-tu, voyageur, des pays et des gares?
> Du moins as-tu cueilli l'ennui, puisqu'il est mûr,
> Toi que voilà fumant de maussades cigares,
> Noir, projetant une ombre absurde sur le mur?

But the conclusion is flat:

> Si je me sens puni, c'est que je le dois être,
> Ni l'homme ni la femme ici ne sont pour rien.
> Mais j'ai le ferme espoir d'un jour pouvoir connaître
> Le pardon et la paix promis à tout Chrétien.

16 For example, *Purgatorio*, III, 79-84; Verlaine, Pléiade, 1133.

Instead of Baudelaire's great apostrophe to fate and experience, we are fobbed off with a pious banality which could be found in any devout pamphlet. Other pieces, detailing the poet's struggle with temptation, are better: VII, "Les faux beaux jours," VIII, "La vie humble," IX and X, a search for spiritual refuge in the historic past – the seventeenth century, the Middle Ages:

> Ô n'avoir pas suivi les leçons de Rollin,
> N'être pas né dans le grand siècle à son déclin,
> Quand le soleil couchant, si beau, dorait la vie ...

The lines are of high quality. Elsewhere, however, as in XX, "L'ennemi se déguise en l'Ennui" (an inferior treatment of a Baudelairean theme), or XXIV, "L'âme antique était rude et vaine," thought and style break down completely. What is the point of comparing Hecuba and Niobé as tragic mothers with the Virgin Mary and giving the latter the preference on the grounds that "Toute la Charité ruisselle des sept Blessures de son cœur"? Rancid piety of this sort has nothing in common with the great prison verse, and the impartial reader, seeking poetry and not a sermon, remains unconvinced.

The poems to Mathilde and Georges – V, XV, XVIII – are good enough in their way, but only when we forget the circumstances for which they were composed. It will perhaps be argued that a poet's work ought to be accepted at face value: if he describes in haunting terms his sorrow and loneliness when his wife walks out and his son is kept from him, should we ask for anything further? I think we should. Verlaine chose the ground himself: a lyric celebration of personal grief. And one of the first requisites of grief is that it be genuine. He claims our sympathy; we have a right to know on what grounds. And when we discover that his wife did not desert him – quite the contrary; that his son was not sequestrated but that he abandoned the child for Rimbaud and then Létinois; when we find that at the time he published his lachrymose complaints he was at Juniville with Létinois – when all this is apparent, we feel that we have been taken in. Had Mathilde read the poems, believed them, and offered to return to him, she would have put him to serious embarrassment; he would certainly have found some excuse for refusing. His laments may be self-deceptive rather than hypocritical – that is, they are not *consciously* false; but is an unconscious liar much better than a knowing one? In v, he praises Mathilde's eyes because they have the power of saying "Enough!" to male desire – a strange sentiment under his pen; and the sixth line, describing her as a *maternelle endormeuse des râles* shows what he expected from her as a wife: a martyr like Elisa. The fifteenth poem, beseeching pardon, referring to her as "ma sœur qui m'avez puni," is a piece of smooth masochism, with no admission of personal faults. He blames his sufferings on her by implication; he was not yet ready to admit any responsibility for the disaster of his marriage; and xvii and xviii continue the same theme. As for xvi, "Ecoutez la chanson bien douce," it is exquisite. But again, we have to forget the context from which it sprang.

The central panel of *Sagesse* culminates in "Mon Dieu m'a dit." Verlaine seems to have thought that that supreme moment needed a preface, and he wrote three poems to introduce it. They are passable, although the ode to the Virgin, "Je ne veux plus aimer que ma Mère Marie" is not entirely free from conventional sentiment and thread-bare diction. I have already discussed the ten sonnets of "Mon Dieu m'a dit." They are usually considered the summit of Verlaine's work, both in style and content, and this opinion is well founded. Certainly they occupy a commanding situation in the history of mystic literature. Their piety, it is true, may not be quite above suspicion. Knowing Verlaine, we cannot help wondering how much genuine faith they reveal. Are they not, perhaps, one more illustration of his incorrigible weakness, his flight from reality, with God in the place of Elisa, Mathilde, or Rimbaud? There is even a hint of exhibitionism at times, something like a "Listen to me, for I have sinned!" A poet is seldom a reliable guide to faith: he is less interested in the truth or falsity of a doctrine than in how it corresponds to his own emotional state, and this is truer of Verlaine than of nearly anyone else. The true mystic seeks something more in religion than a refuge from personal maladjustment. All these reservations, however, cannot dim the glowing, mounting ecstasy of Verlaine's achievement. If the cycle is not his most popular work, that is because it is not his most original. In venturing onto mystic ground he was no longer unique: he challenged comparison with some very formidable rivals. *Fêtes galantes* and *Romances sans paroles* contain poetry only he could write: in *Sagesse* he wrote what other men have done equally well. But it is a question whether anyone else has done much better, has produced 140 consecutive lines of such pure verse, without one false note, one blemish of style or prosody.

The first poem of the closing section sets the tone – peace and salvation:

> Le Sage peut, dorénavant,
> Assister aux scènes du monde ...
> Il ira, calme, et passera
> Dans la férocité des villes ...

The poet has reached his goal. And then in the next item, "Du fond du grabat," the massive symphonic movement we have been following breaks up in a dazzle of scattered harmonies. Nothing could better illustrate the capricious, intimate nature of Verlaine's genius. He was incapable of prolonged inspiration: the conclusion of *Sagesse* is not a triumphant coda in the manner of the *Paradiso*, but a series of fragments, a failure from the point of view of design. Fortunately it is a failure of small importance, given the beauty of the bits and pieces. In some ways it is almost advantageous, as though some elaborate piece of jewellery had suddenly disintegrated into a heap of brilliant stones. We can handle and admire them with no thought of the pompous setting for which they were intended.

The cause of this abrupt collapse was Rimbaud – not surprisingly, considering how his memory obsessed Verlaine during the composition of *Sagesse*. He had already troubled the groping piety of the opening section, first in "Malheureux! tous les dons":

> La malédiction de n'être jamais las
> Suit tes pas sur le monde où l'horizon t'attire ...

And again in the "Qu'en dis-tu voyageur?" which immediately precedes and which also apostrophizes him directly:

> Toi qui rêvais (c'était trop excessif, aussi)
> Je ne sais quelle mort légère et délicate!
> Ah toi! l'espèce d'ange avec ce vœu transi!

Both poems, together with "Du fond du grabat," were written almost simultaneously – September-October 1875 at Arras; in all three Rimbaud symbolizes adventure, movement, the seduction of far-off horizons – just as Mathilde, wife and mother, represented permanence and safety, the qualities Verlaine also sought in the Church. The spiritual drama of his life, the fluctuation between opposites or "parallels," existed before he met either Rimbaud or Mathilde, and was finally polarized around their figures. Even when he implored Mathilde's forgiveness, he was thinking of Arthur's dynamism – which, eight years later, he frankly exalted in the "Laeti et errabundi" of *Parallèlement*. The demi-god had vanished in seascapes and tempest like his own "bateau ivre"; Verlaine was left a prey to the torment of those who remain behind, a traumatic blend of lucid memory and vague surmise. He knew the face and the body, the speech, the habits of thought and mind; but this clear vision was hemmed in by darkness: in what unknown circumstances was Arthur now moving; amid what new faces and obscure surroundings, what complications of suffering, triumph, friendship, or passion? The questions throughout "Qu'en dis-tu voyageur?" are obsessive and agonized, not rhetorical: "A-t-on assez puni cette lourde innocence? Qu'en dis-tu? L'homme est dur, mais la femme? Et tes pleurs, qui les a bus? Et quelle âme ... console tes malheurs?" Verlaine might boast his own faith, pray for Rimbaud's conversion, shake his head in rueful disapproval through all three poems, hope that his ex-friend might someday find peace in Christ. The old seduction was stronger than any religious convictions, and breaks out in a dozen places in "Du fond du grabat":

> Le vent du coteau,
> La Meuse, la goutte

Qu'on boit sur la route
A chaque écriteau,
Les sèves qu'on hume,
Les pipes qu'on fume!

...

Voyageur si triste,
Tu suis quelle piste?

"À propos d'Arthur Rimbaud," he noted as he completed "Malheureux! tous les dons." And then he added: "Après coup, je me suis aperçu que cela pouvait s'appliquer à 'poor myself."[17] The same is true of "Du fond du grabat" and of "Qu'en dis-tu voyageur?" – he was addressing Rimbaud, and also that part of himself Rimbaud had unchained. And the vision of Arthur is even more precise in the tenth poem of this concluding section:

La tristesse, la langueur du corps humain
M'attendrissent, me fléchissent, m'apitoient.
Ah! surtout quand des sommeils noirs le foudroient,
Quand les draps zèbrent la peau, foulent la main!

In the original manuscript of *Sagesse* this piece was to have been followed by "Ce soir je m'étais penché sur ton sommeil," the poetic rendering (1872) of their nights in Paris and Brussels. Both sonnets are good examples of Verlaine's genius: a whispering profundity combined with the ability he often showed to transfigure even the most trifling details (like the sheets which "zèbrent la peau, foulent la main") – qualities which distinguish him from all other poets. But what a strange aberration to include the sonnets in a book like *Sagesse*![18] They show how, as he concluded the volume, he forgot the original plan and surrendered to pure lyricism.

This is just as evident in poems III-VII – "L'espoir luit," "Un grand sommeil noir," "Le ciel est par-dessus le toit," etc. They

17 Verlaine, Pléiade, 1118-19.
18 He seems to have felt the inconsistency himself because in preparing the manuscript for the press, he replaced "Ce soir je m'étais penché" by the relatively mild "La bise se rue à travers." Verlaine, Pléiade, 1133.

were written in 1873, before his conversion, and thus have nothing to do with the religious themes of *Sagesse*. Numbers XIII-XVII (England, 1875-76) recall the *Paysages belges* of *Romances sans paroles*: exquisite bits of nature description – sea, sky, woodland. London inspired XIV, another example of the city theme he admired in Baudelaire. The subject is night instead of dawn; otherwise the tone is not unlike Wordsworth's sonnet on Westminster Bridge:

> Il semble ici qu'on vit dans l'histoire.
> Tout est plus fort que l'homme d'un jour ...

XVI is not as good, and hardly measures up to the "Tableaux parisiens" of *Les Fleurs du mal*. The same applies to XX, a rather long-winded pastiche of the "Epilogue" to Baudelaire's prose-poems. The last number of the section, and the conclusion to *Sagesse* as a whole, "C'est la fête du blé," is a beautiful fusion of religious themes and scene-painting. It was written at Fampoux in 1877, during the harvest season. There is a hint of Leconte de Lisle's "Midi" here and there. But the texture of the lines has a richness beyond anything the Parnassian ever wrote:

> Tout bruit, la nature et l'homme, dans un bain
> De lumière si blanc que les ombres sont roses ...

– The "impressionist" Verlaine once more, transcribing in verse the effects of a Monet or a Pissaro. The poem is a curious prelude to his own attempt at farming three years later.

Had he lingered much longer over *Sagesse* he might have ruined it. Most of the best poems (37 out of 57) date from before 1877; and as time passed, his Catholic piety became intolerant and dogmatic: moderation was never one of his virtues. Examples are the sonnet on the expulsion of the Jesuits from France (1879), and the eleventh and twelfth poems of the first section – satires on the free-thinkers and anti-clericals of the period: "petits amis," he says, "qui sûtes nous prouver par A plus B que deux et deux font quatre." The *Voyage en France par un Français* is an even more deplorable example of this tendency. He had been working at it for five or six years (it was the "patriotic book" he mentioned to Delahaye in 1875), and he finished it at Juniville in 1880. Even as propaganda it is a lamentable performance, an hysteric attack on Republican France in the name of the Church and the monarchy. Contemporary French literature itself is not spared; we cannot know what he said of the poets – that chapter is lost – but we have a detailed castigation of the great novelists of the period (Flaubert, Goncourt, Zola, Daudet) carried out with the intransigent zeal of a curé writing in some backwoods parish. Their books, besides overflowing with "horrible" sensuality (under the influence of religion, Verlaine sometimes lacked not merely humour, but even common sense) are anti-clerical and ought to be suppressed. The French Revolution is denounced as the source of all evil: it unleashed the Seven Deadly Sins which "se ruèrent de tous côtés et s'installèrent dans chaque fonction publique"; universal suffrage and freedom of the press are works of the Devil. "Du temps que la France avait un roi, ce roi la représentait dans tout ce qu'elle avait de noble et d'élevé, dans la pensée et dans l'action, tête solide et cœur vaillant."[19]

This royalist bias, rooted as it is in French history, is hard for a Catholic of any other nationality to understand. When the kings of France united the country during the Middle Ages and the Renaissance, they worked (despite occasional friction) in alliance with the Church and enjoyed its support. Louis IX was canonized – the pope gave Louis XI the title of *Rex christianissimus* in 1469 – and when Richelieu and Louis XIV perfected absolutism in the seventeenth century, throne and altar were welded together as the basis of the national life, one implying the other. The memory of that politico-religious monolith has haunted French conservative thought ever since. Ultra-Catholic groups in France still tend to be royalist, and *vice versa*; the foreigner who frequents them is often surprised to find elderly ladies and intense young men sighing for the Grand Siècle and toasting "le Roi." The phenomenon is especially potent in times of disaster when there is talk of "traditional values." Present difficulties are attributed to scientific rationalism, the execution of Louis XVI, the separation of Church and State, or the works of Voltaire, André Gide, and M. Jean-Paul Sartre. The years following 1870 were just such a period; the

19 *CML*, I, 346, 405.

extreme right was particularly clamorous and even had a candidate for the vacant throne – Charles x's grandson, the Comte de Chambord, who had lived in exile since 1830. There was a royalist majority in the National Assembly of 1871, and for a time a restoration appeared certain. But Chambord proved even more stupid than his ancestors, and by insisting on the old Bourbon flag instead of the tricolour, he ruined his chances. The Republicans seized their opportunity. From 1875 on, the elections returned ever larger numbers of leftist candidates, and since the monarchists had leaned heavily on the Church, the tone of the Chamber became more and more anti-clerical. The Jesuits were expelled in 1879 (hence Verlaine's poem); for the next thirty years the struggle continued bitterly, reaching a climax during the Combes administration of 1902-5, when an effort was made to root Roman Catholicism out of French life.

Since he had been saved from his youthful "errors," Verlaine considered himself fit to join this battle on the side of the angels. He wanted to play the role of a Catholic publicist, like Joseph de Maistre or Louis Veuillot. The fact that his past disqualified him and that a sincere and silent piety was his proper role, never entered his mind. He was always blind when his whims were in question. Like all the emotionally retarded, he had a craving for absolutes. During his years with the Parnassians he had been the most extreme of them all (which is why the Parnassian items of *Poèmes saturniens* read almost like parodies); later on, in 1871, he was not content to be a simple Republican like Blémont and Lepelletier, but became a Communard as well. And now that he was a Catholic, mere devotion was not enough. He turned ultra, and swallowed the absolute monarchy along with the absolute Church: "un régime," he wrote of pre-Revolutionary France, "que je voudrais voir reparaître jusque dans *tous* ses précieux détails."[20] Fortunately for him this desire was unrealizable: one of the *précieux détails* consisted of burning sexual deviates alive. Had he forgotten the fact, or never known it?

As things stood, the *Voyage en France* was too violent for even the Catholics. When Verlaine sent the manuscript to the *Revue du*

20 *Œuvres posthumes* (Messein, 1911), I, 216-17.

Monde catholique in 1881 it was rejected as not being in the spirit of the periodical. A number of sonnets, written at the same time and in the same style, attacking the politicians of the Third Republic (Grévy, Ferry, Paul Bert) fared no better. They were not printed until 1896, in *Invectives*. He could not write convincing prose, and to think of himself as a "Christian Juvenal" was pure illusion.

While he was engaged on these projects, the farm at Juniville was not prospering. Even though Verlaine was no farmer, Lucien and his father had grown up on the land; it is surprising that they could not make a success of an enterprise which, by comparison with the small property they had lived on up to that time, was something of a windfall. Perhaps that is the explanation: Létinois did not know how to manage a large holding and lost his head. It has been alleged that he wanted to add to the land and that he bought further acres and incurred obligations which, owing to a bad harvest in the autumn of 1881, he could not meet. The property had been bought in his name, with a clause guaranteeing Verlaine's rights[21]; possibly this arrangement gave the old peasant too much of a free hand. Anyhow, the place had to be sold in January 1882. The Létinois family took refuge in Belgium, which lends support to the theory that the father had got himself involved in legal difficulties. Verlaine remained at Juniville to liquidate the affair. Elisa had joined him at the first hint of bad news, and together they managed the auction. The property brought 15,000 francs – just half what it had cost.

It was another failure, and for the same reason as all Verlaine's failures: his dreams never corresponded with reality. But he had no regrets:[22]

> Notre essai de culture eut une triste fin
> Mais il fit mon délice un long temps et ma joie;
> J'y voyais se développer ton être fin dans ce bon travail ...

21 Delahaye, *Verlaine*, 291, says this was done for fear the Mautés might try to seize the property; Lepelletier, *Paul Verlaine*, 423, declares that there was no danger, and that had there been, why not buy in Mme Verlaine's name? He draws no conclusions, but he is clearly hinting at Verlaine's mad infatuation for Lucien. Verlaine probably intended the arrangement as a further proof of his affection.
22 Verlaine, Pléiade, 452.

Meanwhile, he had to rearrange his life yet once more. He went up to Paris with Elisa in the summer of 1882 and re-established contact with some of his friends. He could not teach in France; he lacked the necessary diplomas. But there was his old position at the Hôtel de Ville. The disasters of 1871 were long past; he decided to get himself reinstated. At first this did not seem impossible. Lepelletier was devoted to him, and through eight or ten years of hard work had achieved something of a position in the world of Parisian journalism. He was also on the best terms with Charles Floquet, Prefect of the Seine, and J. de Bouteiller, Chairman of the Paris Municipal Council. He persuaded them to consider Verlaine's application favourably, and with support like this, success appeared certain. For the next few months, Verlaine got together a file which included certificates of good life and morals from the mayors of Fampoux, Jehonville and Arras. But the affair lapsed mysteriously, and ended in a refusal. Lepelletier blames this failure on Floquet's resigning at the critical moment, on Verlaine's old association with the Commune, and on the Brussels scandal: "la légende de Belgique, le jugement de la justice belge mal lu, ou pas lu du tout."[23] Had he been given some hint of the truth? It was extremely unpalatable. On October 31, 1882, the very day he left the Prefecture, Floquet wrote to Brussels for information about Verlaine's trial. The reply reached his successor, Louis Oustry, a month later (it is dated November 28): "L'instruction de l'affaire ... nous révèle la moralité plus que douteuse de ce personnage. En effet, le juge d'Instruction de Bruxelles ayant ordonné la visite corporelle du prévenu par les docteurs Semal et Vleminckx, ceux-ci firent un rapport en ce sens que Verlaine portait sur sa personne les traces de pédérastie active et passive."[24] By implication, therefore, Verlaine had tried to murder Rimbaud for homosexual reasons. With a document of this sort before him, Oustry had no

23 Lepelletier, *Paul Verlaine*, 127.
24 Quoted by Martin, "Verlaine et Rimbaud." Floquet had been elected to the Chamber of Deputies on October 22, 1882, which necessitated his resignation as Prefect. Louis Oustry was nominated to succeed him on October 30, and presumably took up his functions next day. See *Bulletin municipal officiel de la Ville de Paris* for the year 1882.

choice but to veto the poet's application, and Floquet would doubtless have done the same thing in his place.

This fiasco was the equivalent of a rejection by regular society. And just at this moment another and much graver disaster occurred. Lucien Létinois had been working in an industrial plant at Ivry, in the Paris suburbs. On April 3, 1883, he caught typhoid, and four days later he was dead.

Added to the Juniville failure and the civil service refusal, this stroke broke Verlaine's will and goes a long way to explaining the deliberate squalor of his life henceforth. He was frustrated on all sides. Yet, stunning as the blow was, it at least spared him the agony of an inevitable rupture. His relations with Lucien could not have gone on much longer as they were. The boy had become a man, and he was growing tired of his mentor's obsessive friendship. For four years, Verlaine had fussed around him like a broody hen. There were the months at Rethel, then the English interlude and the confession scene in London. And in the autumn of 1881, when Lucien was drafted, Verlaine paid the 1500 francs which reduced his service to a year, and got a room near the camp at Châlons so that he could see him every day. Later still, after the Juniville liquidation, Létinois found a job as supervisor in a school at Boulogne-sur-Seine. Verlaine went to live in the town, and when the Ivry offer came up, substituted for him so that he could accept it. The young man was tied down and blackmailed by affection. Wherever he turned, there was the same dominating benevolence, the same oppressive kindness. He might have stood it better had the results been good, but they were not. Teaching in England (Verlaine's idea) ended in humiliating dismissal. The farm went bankrupt. From being small but solid cultivators at Coulommes, the Létinois found themselves crowded into a tiny flat at Ivry. Lucien began to view his old master with some disillusionment: "Je lui ai beaucoup de reconnaissance," he told Delehaye, "et je l'aime beaucoup à cause de sa bonté pour moi, de son affection très grande, malgré ses défauts, malgré sa légèreté et ses émotions continuelles ... Si je ne l'aimais pas, je ne vaudrais pas cher, si je l'accusais je serais injuste, puisque ses intentions étaient bonnes ... Ce qui est sûr, c'est qu'il eût mieux valu pour nous ne pas le trouver sur notre chemin."[25]

He was reassessing his early fascination, and the pride and gratitude he had felt when Verlaine first noticed him were becoming tinged with impatience. He was, after all, rigorously normal, a healthy peasant. He had little more tolerance than Rimbaud for Verlaine's sentimentality – his "eternal emotions" (the phrase suggests a good deal). And during their eighteen months at Juniville the poet's exaggerated affection had caused talk: "Cette vive amitié entre un homme de quarante ans et un jeune homme de dix-huit était ... le sujet de toutes les conversations. Il y avait là certainement quelque chose d'anormal. On accusait ouvertement les deux amis de sodomie, et les mauvaises mœurs de Verlaine étalées plus tard au grand jour (lors de son second séjour à Coulommes) confirmeraient assez ces dires."[26] Hints of this gossip perhaps reached Lucien, and he may also have reflected, after the event, on the Christmas episode in London. Verlaine's motives were clear enough to be guessed at, even by a person of limited intelligence. There must have been times when Lucien – when Verlaine himself – realized that the situation could not be indefinitely prolonged. The English girl had been only a first alarm. Some day the young man would meet a woman to whom no objection could be made. What role would Verlaine play in the new household? What would a wife think of this ambiguous "father-in-law," forever scribbling poems and hanging about the house? As he followed Lucien's coffin to the grave, Verlaine found a certain consolation in the thought that if he had never possessed the boy, no woman ever would:

> Tout en suivant ton blanc convoi, je me disais
> Pourtant: C'est vrai, Dieu t'a repris quand tu faisais
> Sa joie et dans l'éclair de ta blanche innocence,
> Plus tard la Femme eût mis sans doute en sa puissance
> Ton cœur ardent ...[27]

25 Delahaye, *Verlaine*, 312-13.
26 This testimony, dating from 1885-90, was printed by Coulon, *Verlaine, poète saturnien*, 246-47.
27 Verlaine, Pléiade, 449.

Lucien was buried in a white coffin, "comme pour une jeune fille," as Verlaine pointed out to Delahaye, who had come to the funeral. "Et lui, certes, le mérite! ... Combien en est-il cependant, qui, à son âge?"[28]

But at best this was a negative consolation. Lucien's death very nearly destroyed Verlaine's will to live. He had met him at the moment of *Sagesse*, when his religious faith was still strong; had tried to love him in accordance with the strictest moral principles, and, up to a point, had succeeded. And now everything was over – through no fault of his, but through the impersonal agency of disease. It was one of those shattering experiences the Existentialists call "absurd," a proof that guilt and innocence, vice and virtue, are alike on the inhuman scale of destiny.

And it was all the more unfortunate inasmuch as, at that moment, he was well on the way to remaking his existence. His failure with the Hôtel de Ville was disappointing but not fatal. He still had a number of trumps in his hand which were continually increasing. Elisa, when they reached Paris together in July 1882, had enough money left to keep them for some years. She took an apartment at 17 rue de la Roquette, which Delahaye describes as well lit and comfortable. The family furniture (armchairs covered in spotted velvet imitating leopard skin, an oil portrait of Captain Verlaine in uniform, a portrait of Elisa) though somewhat the worse from the numerous moves through which it had gone, was presentable; and Elisa, delighted to be living with her son again, was cheerful and active. She used to play ball with the girls and teachers of a neighbouring school, and when Verlaine's friends came to see him she stuffed them with lumps of sugar, a sovereign remedy against sore throat.[29] The visitors were numerous, and they were not just old friends; they included members of the rising generation – Léon Trézenic, Charles Morice, Ernest Raynaud, Jean Moréas, Maurice Barrès – founders of literary reviews, writers of new books. They represented the future, and unlike their predecessors – Leconte de Lisle, A. France, Goncourt, Alphonse

28 Delahaye, *Verlaine*, 329.
29 *Ibid.*, 324-25.

Lemerre – they found the scandals of Verlaine's life irrelevant by comparison with his poetry.

For they had all read him, had been reading him for years. His disappearance from the literary scene a decade before had been a personal eclipse only; his books remained behind, alive and radio-active, constantly attracting new readers. And the literary atmo-sphere was changing in his favour. People were growing tired of Leconte de Lisle's Parnassianism and Zola's Naturalism; literary history calls the new movement Symbolism; an exploration of the psyche, a preoccupation with sensation and suggestion, the very qualities which distinguish *Poèmes saturniens*, *Fêtes galantes*, *Romances sans paroles*, and *Sagesse*. Mallarmé had begun his famous receptions in the rue de Rome, and he had long been Verlaine's friend and admirer. And there was the influence of Baudelaire. As the century waned, it was becoming obvious that *Les Fleurs du mal* was not just another eccentric volume, but a turning point in po-etic technique and feeling; in both respects Verlaine was emerging as the master's greatest disciple, continuing his innovations and adding new harmonies of his own. The world of letters had a place ready for him in 1883; nothing less than that of master of the new school.

His ardent young visitors were one sign of this; another was the welcome he found in avant-garde periodicals such as *Paris-Moderne*, *La Nouvelle Rive Gauche*, *Le Chat Noir*, and *Lutèce*. Their circula-tion might be small, but it was deep; they were read by those who counted. On July 25, 1882, within weeks of Verlaine's arrival in the capital, *Paris-Moderne* published two of his poems, "Le Sque-lette" and "Et nous voilà très doux" under the heading "Poems from *Jadis et Naguère*" (thus giving the title of his next collection). "Art poétique" followed on November 10 and caused a sensation. Charles Morice, another rising poet, criticized it severely and Ver-laine replied in an article (*La Nouvelle rive gauche*, 15-22 décembre 1882). This exchange brought about a meeting, and Morice be-came one of his greatest admirers.[30] Verlaine was even asked to

30 Charles Morice wrote the first full-length study of Verlaine, *Verlaine, l'homme et l'œuvre*, 87 pages.

baptize the new movement. The Symbolists had been labelled "decadent" by traditionalist critics of the period like Scherer and Brunetière, and needed a rallying cry against the Philistines. Verlaine advised them to counter-attack by taking "decadence" as their slogan: "On nous l'avait jetée comme une insulte, cette épithète; je l'ai ramassée comme cri de guerre," he told Jules Huret.[31] The word had been bandied about for some years, particularly in connection with Baudelaire. It was one of the accusations levelled at him during his lifetime, and Théophile Gautier had raised it to something like a doctrine in the preface he wrote for *Les Fleurs du mal* in 1868 – analysing the seductive beauties of artificiality and perversion, equating nineteenth-century Paris with decadent Rome. The poets of the eighties found these ideas alluring; to please his young friends, Verlaine summed the matter up in a sonnet, "Langueur," which appeared in *Le Chat noir* on May 26, 1883:

> Je suis l'Empire à la fin de la décadence,
> Qui regarde passer les grands Barbares blancs ...

There is a touch of parody in the lines, but it is so good-natured as to be almost sincere. Echoes of "Langueur" occur in the novels, poems, plays, and essays of the next twenty years: it became a cornerstone of the *école décadente*, which soon had its own periodicals – *Le Décadent* and *La Décadence* – both founded in 1886 and both claiming descent from Baudelaire and Verlaine, "nos dieux," as an enthusiastic editorial put it.[32]

It was through contacts with literary groups of this sort that Verlaine met his future publisher, Léon Vanier. Like Alphonse Lemerre in the days of *Le Parnasse contemporain*, Vanier was founding a house to specialize in editions of contemporary poetry, and in March 1884 he brought out Verlaine's *Les Poètes maudits*, essays on Corbière, Mallarmé, and Rimbaud.[33] The volume was slim, but it was a date in French literature nonetheless – not because of

31 *CML*, II, 1762.
32 Maurice du Plessis, *Le Décadent*, January 31, 1888.
33 *CML*, I, 465-99.

its critical merits (which are small), but because the essay on Rimbaud included poems like "Voyelles," "Les Chercheuses de Poux," and "le Bateau ivre," which Verlaine had learned by heart or kept among his papers. With the passage of time he had forgotten Rimbaud's insolent sadism, the Brussels tragedy, the episode at Stuttgart and the later attempts at blackmail. He remembered only the ecstatic chaos of those two years in Paris, Brussels, and London, when life and poetry had an intensity and a depth he never found again, not even at the moment of "Mon Dieu m'a dit." And so it was to be henceforth: *Les Poètes maudits* resumes openly the Rimbaud theme which had even pierced the pious texture of *Sagesse* and which rapidly became one of Verlaine's main inspirations.

We find it once more in *Jadis et Naguère*, completed in 1884 and published by Vanier the following January. It contains the *récits diaboliques* of the prison months in Brussels and Mons; they are grouped at the end under a prologue describing them as "fantômes moroses." It is a pity that, "Crimen Amoris" apart, they are such poor stuff, for they occupy over a quarter of the book and weigh it down badly. Taken as a whole, *Jadis et Naguère* is clearly a mass of odds and ends dumped together with even less care for unity than *Sagesse*. If Rimbaud is the main theme, that is only because there are more poems about him than about anything else; the rest of the content is entirely heterogeneous. Almost none of it, not more than half a dozen of the forty-six items, dates from the time of publication. Most of the poems, including those on Rimbaud, belong to the sixties and seventies: contributions to reviews, youthful outpourings of a humanitarian sort ("Le soldat laboureur," "Les loups," written with a socialist volume in mind, *Les Vaincus*), a one-act play ("Les Uns et les Autres") dating from 1871 in the style of *Fêtes galantes*; and while some of them, such as "Art poétique," are very fine, there is an over-all impression of waning creative power. *Jadis et Naguère* has none of the originality of *Fêtes galantes* or *Romances sans paroles*, nor the sustained power of the best parts of *Sagesse*.

Nevertheless, it did a good deal towards consolidating Verlaine's growing fame. As far as the public was concerned, its very lack of originality was not altogether a defect. Turning its pages, the readers of 1885 were able to recognize certain characteristics of the poet they already knew; echoes of *Fêtes galantes* in "Les Uns et les Autres," of *Romances sans paroles* in "Art poétique" and "Langueur," of the Rimbaud scandal in "Vers pour être calomnié" and "Crimen Amoris." And just at this moment they were helped to a truer appreciation of Verlaine by praise from an unexpected quarter: J. K. Huysmans' novel *A Rebours* (May 1884). Up to that time, Huysmans had been a disciple of Zola, writing studies of manners like *Les Sœurs Vatard* and *En ménage*. His new volume was a complete break with Naturalism, and showed the way literary currents were changing. It was less a novel than a series of essays on art and literature, tied together by the personality of the critic-hero, Des Esseintes. In chapter xv, dealing with contemporary French poetry, Verlaine's qualities are set forth with enthusiasm and precision: "Des Esseintes retrouvait ... un talent déjà profondément imbibé de Baudelaire ... *La Bonne Chanson, les Fêtes galantes, Romances sans paroles* ... *Sagesse* renfermaient des poèmes où l'écrivain original se révélait ... Il avait pu exprimer de vagues et délicieuses confidences, à mi-voix, au crépuscule. Seul, il avait pu laisser deviner certains au-delà troublants d'âme, des chuchotements si bas de pensées, des aveux si murmurés, si interrompus, que l'oreille qui les percevait, demeurait hésitante, coulant à l'âme des langueurs avivées par le mystère de ce souffle plus deviné que senti."[34]

A Rebours appeared at the right moment, in time to take advantage of the growing interest in Symbolism and Decadence. It is one of those pieces of intransigent eccentricity which becomes a Bible for young writers[35]; its paradoxical brilliance was fascinating, and as a novel it had an advantage over poetry and criticism – it was widely read. No other book, perhaps, did more for Verlaine's fame.

His position during the early eighties, in brief, was rapidly

---

34 J. K. Huysmans, *A Rebours*, 280-81.
35 See, for example, Georges Rodenbach's article "La Poésie nouvelle. A propos des décadents et des symbolistes," *La Revue bleue*, 4 avril 1891: "Ce livre de M. Huysmans ... devint un programme involontaire, la loi et le code, le texte de ralliement, l'hymne des enrôlés pour l'art neuf."

becoming excellent: poems, articles, a volume of criticism, a volume of verse, discriminating praise from the best judges, adoration from the young. Musicians were becoming interested in his work. In 1883 and 1885 Charles Bordes and Ernest Chausson wrote accompaniments for several pieces from *Poèmes saturniens* and *La Bonne Chanson*, an example followed later by Debussy and Fauré.[36] By comparison with all this, the civil service fiasco and even the Brussels scandal were of small importance. He had only to go on writing and wait for fame; he was very nearly famous already. The way he threw away his chance, almost ignored it, is proof of what a shock Lucien's death had been.

> Cette adoption de toi pour mon enfant
> Puisque l'on m'avait volé mon fils réel,
> Elle n'était pas dans les conseils du ciel,
> Je me le suis dit, en pleurant, bien souvent ...
> Cette adoption fut le fruit défendu;
> J'aurais dû passer dans l'odeur et le frais
> De l'arbre et du fruit sans m'arrêter auprès.
> Le ciel m'a puni ... J'aurais dû, j'aurais dû!

Lucien's disappearance had been a final disaster, coming after so many others and producing a cumulative effect.

In July 1883, he persuaded Elisa to buy the Létinois farm at Malval, near Coulommes (Lucien's parents had decided to give up farming and remain at Ivry), and moved there with her in September. He had visited the place several times with Lucien; the boy had grown up on the property and house and land were still alive with memories of him. And with a sort of premeditated sadism, Verlaine set about defiling this image. It was a posthumous revenge: against Lucien, whom he had never possessed; against God, whom he had tried to obey; against himself for his own chastity and self-restraint. He began drinking with a concentrated frenzy unparalleled since his last months with Rimbaud; he gathered into the house every pervert, tramp, and delinquent he could pick up on the roads or invite down from Paris. The locals were scandalized. Within a short time he was known throughout the district by a filthy nickname, but he was too desperate to care.

36 Porché, *Verlaine tel qu'il fut*, 273.

It was a header into the cesspool, an abasement so utter that even Lucien's death does not explain it completely. The boy's disappearance, like the other mishaps of Verlaine's life (the death of his cousin, of his aunt, the loss of Rimbaud) acted on his eternal moral disorder – the terror of reality, the craving for escape – gave him the excuse he needed for dropping a veil of alcohol between himself and existence. The phenomenon is always the same, from his adolescent debauches at Jehonville to his legendary dipsomania in the Latin Quarter.

Money began cascading through his hands. He treated whole barrooms to drinks, bought one of his dubious companions a merry-go-round for 1500 francs, and once at least was rolled by two toughs he had propositioned, and left with empty pockets in a ditch. The remains of Elisa's fortune were finally dissipated; she signed Malval over to him in April 1884. A year later he sold it for half its value and squandered the money. When Elisa, appalled at the prospect before them, tried to resist his demands, he became so violent that he roused the village. The scenes resemble those Victoire Bertrand described. In January 1885, Elisa had to take refuge with her next-door neighbours, a Belgian couple called Dave. And precisely then Verlaine learned that Mathilde, taking advantage of changes in the legal code, had divorced him. He went to Paris on February 9, 1885, perhaps hoping to see her. He was not successful, and returned to Malval drunk. He found that Elisa had come to the farm during his absence to get some clothing. For reasons which only his drunkard's brain could understand, this discovery made him furious. He burst into the Dave's house and seized his mother by the wrists: "Si tu ne reviens pas chez moi immédiatement, je te tue!" (He always maintained that he said "Je me tue," which is perhaps true; the two expressions are easily confused. Perhaps, as in the scene Victoire Bertrand records, he said both.) Dave later testified that he also drew a knife from his pocket, another likely detail. The Belgian threw him out, and there might have been no sequel had not Verlaine, with the cross-grained obstinacy he showed at times, gone to the police next day and laid a complaint charging his neighbour with breaking and entering. Dave then accused him of attempted murder.

The case came before a court at Vouziers on March 24, 1885. Elisa did what she could to disculpate her son, but in common decency she had to give Dave some support, and witnesses were summoned from Coulommes who had a good deal to say about Verlaine's debauched habits generally. He was sentenced to a year in prison and a fine of 500 francs.

Discharged on May 13 after serving about six weeks of the sentence, he lapsed into sheer vagabondism. Elisa had gone to Fampoux; the farm at Juniville had been sold and the proceeds squandered, Malval likewise. There was no valid reason for Verlaine to return to the Coulommes district, where he was known as a drunk, a pervert, and a jailbird. Yet return he did; for nearly a month he wandered the roads, a sinister figure in top hat and fur-trimmed overcoat (no costume for June, but it was all he possessed and he could not remove it since he had no shirt), depending on hand-outs for food and liquor. In a short account he wrote of the adventure, *La Goutte*, he says that he hoped to collect some money still owing from the Juniville sale. The notary was absent when Verlaine reached his office, and whether anything was ever paid is unknown; probably not. His true reason for coming back was deeper. He knew the universal reprobation in which he was held; his visit was a self-imposed penance, a voluntary submission to insult and contempt. Besides satisfying his old guilt-complex (sharpened as it was by mistreatment of Elisa and Lucien's death), he was able to collapse voluptuously into remorse and irresponsibility. Some of the details he records show clearly the relish he took in his own degradation – a night in a tinker's cart, the charity he received from a fellow tramp. He had reached rock bottom and could sink no lower.[37] To a mind like Verlaine's, haunted by insecurity, this realization brings a kind of peace. The three or four squalid weeks on the road were a prelude to the ignominy of his last years, and he never recovered from them.

37 "La Goutte," *CML*, I, 605.

9/Latin Quarter legend/
Last years, last works

THE COUR SAINT-FRANÇOIS opens through a *porte-cochère* at 5, rue Moreau, and has changed little with the passage of eighty years. Heavy iron gates, never closed, their lower rungs dissolving in the rust of a century, lean against the walls of the entry; beyond stretch a hundred yards of irregular cobblestones, with houses on either side and the sombre brick vaults of the elevated railway barring the far end. The place is a little less squalid than it used to be. Trains passing to the Bastille are now electrified and no longer stain the façades with smoke, and during the day the shopkeepers of the quarter use the narrow space to park their vans and automobiles. But the essentials remain unaltered and give an impression both gay and sordid, like a wink from an inebriated tramp. The Hôtel du Midi is still doing business at no. 6; its clients still live on the edge of the law and have good reason for disliking curious visitors. Anyone strolling there, seeking memories of Verlaine, receives ambiguous looks from doors and windows. The poet's sojourn only lasted a few months, but nothing better suggests the atmosphere of his last years than this curious dead end.

He arrived with Elisa about the middle of June 1885. His room was on the ground floor, at street level; his mother lodged above him on the first. He had written her at Fampoux when he tired of vagabondage and she had joined him at once. Why he chose the Hôtel du Midi, how he even knew of it, is a question. Perhaps from some of his disreputable acquaintances in the Paris under-world. The house was a brothel, catering to a motley clientèle of pimps and prostitutes, unemployed workers, drug-pushers, ex-convicts, all the social wreckage that drifts into a placid slum to fester and sink. To this point had maternal affection brought Elisa. Her fortune had shrunk to a few bonds (20,000 francs' worth, which she prudently stuffed into her mattress). Nothing remained of the modest affluence of the past but the oil portrait of the Cap-tain and a family plot in the cemetery at Batignolles. Verlaine's previous disasters had been cushioned by money. He had always known where to find shelter and enough cash to pay his bills. Now he was reduced to indigence and had dragged his mother down with him.

To make matters worse, the results of years of debauchery were coming home to roost. In September he had his first attack of the hydarthrosis of the left knee which rapidly became chronic. It is one of the least pleasant manifestations of tertiary syphilis, marked by stiffening and swelling of the joints.[1] He was soon immobilized in bed, his leg in a "gutter." He remained so for over four months, and meanwhile Elisa came down with pneumonia. At her age and in her wretched circumstances the case was hopeless. Paul tried to have himself carried up to her room, but the operation proved so agonizing that it had to be abandoned. On January 21, 1886, she died. We have a pencil sketch of her, taken on her death-bed. The face expresses tenderness and complete peace; she had done what she could, come to her son whenever he called her, followed him from bourgeois comfort at Batignolles to a bawdy-house in the slums. And she would have gone on longer, forever it seems, and spent more time and money had she possessed them. But both had run out. Death cancels all engagements, even such an engage-ment as her love for Paul. The coffin could not be got down the

---

1 Verlaine appears to have contracted syphilis in London during his stay there with Rimbaud in 1873 (another sidelight on the kind of life they led together.) "Ne crains pas les femmes," he wrote Philomène on November 27, 1893, dur-ing his lecture tour. "D'ailleurs, Londres m'a porté malheur, il y a vingt ans, sous ce rapport." *Correspondance*, II, 308.

stairs and had to be lowered through a window. From his bed Verlaine watched it descend, and that was the last he saw of his mother.

No French funeral can take place without a representative of the family to lead the mourners and receive the condolences of those present. This was even truer in 1886 than it is now. Since Verlaine was helpless only one person was eligible – his ex-wife, the mother of his son. It was a devastating irony, and what Elisa would have said had she known can only be imagined. The funeral was a lonely affair. Mathilde saw none of Verlaine's old friends or anybody she knew, and drove out to the cemetery in a hack with two very common women whose conversation was liberally spiced with the word *merde*. One of them declared that Elisa contracted pneumonia when Verlaine sent her out on a cold night to get him tobacco in the Place de la Bastille.

It was not known what property the mother had left. Her only source of income appeared to be a small pension as an officer's widow. Nevertheless, Mathilde sent her lawyers to seize whatever could be found. Her action has naturally aroused a good deal of indignation; she was stripping Verlaine of what little he still had. Her own conscience seems to have troubled her a bit, for she takes care to note in her memoirs that learning of his poverty "je lui en fis remettre une grande partie, contre reçu que j'ai toujours," and that his subsequent descriptions of her as a grasping harpy were untrue.[2] The receipt has never been found. Was she lying? On the whole, unless snobbery was involved, she was not the sort of person who brazenly perverts the truth, whereas Verlaine's mendacity is legendary. Nevertheless, there is something questionable about her story. If she still had the receipt, she should have produced it. But let us be just. Lying or not, no ex-wife ever had a better excuse for being unpleasant. Verlaine had given her a child and then deserted her, first for Rimbaud, then for Létinois. She knew that he had spent large sums on both. Elisa had told her that the Rimbaud spree cost 30,000 francs, and, though she did not

2 Mathilde, *Mémoires*, 255.

know all the details of the farm at Coulommes until she read Le-pelletier's book, she must have suspected that it had been an expensive business. "Je trouve fâcheux que cette paternité adoptive ait fait oublier à Verlaine son fils veritable, et qu'il ait acheté, au nom du père Létinois, une propriété qui eût dû revenir à Georges un jour."[3] During all this time, furthermore, not a franc of her 1200-a-year alimony had been paid. Mme Mauté, always Verlaine's friend, had died in 1884; Mathilde and her father decided that the situation would have to be remedied. Their attitude had understandably hardened since Verlaine decamped with Lucien in 1879. He was incorrigible; when would he take up with somebody else? Supposing Elisa to have left anything, it would certainly be dissipated in a very short time. The money squabbles at the end of a marriage are always ugly, and Mathilde behaved like thousands of other women caught in the backwash of a divorce. Her conduct was hardly noble; but, if only for Georges' sake, she had some justification.

Curiously enough, it was owing to Verlaine himself that she got anything at all. Elisa had never spoken of her bonds, not even to her son, and it was the hotel-keeper, Chanzy, who, profiting by long experience in such cases, rummaged in the mattress and found the packet. When the Justice of the Peace for the Twelfth Arrondissement, acting on behalf of Mathilde's lawyers, came to the Cour Saint-François, Verlaine handed him the bonds quite spontaneously. The official was impressed, and called him an "honest man"; Chanzy (to whom he owed 1825 francs for board and room) told him that he was a "bloody fool." It was one of those theatrical gestures Verlaine liked to make, an emotional luxury, and as things stood it was rather ill-timed, for he was now reduced to 805 francs and nothing more.[4] With Elisa's death his life entered its final and legendary phase. Even people who have never read a line of his verse know the picture: the great lyric poet, the modern Villon, living in a slum with prostitutes and de-

3 *Ibid.*, 240.

4 In February 1886, his aunt Rose Dehée died and left him 2400 francs. See his exposé of his financial position to Léon Vanier, letter of 26 janvier 1887, *Correspondance*, II, 63.

linquents, or recovering from an attack of *delirium-tremens* in the charity ward of a hospital.

The legend, for once, is substantially accurate. His mother had not been dead a month before he took up with a strumpet, Marie Gambier, one of the girls in the hotel. She was a cheerful redhead who "did" the Bastille and the Boulevard Richard-Lenoir. Verlaine later put her into a poem and a short story. She stayed in his room, leaving every evening at seven for her stint of the sidewalk; the poet remained in bed writing until she got back. She was a pretty slut, and like all the hyper-sensitive he was keenly alive to the charm of physical beauty. As Baudelaire knew, beauty is an enigma: its drug-like power demands an answer, and none has yet been found but sexual possession. Though sexual possession never solves the riddle, men have no other choice but to keep trying it. If they are Baudelaires and Verlaines, led by the mind as much as the body, the resulting frustration is another and equally tantalizing mystery. When Marie returned to the hotel drunk with a black eye she was still desirable; her squalid promiscuity pandered to Verlaine's masochism; there was a vicarious thrill in a body that had belonged to so many other men. "O ce corps! O, du col aux orteils, cette blancheur de lait sur du marbre rose ... cet embonpoint charmant, tout au plus à fossettes vers les endroits juste qu'il faut, cette harmonie des seins, et du ventre et des cuisses!" – "Heureux, oui! car malgré la plus que médiocrité, le presque bassesse de sa 'conquête', jamais il n'avait été aussi bien traité de toutes les façons qu'à présent, jamais il n'avait aussi, jamais, mon Dieu! éprouvé un sentiment plus tendre, reconnaissance, estime partielle et piété, admiration humble, enfin, du corps, instrument parfait de tant de belles joies!"[5]

Marie was good-hearted after the unthinking fashion of her kind. She nursed Verlaine through a couple of attacks, even had a certain affection for him. He was a semi-invalid, and he looked a wreck, but he was also a "Monsieur," much above her class, and this flattered her. (She had been a drudge in Amiens, seduced by a cavalryman on leave and then abandoned.) All of which did not

5 "Deux Mots d'une fille", *CML*, II, 242, 247-48.

prevent her from deserting him four months later, in May, to go off with a cooper who had long been her *amant de cœur*.

This brief affair was typical of those that followed. Verlaine relapsed into his adolescent craving for tainted sex, the more tainted the better. Among the Germaines, Andrées, Suzannes, and a host of other professionals, two figures stand out: Philomène Boudin and Eugénie Krantz. Now with one, now with the other, he spent the rest of his life. Both had taken their baptism of fire under the Second Empire and were long past their prime. Philomène (also known as "Esther") was an overblown brunette, easy-going, sluttish, like most prostitutes slightly paranoiac, fond of Verlaine in her way but also of the money she could get out of him, and capable of sudden and gluttonous passions for a pimp or a chance client. Verlaine loved her with senile violence. He wrote verse to her, even offered marriage – he, who had been devoutly outraged only a few years before when Mathilde divorced him and married Delporte. "Quant au mariage, si tu parles sérieusement, tu m'auras fait *le plus grand plaisir de ma vie*, et nous irons chez M. le Maire quand tu voudras. C'est d'ailleurs le plus sûr moyen de t'assurer quelque chose de fixe après ma mort ... Je n'aime que toi et combien!"[6] Her infidelities made him suffer and he separated from her more than once; but the break was never definite. "Chérie, trop! C'est la mort dans l'âme que je t'écris ceci ... tout m'indique que tu as un amant, que tu demeures avec lui et qu'il se *fout* de moi, comme de toi. A ton âge, on n'a pas *pour rien* des amants de 29 ans! Je suis écrasé de chagrin ... Toi, qui ne m'aimes ... que pour mon argent, pour qui je ne suis qu'un miché, qu'un client, qui suis le monsieur qui t'entretient, tandis que d'autres sont tes amants – tu l'as dit à quelqu'un ..." And then, with a characteristic shift of purpose: "Si nous devons vivre ensemble, marions-nous ... Et la confiance revenue sur preuves, je saurai te rendre la plus heureuse des femmes ..."[7]

These letters recall the contradictions of his missives to Rimbaud. Philomène exploited his psychic weaknesses in much the

6 *Correspondance*, II, 304-7, letter of 25 novembre 1893.
7 *Ibid.*, 4 décembre 1893, 319; during a lecture tour in England.

same way, and her hold on him was very strong. A sketch he made at this time (it is dated London, November 30, 1893, just five days before the above letter) shows the kind of satisfaction she provided: Verlaine kneels before her, hands clasped, imploring pardon; she remains haughty and unmoved, like a severe governess. Only the traditional hairbrush is lacking.[8] A few days later (December 5), he was writing incoherently to his friend F. A. Cazals for further information. "La (the) question est l'éternelle Esther (a badname [sic]. I prefer Philomène) ... Je suis jaloux à en mourir, si je m'étais avisé de rompre avec cette trop aimée bizarre et savoureuse middle aged woman! Est-ce vrai qu'elle me trompe et m'exploite dans les grands prix? Tu peux le savoir et me le dire."[9]

Even when he informed Eugénie of the rupture (in a second letter written the same day) and asked her to meet him on his return to Paris, he confessed his passion for the other. "Je me sépare d'Esther avec un gros chagrin. J'aime et j'aimerai toujours cette femme-là. Mais elle m'est dangereuse et mon parti est bien pris. Toi, je t'aime aussi. Tu as toujours été bonne pour moi et je travaille bien seulement avec toi ... A demain et nous ferons un bon petit dîner ... avant de faire dodo."[10] Eugénie happened to be in possession when he died, and could therefore attend his funeral in an almost official capacity. Had Verlaine lasted a bit longer her place might have been taken once more by Philomène.

It would perhaps have been better so, for Eugénie was even less attractive than her rival. Just as promiscuous and unbalanced (there was a pimp in her life too, and half a dozen lovers for whom on occasion she abandoned Verlaine), she had another fault besides, the most tedious of all in a whore: a passion for respectability. She demanded consideration; she "wasn't one of those women"; because she did a little work for a department store, La Belle Jardinière, and kept a sewing-machine in her room, she wanted to be taken for a virtuous seamstress. She nagged Verlaine, tried to hold

8 Reproduced in Bornecque, *Verlaine par lui-même*, 162.
9 Georges Zayed, *Lettres inédites de Verlaine à Cazals*, 279.
10 *Correspondance*, II, 321-22.

him to his table and make him write (she had discovered that a few lines of verse would bring cash at Vanier's office); she inspected visitors and kept out undesirables – which meant anybody unlikely to bring money to the house.

During a dispute her innate vulgarity would explode like a bursting sewer: "Elle était en train de se faire crever ... à travailler comme une bête, pour nourrir, pour soigner un fainéant ... pire qu'un fainéant, un maquereau ... un homme qui n'avait pas honte de se faire entretenir par une femme ... Oh! le travail ne lui faisait pas peur ... elle avait toujours travaillé, elle travaillerait encore" – here a tragic gesture towards the sewing-machine – "si elle n'avait pas à soigner un type qui s'était fricassé le tempérament à faire des orgies avec des traînées ... qu'il regrettait du reste, avec lesquelles il conservait des accointances ... elle le voyait bien ... elle était malade, mais elle avait des yeux ... elle n'était pas une poire, elle était une honnête ouvrière!" Verlaine had told her about his marriage, and in moments of ill-humour she took the wife's part. Most prostitutes of her sort proclaim a loud reverence for abstract virtue: "Tout de même ... si ce n'était pas malheureux! ... une jolie jeune fille, bien élevée, dans une bonne famille, et mariée à un brutal, à un soûlard! ... Elle aurait voulu être là, injurier ce méchant, lui taper dessus!"[11] Her very brutality explains her hold: she played on Verlaine's masochism even more surely than Rimbaud or Philomène had done, and she liked alcohol as much as Verlaine did himself: "Tu bois, c'est hideux! presque autant que moi," he wrote in a poem to her: "Je bois, c'est honteux, presque plus que toi."[12] Whenever he was in funds they got drunk together, ending in a bout of furious love-making or an equally furious spat, to an accompaniment of curses, blows, and broken crockery.

These debauches alternated with periods of hospitalization. It has been calculated that Verlaine spent half of the last nine years of his life in various hospitals: Tenon, Broussais, Cochin, l'Asile de Vincennes, Saint-Antoine, Saint-Louis, Bichat.[13] The sojourns

11 Delahaye, *Verlaine*, 531, 533.
12 *Chansons pour Elle*, XII, Verlaine, Pléiade, 718.
13 See the list given by Richer, 78-9.

varied from four weeks to six months. At first he did not like the idea. The word hospital had a bad connotation at that period; it meant that a person was too poor or too solitary to be taken care of at home. Dying in hospital was synonymous with dying in the poor-house. But when his hydarthrosis was further complicated by inflammation and a running ulcer, he had to yield to the advice of Dr. Louis Jullien, who had been attending him in the Cour Saint-François. He was admitted to the Hôpital Tenon on July 22, 1886. Within a few weeks the regularity of life in the wards, the warmth, the attention, the decent food, so delighted him that far from wanting to leave he was afraid of being put out.[14] In the end he got into the habit of returning whenever he was in difficulties: once more in 1886 (November), five times in 1887, once in 1888, twice in 1889, three times in 1890, twice in 1891, twice in 1892, once in 1893 (from June to December), and twice in 1894. His charm worked on the doctors: we begin to hear of "dear Dr. Jullien," "dear Dr. Chauffart" in the letters. "Si bon, si gentil, d'ailleurs, le docteur Chauffart, et tout son personsel! Je suis l'enfant gâté de la boîte," he wrote from Broussais in 1893.[15]

He was becoming so famous, indeed, that even the world of medicine was aware of the fact. Besides the articles in the *avantgarde* literary reviews, important critics were beginning to appreciate his work. Lepelletier, whose word now counted for something in the offices of *Le Réveil* and *L'Echo de Paris*, never ceased writing in his favour,[16] and on January 7, 1888, Jules Lemaître, the most influential pundit of the time, published a lengthy study in *La Revue bleue*, "M. Paul Verlaine et les poètes 'symbolistes' et 'décadents'." Lemaître was a professional and he could never resist the temptation to be sprightly; his article is flippant and inadequate, but it is also favourable, and coming from such an authority it did much to enhance Verlaine's reputation. There are

14 Cazals and Le Rouge, *Les Derniers jours*, 66.
15 Letter of 29 juillet 1893, to Carton de Wiart, quoted by Porché, *Verlaine tel qu'il fut*, 289.
16 See Verlaine's letters to him: 13 décembre, 1886, octobre 1887, avril 1888, février 1889.

quotations from all his books and *Sagesse* is singled out for special praise: "M. Paul Verlaine a avec Dieu des dialogues comparables (je le dis sérieusement) à ceux du saint auteur de l'*Imitation* ... Je crois bien que les derniers sonnets contiennent quelques-uns des vers les plus pénétrants et les plus religieux qu'on ait écrits ... Avez-vous rencontré, fût-ce chez sainte Catherine de Sienne ou chez sainte Thérèse, plus belle effusion mystique? Et pensez-vous qu'un saint ait jamais mieux parlé à Dieu que M. Paul Verlaine? A mon avis, c'est peut-être la première fois que la poésie française a véritablement exprimé *l'amour de Dieu.*"[17]

The limping wreck who turned up regularly at the admission desk of Broussais or Tenon might look like dozens of other derelicts, but he was Paul Verlaine, a poet whose name was being acclaimed both in France and abroad. Although he failed to get even one vote when he set up as candidate for the Académie Française in 1893, he was elected "Prince of Poets" to succeed Leconte de Lisle the following year. One hundred and eighty-nine writers (poets and critics) were consulted, and since some of them proposed more than one name, the total number of opinions expressed was about four hundred. Verlaine obtained a majority of seventy-seven over any other contestant. The result, as Pierre Martino says, was not very conclusive; most of the voters preferred the surviving poets of the Parnassian school – Heredia, Sully-Prudhomme, Coppée, Dierx, Mendès – who together polled a hundred and twenty-five votes. The title was only an expression of opinion; it had nothing official about it. Nevertheless, it was now Verlaine's, and granting that the writers questioned were competent judges, then contemporary opinion at its best considered him the greatest living French poet.

Meanwhile, his celebrity abroad was reaching huge proportions. In the eighties and nineties literary groups all over Europe were becoming interested in contemporary French poetry; particularly the work of Baudelaire, whose reputation was now well on the way to the apotheosis which, in 1917, marked the fiftieth anniversary of his death. The movement had been in progress

17 Reprinted in *Les Contemporains*, IV, 93-95. See also Martino, *Verlaine*, 200.

since at least 1862, when Swinburne published a study of *Les Fleurs du mal* in England; Verlaine had long been recognized as Baudelaire's greatest follower and benefited from the master's posthumous glory.[18] In 1892, young admirers in Holland asked him to lecture at Amsterdam, and in 1893 he received similar invitations from Belgium and England. He talked about poetry, his own and the Symbolists'. The texts of these lectures were not worth much, his delivery poor, and his voice far too low to be effective from a platform. And it was never certain in what state he would arrive, or whether he would arrive at all. He had an embarrassing habit of disappearing into a bar or a house of ill fame just as the audience was assembling; his sponsors were frequently obliged to make frantic searches through dives and pothouses to get him back to the lecture hall in time. All this was particularly disconcerting in Catholic Belgium, where one of his great attractions was his religious poetry, and where a good part of the audience came to hear a repentant sinner. Nevertheless, the lectures were on the whole successful. Favourable reviews appeared in the press and the fees he received were excellent. The Belgian and Dutch ventures brought him 600 francs each (about $120), and in England (where he spoke four times – at Oxford, at Manchester, and twice in London) he was paid 1455, nearly $300 – nineteenth-century dollars. Obviously he had nothing to complain of, the more so as each trip to foreign parts increased his prestige at home.

"Messieurs," Dr. Chauffart would say to his interns when they reached Verlaine's bed during the morning visit, "voici un grand malade ... et un grand poète, le plus grand poète catholique du siècle," and then proceed to discuss *Romances sans paroles* or *Sagesse*.[19] Most of the young men had heard of Verlaine or read his verse, and they were impressed; their attitude was deeply

18 His affiliation with Baudelaire was often noted: Huysmans, *A Rebours*; Albert Giraud, "Les Poètes baudelairiens," avril 1888, *La Jeune Belgique*; Jules Tellier, *Nos Poètes* (1889); E. Verhaeren, "Paul Verlaine," *La Revue blanche*, 15 avril 1897. At the end of the century his popularity sometimes outranked Baudelaire's: in the famous inquiry carried out by *L'Ermitage* (February 1902), "Quel est votre poète?" many writers and critics preferred him to Baudelaire.

19 Cazals and Le Rouge, *Les Derniers jours*, 46.

respectful. Meanwhile other visitors were arriving in crowds. His friends and disciples had never deserted him. The two years of disorder following Létinois' death had not affected his position in literary circles; he was no sooner back in Paris than his admirers sought him out again. Even when he was bedridden at the Hôtel du Midi they came to sit in his room despite the nightmare squalor of the place, and there was always a group around his table at any café he frequented – the François Ier, L'Académie, La Chope Latine, le Procope, le Café Voltaire, le Chat Noir, Le Divan japonais, etc. At the Soleil d'Or one of the entertainers, Dalibard, used to imitate his walk and recite extracts from his poems to the immense enthusiasm of the audience. In hospital he held veritable receptions. Men and women who were already famous or on the way to becoming so crowded around his bed: Moréas, Barrès, Rachilde, Anatole France (they had made up their old feud), Ghil, Huysmans, Forain, Viélé-Griffin, Mallarmé, Pierre Louys, André Gide. An American lady sent him orchids. His glory was reaching out towards the twentieth century, and the dullest intern could not be insensible to such prestige. The hospital authorities began relaxing their rules in his favour. They gave him a lamp and allowed him to work after curfew, to receive visitors whenever he wished, to take them out into the garden and talk beneath the plane-trees. Verlaine was aging fast. Looking at his portraits, most of which date from his last ten years, it is difficult to realize that he was only fifty-two when he died; he appears sixty or seventy. Yet his very ruin was impressive. The beard, the splendid forehead, and the slanting eyes made him look more and more like Socrates. Everybody noticed it;[20] under the plane trees, listening to him as he sat in his hospital robe, his friends had the impression of taking part in a Platonic dialogue. These sessions became famous, an indispensable part of the literary scene. In the end, as François Porché says, the hospitals would almost have fought each other for the privilege of receiving him.

Another detail is even more revealing: the police themselves

20 "Der bizarre Sokrateskopf" as Kessler calls it, 11.

were impressed by his fame, although he did not know it. The
Prefect, M. Lépine (another of his admirers) gave strict orders to
all Latin Quarter patrolmen that on no account were they to
arrest Verlaine, whatever he did.[21] The Third Republic had its
defects, but disrespect for literature was not one of them.

For all these reasons, the squalor at the end of his life was more
glamorous than real. He knew bad days; in September 1887 he
was on the point of starving to death – or so he said. But friends
intervened (one of them was Coppée, who sent him 50 francs);
they intervened more and more frequently with the passage of
time. Verlaine was one of those fortunate men to whom people
give money as readily as to a child. Everybody recognized that he
was irresponsible; they were not even much offended when he
squandered whatever he received on drink and women. Poverty
became another part of his legend, like a joke in the repertory of a
musical comedy star. One almost gathers that affluence would
have made him less attractive. He was constantly begging for
ready cash and he seldom met with a refusal. Vanier bought his
poems piece-meal, so many verses at a time; the poet would send
Philomène or Eugénie – whichever happened to be in favour at
the moment – with a sonnet and a request for cash: September 24,
1890: "Mlle Krantz, qui est digne de toute confiance, que j'aime
beaucoup, qui m'empêche de faire des sottises et qui prend soin
de moi et de mes affaires d'une façon admirable, veut bien se
charger d'aller quérir de vous cent sous qui me sont indispensables." – March 17, 1891: "Très malade, je prie Mme Philomène
en qui j'ai *justement* mis toute ma confiance, de bien vouloir passer
chez vous et d'y toucher le plus d'argent possible, cent francs au
moins." – July 13, 1893: "Voulez-vous, contre ces 30 vers *très
chics*, remettre à Philomène cent sous." – July 28, 1893: "Voulez-
vous régler, à ma *femme* Philomène, les deux pièces de vers qu'elle
vous portera." – August 9, 1893: "Voici de très beaux vers qui
méritent bien double paye. Double paye ou non, veuillez remettre
à Mlle Philomène la somme." – February 24, 1895: "Voici 30

21 Cazals and Le Rouge, *Les Derniers jours*, 46.

vers que je crois dignes des 10 francs qui me sont indispensables ...
Je vous serai donc obligé de les régler entre les mains d'Eugénie."[22]

Finally, in September 1894, at the moment of Verlaine's election as Prince of Poets, Maurice Barrès organized a committee of fifteen people who agreed to give him 10 francs a month each. It included some society leaders (a duchess and two countesses), and a group of authors and critics of the period such as Henri Bauer, François Coppée, Léon Daudet, Jules Lemaître, Octave Mirbeau, Comte Robert de Montesquiou-Fesenzac, and Barrès himself.[23] Although some of them paid irregularly, Verlaine was never again in complete indigence. His books were beginning to sell; magazine editors were always ready to buy his contributions, sometimes at fairly high rates.[24] And in addition the Ministère de l'Instruction publique allowed him 1500 francs in three instalments during 1894-95. He also found a patron in Montesquiou-Fesenzac, a characteristic figure of the period, one of those brilliant eccentrics lucky enough to live at a time when mere eccentricity could still attract attention. Great wealth, a title, a taste for the arts and a talent for epigram gave him a position his merits hardly deserved (he wrote a certain amount of trivial verse), and two or three novelists paid him the doubtful compliment of writing his peculiarities into the heroes of their books.[25] There was always a hint of condescension in his attitude towards Verlaine, but he seems to have realized that his own position was nothing but fashionable notoriety and that his chief claim to fame would someday depend on the kindness he had shown a greater man. Between 1892 and 1895 Verlaine sent him (or his secretary Yturri) some thirty letters, all containing requests for money or thanks for receiving it.

22 *Correspondance*, II, 166, 175, 227-29, 252.
23 Porché, *Verlaine tel qu'il fut*, 301.
24 All this money was squandered at once. "Il fait une noce effroyable, l'auteur de *Sagesse!*" Deschamps, editor of *La Plume*, wrote René Ghil in 1890. "Je lui ai donné en une semaine 600 francs. Il a tout mangé! Je vais serrer la vis." (Quoted by Coulon, *Verlaine, poète saturnien*, 223.) In a police report in the Verlaine file at the Préfecture dated May 9, 1892, we are told that Verlaine "fait sa fréquentation habituelle des filles publiques et passe pour être un alcoolique."
25 Huysmans, *A Rebours* (Des Esseintes); Jean Lorrain, *Monsieur de Phocas* (Freneuse), *Les Noronzoff* (Prince Vladimir Noronzoff); Marcel Proust, *A la Recherche du temps perdu* (Charlus).

From *Jadis et Naguère* until his death, the poet wrote more than at any other time in his life; his output during these years accounts for two-thirds of his total work. There are fifteen collections of verse and a large quantity of prose (short stories, book reviews, lectures, autobiographical writings, critical studies). Were all this equal to his first books it would make him one of the greatest writers of all time, but unfortunately such is not the case. The waning creative power noticeable after *Sagesse* becomes more and more pronounced until in the end he was little better than an ink-stained hack who had outlived his talent.

To take the prose first. If it is not bad it is mediocre, of no interest except for the light it sheds on the man who wrote it. Thus one short story, "Pierre Duchatelet," is a further revelation of his self-deceptive powers; he tells of his life with Mathilde in 1870 and asserts that she left him because he enlisted to fight the Prussians. In "Louise Leclercq" he identifies himself more or less with the heroine, who, despite a strict Catholic upbringing, deserts her parents and elopes to Brussels with a lover. Echoes of the adventure with Rimbaud may be heard here and there. "Rampo" (also entitled "Charles Husson") has a curious homosexual twist which probably records one of the author's own experiences, for despite his relations with Philomène and Eugénie, he had not dropped less orthodox activities. "Deux mots d'une fille" sketches the Marie Gambier episode; it is perhaps the least worthless of these tales. But though it contains an interesting picture of slum life during the eighties, it is no masterpiece. The "Mémoires d'un veuf" (1882-86) arc attemps to rival Baudelaire's prose poems and fall lamentably short of their models. Verlaine, so sure of himself in verse, had no idea how to handle prose; he thought he was being original when he adopted a far-fetched vocabulary and embarrassed his meaning with elaborate inversions. "Bons bourgeois" is worth looking at because it commemorates a scene with M. Mauté during dinner in the rue Nicolet; "A la mémoire de mon ami," which I have already discussed, evokes the ghost of Lucien Viotti and proves the depth of the poet's affection for his dead friend; "Du Parnasse contemporain" is a brief account of the Parnassian group before the break-up of 1870. The only merit of *Les Poètes maudits, deuxième série* (1888) is the self-portrait entitled "Pauvre Lélian," an anagram for Paul Verlaine which has stuck to him ever since. *Madame Aubin* (1886) is a grotesque attempt at a one-act play. *Les Hommes d'aujourd'hui* (1885-93) contains twenty-seven insignificant studies of contemporary authors. As for *Mes Hôpitaux* (1891), *Mes Prisons* (1893), and *Les Confessions* (1894-95), though they are autobiographical documents of first-rate importance, they have nothing else to commend them. As a prose writer, Verlaine must be pronounced an unqualified failure.

The volumes of poetry have greater value, even if none of them reach the level of the first collections. *Amour* appeared in March 1888. Its earliest verse dates from ten or fifteen years before (some was intended for *Cellulairement*). Other pieces were written at Stickney and Bournemouth; the Lucien Létinois cycle was composed between 1881 and 1887. The results are somewhat uneven. The religious poems ("Prière du matin," "Bournemouth," "There," "Un Crucifix," "Paraboles," etc.) have a tone of gentle melancholy and smooth resignation which, though fine enough, is a bit insipid by comparison with *Sagesse*. "Ecrite en 1875" reads at first like a piece of pure fantasy, the evocation of a blissful and imaginary state:

> J'ai naguère habité le meilleur des châteaux ...
> Une chambre bien close, une table, une chaise,
> Un lit strict où l'on pût dormir juste à son aise ...
> Et je n'ai jamais plaint ni les mois ni l'espace,
> Ni le reste, et du point de vue où je me place
> Maintenant que voici le monde de retour,
> Ah! vraiment, j'ai regret aux deux ans dans la tour!
> Car c'était bien la paix réelle et respectable ...

With something of a shock, the reader discovers that Verlaine is describing life in the penitentiary at Mons. The child had found repose there and freedom from all duties, a discipline imposed and accepted in return for certain benefits: regular meals, decisions made by others, the future provided for, all the problems of the world, in short, excluded behind iron and masonry. In its way the place was not unlike the Esplanade at Metz, and, later, the charity wards. It is not surprising that Verlaine got 175 days off for good behaviour.

The poems to Mathilde (he was still thinking of her, even at this late date) show him, as ever, in the most favourable light. He had had the first of them, "A Madame X," in his baggage since 1873; deciding to print it in *Amour* he thought it needed some accompaniment, and therefore added "Un Veuf parle," "Il parle encore," "Ballade en rêve," and "Adieu." They have a becoming sadness, laced here and there with references to Georges. The whole situation was a wonderful excuse for self-pity:

> O Jésus, vous voyez que la porte
> Est fermée au Devoir qui frappait,
> Et que l'on s'écarte à mon aspect ...

The poem is dated 1879, and remembering Verlaine's conduct at that time, we are staggered by such lachrymose hypocrisy. Or was it hypocrisy? Obviously, he believed what he was saying – at least while he said it.

These pieces of lush contrition are followed by twenty-five other poems to Lucien Létinois. I have little to add to my discussion of that unsavory episode. Even granting that Verlaine's affection for the young peasant was "pure" in a technical sense, the constant references to him as "my son" and the eternal chatter about God and redemption are nonetheless very tiresome. The poems leave a bad taste in the mouth; they cannot be taken at face value. The fifth is the best, perhaps because Lucien is not specifically involved:

> J'ai la fureur d'aimer. Mon cœur si faible est fou.
> N'importe quand, n'importe quel et n'importe où,
> Qu'un éclair de beauté, de vertu, de vaillance
> Luise, il s'y précipite, il y vole, il s'y lance ...
> Puis, quand l'illusion a replié son aile,
> Il revient triste et seul bien souvent, mais fidèle,
> Et laissant aux ingrats quelque chose de lui,
> Sang ou chair ...

Ah, ses morts! Ah, ses morts, mais il est plus mort qu'eux! ...
Il rêve d'eux, les voit, cause avec et n'en sort,
Plein d'eux, que pour encore quelque effrayante affaire.
J'ai la fureur d'aimer. Qu'y faire? Ah, laisser faire!

The poem appeared in *La Revue contemporaine* on October 25,
1885 – more than two years after Lucien's death – and must therefore have been written just after Verlaine moved to the Cour
Saint-François. No one has better expressed the monomania of a
fixed idea, nor the ignominy of aging flesh forever goaded by desire, a spectacle both ludicrous and tragic, one of the basic miseries
of our human condition. The poem stands out in the Lucien cycle
like a gout of blood on synthetic velvet; it may not even refer to
the boy at all. What appalling figures move obscurely behind the
lines?

There is one point about the Verlaine of *Amour* – and of all
these last volumes – which should not be missed. Hand and brain
might falter, but he was still, if only by fits and starts, a consum-
mate master of the mere technique of poetry, the hammering of
words and syllables into harmonious patterns. We are often so
preoccupied with inspiration, feeling, and content that we forget
this indispensable talent, without which all else is vain. The sonnet
"Parsifal" (in *Amour*) is a good illustration of these elementary
truths. It was first published in the *Revue wagnérienne* (January
1886) along with several other poems, one by Mallarmé, in honour of Wagner. As an example of sheer poetic sorcery it is un-
rivalled – from the "Parsifal a vaincu les filles" of the first line to
the splendid hiatus of the last: "Et, ô ces voix d'enfants chantant
dans la coupole!" Verlaine was to repeat the miracle several times
before he died. Such poems are fine stones in the desert of his
later work.

For desert most of it is, although an exception must be made in
favour of his next volume, *Parallèlement* (June 1889), the last of his
books deserving serious attention. He had been working on it
since 1885-86, but, as in the case of *Jadis et Naguère*, a good deal
was composed much earlier. There are four parts, *Les Amies*,
Filles, *Révérence parler*, and *Lunes*; the latter is longer than all the

others combined, and contains the best verse and also the most recent, written within a few years of publication.

Les Amies is a reprint of the six Lesbian sonnets issued by Poulet-Malassis at Brussels in 1867. They could now be published in France; censorship under the Third Republic was less severe than during the Second Empire. *Filles* deals with the prostitutes Verlaine knew in the Cour Saint-François and elsewhere (Marie Gambier is the heroine of one poem, "A la Princesse Roukhine"): the entire section has a light-toned, flippant elegance, expressed in lines of five or eight syllables. *Révérence parler*, except for the prologue, was composed in prison for *Cellulairement*. It is charming, and some of the poems, "Dame souris trotte," "La cour se fleurit de souci," "Réversibilités," are among Verlaine's best.

Lunes is more sinister, an exaltation of sexual inversion, dominated by the memory of Rimbaud. As the years passed, even the reservations expressed in *Sagesse* gave way to pure fascination, emerging each time Verlaine wrote of his friend. When he published the *récits diaboliques*, that grotesque indictment of Rimbaud in *Jadis et Naguère*, he felt obliged to preface them with a sonnet "Le Poète et la Muse," an unabashed evocation of the love-scenes in the rue Campagne-Première. From then on all references to Rimbaud show the same unqualified adoration: 1884, *Les Poètes maudits*; 1886, the preface to *Les Illuminations*; 1887, the sketch in *Les Hommes d'aujourd'hui*. One poem of *Lunes*, "Explication," is a pendant to "Le Poète et la Muse," and the "Ce soir je m'étais penché sur ton sommeil" of 1872; the next one, "Autre explication," takes up again the debate between Mathilde and her rival. The manuscript even bears a dedication, later removed, "To Sophie Marie Mathilde Mauté and Arthur Rimbaud," reminiscent of the album scene Delahaye mentions. There is a touch of surrealist horror in the lines, and the style has a concentration unusual in Verlaine; almost as though he had been reading Lautréamont:

> Amour qui ruisselais de flammes et de lait,
> Qu'est devenu ce temps, et comme est-ce qu'elle est,
> La constance sacrée au chrême des promesses?
> Elle ressemble une putain dont les prouesses

> Empliraient cent bidets de futurs foetus froids;
> Et le temps a crû mais pire, tels les effrois
> D'un polype grossi d'heure en heure et qui pète.
> Lâches, nous! de nous être ainsi lâchés!

Rimbaud triumphs once more over Mathilde, his victory being consecrated in the next two poems, "Laeti et errabundi" and "Ces passions." They date from 1888 and 1889, when a false report of Rimbaud's death reached Paris (he did not die until November 10, 1891). Perhaps for this reason Verlaine spoke out more frankly than ever before: "Ces passions" is a curious apology for sexual inversion, and the verse, whatever one may think of the content, is of very high quality. "Laeti et errabundi" evokes in nostalgic detail the adventure of 1871–73:

> Des paysages, des cités
> Posaient pour nos yeux jamais las ...
> Fleuves et monts, bronzes et marbres,
> Les couchants d'or, l'aube magique,
> L'Angleterre, mère des arbres,
> Fille des beffrois, la Belgique ...
> On vous dit mort, vous ...
> Je n'y veux rien croire, Mort, vous,
> Toi, dieu parmi les demi-dieux! ...
> Mort, mon grand péché radieux ...
> Quoi, le miraculeux poème
> Et la toute-philosophie,
> Et ma patrie et ma bohême
> Morts? Allons donc! tu vis ma vie!

When, after 1891, doubt was no longer possible, he very nearly deified Rimbaud: the sonnet of 1893, incorporated into the final edition of Dédicaces, as splendid in its way as Catullus's *Ave atque vale*; the references in *Mes Prisons* and *Les Confessions*; the study published in the English review *The Senate* (October 1895); the "Nouvelles notes sur Arthur Rimbaud" (*La Plume*, October 1895); the "Arthur Rimbaud" of *Les Beaux Arts* (December 1895). And 1895, we should remember, was the last year of his life. The old passion had become part of his legend, simmering in his heart and liable to erupt with unexpected violence: "Une fois, il m'en souvient, chez un marchand de vins de la rue Monsieur-le-Prince, quelqu'un prononça devant le poète le nom d'Arthur Rimbaud," François Porché writes of these years. "La journée était déjà avancée, c'est-à-dire que Verlaine n'en était pas à sa première absinthe. D'un moulinet furieux, il abattit sa canne sur le zinc, et ce qui sortit de sa bouche, à cette minute, est impossible à rapporter. Parmi des hoquets qui s'achevaient en sanglots, au milieu d'un torrent d'injures, cyniquement éclatait l'aveu d'une passion que ni la prison subie, ni les années écoulées, ni la mort même de l'être aimé, n'avaient pu éteindre. Nous assistions à ce délire avec la confusion des fils de Noé devant l'ivresse obscène de leur père. Et nous aussi, nous aurions voulu, sur cette nudité horrible, étendre pieusement un manteau."[26]

On the brink of the grave, Verlaine was the same tormented creature he had always been. *Parallèlement* grew from the ancient lesion, never properly healed, and joined to this was the harrowing contradiction between religious faith and sexual practice with which he had struggled since Létinois' death – if not since his conversion. The most interesting thing about the book, aside from its poetic excellence, is the new way Verlaine accepts his dilemma. There is a note of jocular despair, both cynical and melancholy; an admission of defeat. He now realized that he could not resolve the antinomies of his nature, nor kill one half of himself in favour of the other, and was exhausted with trying. He wrote *Parallèlement* simultaneously with *Amour* and *Bonheur*, to demonstrate how faith and impurity, normal love and abnormal, were parallels, existing side by side in the depths of his being, essential parts of that *homo duplex*, Paul Verlaine.[27] "*Parallèlement* ... d'une extrême et pour ainsi dire ingénue sensualité qui contraste avec le très sincère mysticisme catholique de *Sagesse*," he said[28]; and even when he erased the dedication of "Autre explication" to Mathilde and Arthur he acknowledged its significance: "une note pour les bonnes âmes qui me biographieront quand 'je reposerai dans la mort tranquille'" he told Jules Tellier, thus handing the problem on to

26 François Porché, *L'Amour qui n'ose pas dire son nom*, 39.
27 *Correspondance*, III, 56.
28 Letter to Félicien Rops, 5 janvier 1888, *Correspondance*, III, 313; see also the letter to Dr. Jullien, III, 56.

us.[29] *Parallèlement* is a hymn to the flesh, as represented by both aspects of sexual desire, a parallel with *Sagesse* and *Amour* (as the preface states), "et aussi à *Bonheur* qui va suivre et conclure." And five years later, introducing a new edition: "ce volume-ci est, pour parler comme les bibliothécaires, en quelque sorte l'*enfer* de l'Euvre chrétien."[30] During the 1880s he was attacked by the lascivious renaissance which sometimes accompanies middle age. Besides Marie Gambier, Philomène, Eugénie, Rimbaud's ghost, and the mud-honey of the slums, there was another *grande passion*, in direct line with his old infatuations. It recalls the crises of 1869 and 1871: "J'ai la fureur d'aimer; mon vieux cœur est fou."

Frédéric Cazals was a young painter and journalist of twenty-one, with a shock of black hair, bright eyes, and the cheeky good-nature of a boy who has grown up on the Paris streets and learned to survive with no other resources than his native wit. He mixed with the Decadents and the Symbolists, and contributed to their periodicals, and first met Verlaine in the spring of 1886, at one of the reunions in the Hôtel du Midi to which he was taken by mutual friends. Relations began calmly enough. Verlaine liked him, and Cazals was flattered by the notice of a poet whom all his friends looked on (in their own words) as a god. He ran errands for Verlaine, took his manuscripts to Vanier, came to sit at his bedside, escorted him to cafés, found him rooms, and even lent him money, although he had little enough himself.

But as the weeks passed the great man's affection grew noticeably warmer. He wanted to move to Montmartre, Cazals' quarter, asked to dedicate *Bonheur* to him, made a will in his favour. He was perpetually scribbling enthusiastic notes. Cazals began to lose patience. He was neither a demonic genius like Rimbaud nor a simple-minded bumpkin like Létinois. He saw at once what Verlaine was after; the poet had a notorious reputation, and his attentions were enough to compromise any man. Cazals had no difficulty imagining the snickers and raised eyebrows in cafés and literary circles. Besides wanting to keep his reputation clean, he

---

29 To Jules Tellier, 11 octobre 1887, *Correspondance*, III, 348.
30 Verlaine, Pléiade, 483.

was living with a charming mistress whom he later married and he had no taste whatever for sexual inversion.

The climax arrived on August 20, 1888. During an evening together, Verlaine, after the usual shots of absinth, made his intentions clear. They were met with a resounding snub. Cazals refused in such vigorous terms that the poet had to beat a hasty retreat. "Pardonnez à mes exaltations," he wrote on the 22nd. "Comme c'est au fond tout l'objet de cette querelle, à moins d'être un sot, vous resteriez l'ami de votre P. V."[31] The dash of cold water slowed him down a bit, but he was still Verlaine, with a weak man's inability to resist an obsession, and he soon began again. The first half of 1889 passed in protests and supplications. January 12 (Cazals had missed an appointment): "J'avais comme une idée que tu ne viendrais pas ... Je profite de la triste et attristante occase [sic] (très attristante, je t'assure, surtout après la séance un peu aigre-douce d'hier ...) pour te dire en toute amitié ... que tu serais bien gentil d'être encore plus gentil. Je suis malade, l'avenir m'échappe, je le vois bien, je n'ai que toi d'affection réelle et profonde au monde, et je suis au fond et malgré mes défauts, qui ne sont que des excès de sensibilité, un homme digne qu'on l'aime tout plein, sans réserves ... Je suis, en effet, jaloux, *jaloux* comme un tigre qui serait un agneau ... enragé, de notre belle et noble amitié ... qui est et restera ma dernière passion *humaine* car Dieu m'attire de plus en plus ...."

On January 19 he was in hospital, protesting the blamelessness of his affection: "Mon amitié est pure" – Cazals had obvious reasons for doubting this – "Mon cœur est d'un enfant, d'une innocence absolue. Je n'ai rien de double, je suis naïf comme tout: mais j'ai souffert exceptionnellement et j'ai des cicatrices qui se rouvrent. Ceux ou celles qui me trouveraient ridicule sont des imbéciles qui ne comprennent rien à la vie. Et je dis: venez ... J'ai besoin de votre visite moralement et matériellement. ... Et c'est vrai que je suis jaloux, mais pas comme on l'entendrait. Vous le savez déjà ..."[32] In June, suspicions of Cazals' affairs with women

31 Zayed, *Lettres inédites*, 92.
32 *Ibid.*, 111, 118.

produced a maudlin scribble from a café near the Hôpital Broussais: "Ecris-moi sans plus cachotterie. Des noms, en voici: Diana
auprès delaquelle tu m'as fait faire des commissions, l'as-tu baisée?
Et toutes autres? Je t'ai dit, je suis jaloux, jaloux de l'amitié qui a
des secrets ... Je t'aime de tout mon cœur. Ne sois plus dur à qui
est si doux ... Je pleure en finissant." The "Diana" was Diana
Andrée, an easy-going Bohemian of the period. On June 20, a
fresh explosion, this time because of gossip that had reached him:
"On m'ennuie, on me persécute, de toutes parts, tout en me re-
prochant ma si pure, – enfin! amitié pour toi. – Que je te 'con-
voite', certes ... mais sois témoin que j'ai refoulé tout ça ... En un
mot on nous veut désunir! ... Méfie-toi de tous et de toutes, mais
non de mon caractère horrible, mais, au fond, exquis ... Je suis
capable, tu le sais, de tous les sacrifices, sauf de celui de mon affection qui reste et doit rester jalouse ... Ne la méconnais pas ... Elle
est immense ... sans borne, – énorme ... mais sincère, et je le répète
... si pure."

As the months went on, however, and Cazals remained obdurate, Verlaine had to accept the inevitable. A wistful note creeps
into the letters. He still had hopes, but without much conviction.
In August 1889 he was at Aix-les-Bains, taking the waters in obedience to Dr. Chauffart's orders. On the 26th he wrote an enthusiastic description of Vespers in the local church. Cazals must have
read it with wry amusement, remembering the homosexual attempt of a year before: "L'assistance à la messe est chose exceptionnellement grave ... J'en sors toujours ... meilleur, oui, et résolu
à la vertu ... Ces impressions sont, hélas! fugaces ... Mes chutes
sont dues à quoi? accuserai-je mon sang, mon éducation? Mais
j'étais bon, chaste ... Ah, la boisson qui a développé l'acare, le ba-
cille, le microbe de la Luxure à ce point en ma chair faite pourtant
pour la norme et la règle! ... Je manque de jugement avec tout le
bon sens que j'ai ... Je suis un féminin, – ce qui expliquerait bien
des choses!!"

These exalted sentiments were indeed *fugaces*. Three days later
a statue of Ganymede on the promenade of the bathing establishment excited his verve: "Cette statue ... est jolie et à mon sens très
voluptueuse ... tête fine, cheveux bouclés retombant, corps fluet

mais au point." The legend, he adds, though "perverti et dégradé en passant par l'imagination sensuelle au possible des Grecs" recalls the stories of Moses, Elijah, Enoch, and the Blessed Virgin – whose Assumption is a true "parallel" to the Greek myth. He finally wrote four stanzas on the statue for a second edition of *Parallèlement* and sent them to Cazals on September 10. They hardly correspond with what we know of Moses, Elijah and the Blessed Virgin:

> Eh quoi! Dans cette ville d'eaux,
> Trêve, repos, paix intermède,
> Encor toi de face et de dos,
> Beau petit ami Ganymède? ...
>
> Bah! reste avec nous, bon garçon,
> Notre ennui, viens donc le distraire
> Un peu de la bonne façon.
> N'es-tu pas notre petit frère?

Still later, in a letter of August 30, he enclosed "Rendez-vous" (written two years earlier, in 1887, and also intended for *Parallèlement*). The subject is entirely scabrous.[33]

> Ta voix claironne dans mon âme
> Et tes yeux flambent dans mon cœur.
> Le monde dit que c'est infâme;
> Mais que me fait, ô mon vainqueur! ...
>
> Tu vins à moi, gamin farouche ...
> Rusé du corps et de la bouche ...
>
> Deux, trois ans sont passés à peine,
> Suffisants pour viriliser
> Ta fleur d'alors et ton haleine
> Encore prompte à s'épuiser.
>
> Quel rude gaillard tu dois être
> Et que les instants seraient bons
> Si tu pouvais venir! ...
>
> Je t'attends comme le Messie,
> Arrive, tombe dans mes bras ...

33 *Ibid.*, 139, 140, 174, 187, and Verlaine, Pléiade, 512, 537-38. The poem was later printed (together with "Ganymède") in *Hombres*.

Was it an indirect way of wooing Cazals? If so, the attempt was vain; the young journalist remained as unmoved as ever, and slowly the protestations and the frenzies began to wane. After 1890 their association lapsed into mere friendship. Verlaine relied on Cazals more and more to handle business matters, and even consulted him when he needed advice about Philomène and Eugénie. Cazals was able to exercise his considerable artistic talents on sketches and portraits of the poet. They are excellent, and provide a lively chronicle of his last years: Verlaine in hospital; Verlaine and Eugénie going to market; Verlaine drinking absinth, talking to friends, entering a café, arguing with Moréas, examining prints; finally Verlaine on his death-bed. We usually think of him during this period as struggling from slum to slum with his two bedraggled harridans. In the light of his letters to Cazals it is clear that a fourth figure deserves a place in that strange trinity. The artist was indeed his "last human passion," and perhaps the only one that was not disastrous, thanks to Cazals.

In perspective, *Parallèlement* appears as the eye of a spiritual disturbance which began five or six years before the date of publication and prolonged itself into the final months of Verlaine's life. All his last works have the same orientation: all are "parallels" to one another. *Bonheur* and *Liturgies intimes* continue the mystic inspiration of *Sagesse* and *Amour*, and *Femmes, Hombres, Chansons pour Elle, Odes en son honneur, Elégies, Dans les Limbes*, and *Chair* are about as close to pure lubricity as can be found in literature.

It is a pity that the results, whether mystic or lubricious, are seldom very good. *Bonheur* (1891) is a dreary affair. The dogmatism from which even *Sagesse* is not entirely free now stifles all genuine religious sentiment. We no longer have a mystic revelation but a theological treatise in verse. Old themes crop up like ragged spectres. Mathilde receives a final castigation:

> Démon femelle, triple peste ...
> Gueuse inepte, lache bourreau,
> Horrible, horrible, horrible femme!

As for Cazals, Verlaine tries to sublimate him as he had sublimated

Létinois; he compares him to Christ (the adolescent in "Rendez-vous" was a Messiah too):

> Mais tu vins, tu parus, tu vins comme un voleur,
> – Tel Christ viendra – voleur qui m'a pris mon malheur!
> Tu parus sur ma mer non pas comme une planche
> De salut, mais le Salut même!

Lines like this are further examples of Verlaine's over-free use of religious terms and imagery during the last part of his career. The technique fitted his preoccupation with "parallels," and was widely popular with other writers of the time. René Doumic defined it as "baudelairisme": "cette perversion qui consiste à mêler le catholicisme avec la débauche, et à raviver la sensualité par le ragoût de l'émotion religieuse."[34] When Verlaine used it, however, he was less perverse than sincere. Since his sexual adventures were further symptoms of his basic insecurity and search for reassurance, he genuinely confused them with religious experience; they were in fact part of religious experience as he conceived it. *Liturgies intimes* (1892) has even less interest. It begins with a sonnet on Baudelaire, renouncing him and all his works; which was tantamount to renouncing most of what made Verlaine's own poetry memorable. We need not take such nonsense too seriously. Consistency was never one of Verlaine's qualities, and a few years later he made a handsome apology to his great predecessor, admitting that he owed him all that was deepest in his own poetry.[35]

The erotic works have at least the merit of being outrageous, and the first two collections, *Femmes* (1890) and *Hombres* (1891) are the best. They continue the theme of sexual parallelism: the last poem of *Femmes*, "Morale en raccourci," introduces the first of *Hombres*, "O ne blasphème pas, poète," and makes clear that the second volume was intended as a sequel to the first. Part of *Hombres* was certainly written before 1891. "Dizain ingénu" and "Obscur et froncé" (for which Rimbaud composed the sestet, and which is now printed among his works[36]), date from 1871; Verlaine wrote

---

34 René Doumic, *Les Jeunes*, 248.
35 See *supra*,
36 Rimbaud, Pléiade, 110.

the remaining pieces twenty years later, during one of his sojourns at the Hôpital Broussais. On the whole, these two collections contain his last successful verse, and it has considerable merit. The human race has produced a large amount of pornography, but practically none of it is literature. We read books like *My Secret Life* and *Les 120 journées de Sodome* as documents; they are usually very ill written. Poetry which is both obscene and poetic is even harder to do than prose, but Verlaine turned the trick with amazing skill. *Femmes* and *Hombres* are frank exaltations of the tactile, positive aspects of sexual pleasure, with no hint of remorse or introspection, no effort to make the flesh yield more than it can, above all with none of the prolix and morbid curiosity which spoils so much work of the kind. Add to this a striking felicity of phrase and versification (nowhere is Verlaine's mastery of language more obvious) and the result is an impression of sunny lechery all the more remarkable when we recall the mephitic atmosphere of the period, a time when the sadistic and the epicene were deliberately cultivated: Rachilde's novels and Péladan's, the deplorable works of Jean Lorrain, and even a great part of Huysmans and Zola, with their craze for neurotic aberrations. By comparison with the salacious lunacy of contemporary work like *La Curée*, *A Rebours*, *Monsieur Vénus*, and *Le Jardin des supplices*, Verlaine's lines seem the ebullience of a healthy appetite. We have to go back to the Greeks and Latins to find anything so good in the same line. Pieces like "Goûts royaux," "Hommage dû," "Il est mauvais coucheur," and particularly "Mille e tre" have a sensual elan which it would be difficult to match in any other writer:

> Mes amants n'appartiennent pas aux classes riches :
> Ce sont des ouvriers faubouriens ou ruraux,
> Leurs quinze et leurs vingt ans sans apprêts, sont mal chiches
> De force assez brutale et de procédés gros.
>
> Je les goûte en habits de travail, cotte et veste;
> Ils ne sentent pas l'ambre et fleurent de santé
> Pure et simple; leur marche un peu lourde, va preste
> Pourtant, car jeune, et grave en l'élasticité.

This sensual elan is certainly not matched in the poetry he wrote for his drabs. Eugénie inspired *Chansons pour Elle* (1891), and Philomène is the heroine of *Odes en son honneur* (1893), *Elégies* (1893), and *Dans les Limbes* (1894). Together they share the dubious honours of *Chair* (1895). It is mostly poor stuff, and even the technical eccentricities – the slang, the daring half-rhymes, the dislocated prosody – do not suffice to keep one reading. The same is true of the collections of occasional pieces he turned out at this time: *Dédicaces* (1890–94), *Epigrammes* (1894), *Le Livre posthume* (1893–94), *Invectives* (1896), *Biblio-sonnets*, and *Poèmes divers* (collected and printed in 1913). They are bits and pieces, written by a man who could always turn a stanza and who turned far too many. *Invectives* is a dust-bin of his various manias: fragments of *Cellulairement*, sonnets against the Third Republic and its politicians dating from the period of his royalist fervour. Any political régime, certainly, is a fit target for satire; all are stupid or vicious in one way or other. But to write satire a poet must have a talent for it, and Verlaine had none. Besides which the Third Republic had treated him very handsomely and was soon to pay for his funeral. *Invectives* is not only bad poetry; it is also bad taste. Through all these collections only a few poems arrest the attention, like shells washed up from a dull sea: the sonnets to Villiers de l'Isle-Adam and Rimbaud in *Dédicaces*, the lines to Octave Mirbeau in *Epigrammes*.

The end came suddenly. Ever since 1889, when Dr. Chauffart sent him off to Aix-les-Bains, his hydarthrosis had been complicated by running ulcers, and in December 1895 the leg began to swell. By Christmas he was bedridden in Eugénie's rooms in the rue Descartes (he had been living with her for some months past). On December 30 he sent his last letter to Robert de Montesquiou, written in the mixture of French and bad English he had affected since his years in England: "Nul argent à la maison. Je suis malade comme jamais ... et not a farthing at home and I want remedies and it is necessary to have five. Eugeny, not wistanding all her courage is out of forces and courage. If it were possible to you,

how much thank-full for an immediate money!"[37] Montesquiou
sent him a hundred francs at once.

And at this moment, by some strange alchemy of his being, he
recovered the incomparable manner of the past. For years he had
been writing drivel: pious homilies, lecherous odes to his trulls,
weak satire against men he disliked on principle. His genius seemed
dead, and then suddenly, as eternity engulfed him, he spoke again
in splendid verse – a final poem, "Mort!" The miracle defies all
rational explanation. Perhaps Apollo, as he watched night falling
round this derelict, felt a pang of something like human sorrow;
or perhaps, with typical Greek irony, he wanted to show men
how little their prejudices and their shibboleths count on the scale
of immortality. The gods are always jokers. He touched the fad-
ing brain, and the old fire erupted once more, for the last time;
but there is nothing much finer in all Verlaine's work:

> Les Armes ont tu leurs ordres en attendant
> De vibrer à nouveau dans des mains admirables
> Ou scélérates, et, tristes, les bras pendant,
> Nous allons, mal rêveurs, dans le vague des Fables ...[38]

It was a worthy farewell. On January 5 he was delirious, and on
the 7th he called in the vicar of Saint-Etienne-du-Mont, who heard
his confession. As always, farce and tragedy were grotesquely
mingled. Hearing that he was dying, Philomène tried to see him,
which provoked one of Eugénie's gutter outbursts. She was so
obstreperous that Montesquiou had to reprimand her sharply:
"Vous remplissez une tâche sublime, votre rôle sera immortel,
vous soignez le grand poète Paul Verlaine, on sera obligé de vous
le retirer."[39] Whether she cared anything for sublime tasks, immortality or great poetry is more than doubtful, but Montesquiou
was a count and a millionaire, and whore as she was these facts
impressed her. She had to obey.

There was a brief improvement in the sick man's condition.
When friends came later on he was able to rise and dine with them.

37 *CML*, II, 1750-51.
38 Verlaine, Pléiade, 1039.
39 As Maurice Barrès recalls the incident. Quoted by Richer, *Paul Verlaine*, 90.

But the effort overtaxed his strength. That night, trying to get out of bed, he collapsed on the floor. Eugénie could not move him, and, as she subsequently told Dr. Chauffart, did not like to disturb the neighbours by asking for help. (The excuse is so weak that it must be a lie; she was probably drunk.) She covered Verlaine with sheets and an eiderdown and let him lie. Next day he was only half-conscious. Chauffart tried a few remedies but he saw at once that there was no hope. By seven in the evening, January 8, 1896, Verlaine was dead.

And now the fame that had been gathering around him ignited like inflammable gas. Telegrams arrived from all over the world; wreaths and flowers poured into the rue Descartes. The Ministère des Beaux-Arts paid half the funeral expenses, friends put up the rest. The ceremony was a triumphal procession. A crowd of 5000 people, chanting his verses, followed the coffin from the church of Saint-Etienne-du-Mont to the vault at Batignolles. Everything he had touched was sacred, even Eugénie. A few weeks later the Ministère granted her a hundred francs to cover her incidental expenses. She had explained her financial difficulties, and though the grant was made *à titre rigoureusement exceptionnel*, it was very nearly an official recognition. Nothing could better illustrate Verlaine's prestige than this posthumous care for a battered trollop whose only claim to distinction was that she had been his mistress.

She had other resources as well. There were his papers and knick-nacks which his friends were glad enough to buy; and she laid in a stock of pen-holders from a neighbouring shop and sold them briskly to English and American tourists as "the Master's pen." It was a lucrative trade.[40]

---

40 In an interview, she said she made 835 francs from the manuscripts alone, and "il me reste un *Louis XVII* dont le premier acte est terminé et le second à peine ébauché." Cazals et Le Rouge, *Les Derniers jours*, 98-99.

10/Paul Verlaine

HAD ANYONE PRESENT at the funeral been asked why he admired the dead man, he would probably have answered that Verlaine carried on the work of Baudelaire, added new themes and techniques to French poetry, and freed it from the shackles of tradition. Such was his reputation during his last years: he helped contemporary poets "briser tous les liens qui les rattachaient au passé"; "il brisa ... les cruelles entraves du vers"; "il ouvrit la fenêtre"; he applied fully Baudelaire's theory of *correspondances*, seeking "le nouveau, je ne sais quel art qui serait vaguement des vers, de la peinture, de la musique, ni de la peinture, ni des vers, – quelque chose comme un concert fait avec des couleurs, comme un tableau fait avec des notes, – une confusion voulue des genres, une Dixième Muse."[1]

If we view these opinions nowadays with a rather sceptical eye it is not because they are false, but because they imply a kind of progress: that after Verlaine, and through him, French verse would be better than ever. Eighty years have passed, and such has not been the case. The exact reverse is closer to the truth: Verlaine, with Rimbaud and Mallarmé, was the last great French poet. There have been poets in France since he lived, but none of them reach his stature. Not through lack of talent; they were simply

[1] *Le Décadent* of October 2, 1886, Jean Moréas, Rachilde, *La Nouvelle Rive Gauche*, all as quoted by Martino, *Verlaine*, 188, 193, 201, 189. See also Bonner Mitchell's *Les Manifestes littéraires de la belle époque* for a reproduction of some of these manifestoes.

lesser men. Much the same thing has happened in England, where
Housman and Eliot, brilliant in so many ways, cannot match the
sheer bulk and force of the great Victorians. And when all is said,
were Verlaine's innovations really as extraordinary as his contemporaries thought? Most of them, examined with care, turn out to
be rather trifling: he sometimes composed in lines of 5, 9, 11, 13,
and even 17 syllables, instead of the more usual 8, 10, or 12.[2] It
was the *impair* he recommended in "Art poétique":

> Plus vague et plus soluble dans l'air,
> Sans rien en lui qui pèse ou qui pose.

And in obedience to another precept of the same poem, he demanded greater freedom of rhyme, by which he meant the right
to rhyme weakly or adequately instead of richly.[3]

In some of his best work he follows these rules (if we can call
them that): five of the nine pieces of *Ariettes oubliées* are written in
impair, and the rhymes are often weak – *bois, voix; murmure, future; cœur, langueur; pluie, ennuie* – depending on vowel sounds
alone with no supporting consonant. But his precepts lose something of their force when we discover that three of the other
poems in the same section, including the most "Verlainian" of all
("Il pleure dans mon cœur") are not in *impair* and frequently have
adequate rhymes. And this is true of most of his work: "Mon
Rêve familier," "Chanson d'automne," "Mon Dieu m'a dit," all
of *Fêtes galantes* except three ("Mandoline," "Colombine," "En
sourdine") – verse with less of heaviness and pose than anything
else he produced. The claim that *impair* and weak rhyme can be
used to blur the contours of sense and produce a vague and dreamy
impression is one of those paradoxes a clever man invents and
others believe. Unless a poem is already vague and dreamy, it is
unlikely that any technique will make it so. "Art poétique," as

2 *Impair* is less a rule than a matter of taste. It exists elsewhere in French verse
(La Fontaine), usually, however, in a humorous or satyric context.
3 For the benefit of readers not acquainted with these refinements, *chose* and *pose*,
enfers and *divers, fou* and *sou* are "weak" rhymes; *monotone* and *atone*, where the
final syllable is supported by an identical consonant, are "adequate"; and *destinée* and *matinée*, with two identical sounds, are "rich."

Verlaine himself admitted, was a song; he never intended it to be taken too seriously.

He also liked to override the traditional caesura when he wrote alexandrines. Sometimes it is displaced, falling elsewhere than at the sixth syllable; more rarely deliberately bridged by a single word (*enjambement sur la césure*) as in "Et la tigresse épouvantable d'Hyrcanie" of *Fêtes galantes*.[4] But reverence for the caesura was never an absolute, even in classical days. There may not be an example of *enjambement sur la césure* in Racine, but his tragedies contain numerous lines where the essential pause occurs elsewhere than at the sixth syllable. And for that matter, Victor Hugo had claimed credit for this particular "reform" long before Verlaine wrote ("Réponse à un acte d'accusation"). More important was Verlaine's use of *rejet* or "overflow" at the end of his lines. He was perhaps the first French poet to use this trick with entire success, and it enabled him to obtain effects of great beauty. Of course it had been tried before, notably by the Romantics, but it was employed sparingly and usually smacked of bravado, as in the famous

> Serait-ce déjà lui? – C'est bien à l'escalier
> Dérobé.

Verlaine practised it with a skill so perfect that one suspects it must have corresponded to a fundamental need of heart and ear. And his more experimental work (*Fêtes galantes, Romances sans paroles*) does not contain the most striking examples. They are found in *Sagesse* where they fit the context admirably well, creating a tone of ecstatic adoration, particularly in the "Mon Dieu m'a dit" cycle. The ease and grace of such poems as "Clair de lune," "La Lune blanche," and "Mon Rêve familier," are, I think, more apparent than real. Because such poems express nothing in particular, tell no story, and are mere translations of mood and sensation, we suppose their technique to be as vague, hazy, and harmonious

---

4 The fact that Rimbaud, rebel though he was, and ready for anything adventurous, admired this line shows how unusual it appeared. Letter to Izambard, August 25, 1870, Pléiade, 259.

as the impression that technique creates. But on examination, they turn out to obey most of the regulations, such as alternate masculine and feminine rhymes, and lines of equal syllabification. For this reason alone they are triumphs of poetic art. French prosody is touchy and demanding; a poet who can obey all its rules and still give an impression of shimmering and evanescent reverie is a genius indeed.

There is little else to say of Verlaine as an innovator. When theory was in question he was much less daring, much more of a traditionalist, than his fiery young admirers supposed. For a while, finding himself in the position of a *chef d'école*, he tried to play up. A taste of glory was flattering after so much neglect and so many years of sentimental misfortune. But he was soon shocked by the extreme ideas of his self-named disciples. They began using "Art poétique" as an excuse for discarding rhyme, metre, and prosody in general. He protested vigorously: "Le poème en question est *bien* rimé. Je m'honore trop d'avoir été le plus humble de ces Parnassiens tant discutés aujourd'hui pour jamais renier la nécessité de la Rime dans le vers français, où elle supplée de son mieux au défaut du Nombre grec, latin, allemand, même anglais ... Je résume ainsi le débat: rimes irréprochables ..." And he added later: "Rimez faiblement, assonez, si vous voulez, mais rimez ou assonez. Pas de vers français sans cela."[5]

This was treason to the doctrines he was supposed to represent, and it alienated some of his followers. "Et maintenant je puis ... m'expliquer très court, tout doucement, ... avec de jeunes confrères qui ne seraient pas loin de me reprocher un certain illogisme, une certaine timidité dans la conquête du 'Vers Libre'," he complained in January 1890. "J'aurais le tort de garder un mètre, et dans ce mètre quelque césure encore, et au bout de mes vers des rimes. Mon Dieu, j'ai cru avoir assez brisé le vers, l'avoir assez affranchi, si vous préférez, en déplaçant la césure le plus possible, et quant à la rime, m'en être servi avec quelque judiciaire pourtant, en ne m'astreignant pas trop, soit à de pures assonances, soit à des formes de l'écho indiscrètement excessives. Puis, car n'allez

5 Martino, *Verlaine*, 181, 182.

pas prendre au pied de la lettre mon 'Art poétique' de *Jadis et Naguère*, qui n'est qu'une chanson, après tout, – *je n'aurai pas fait de théorie*."[6] He even added an amusing skit on both himself and his disciples to *Parallèlement*, "A la manière de Paul Verlaine." It is the second poem of the *Lunes* section, and in that sinister context it appears almost sportively hilarious:

> C'est à cause du clair de la lune
> Que j'assume ce masque nocturne
> Et de Saturne penchant son urne
> Et de ces lunes l'une après l'une.

So much criticism from the young ended by nettling him and led to a rupture. He lost interest in the "decadent" school he had baptized. In 1891, when an interviewer (Jules Huret) asked him what he though of Symbolism, he declared that he did not know what the word meant. "Le symbolisme? ... comprends pas ... Ça doit être un mot allemand ... hein? Qu'est-ce que ça peut bien vouloir dire? Moi, d'ailleurs, je m'en fiche ... Certes, je ne regrette pas mes vers de quatorze pieds; j'ai élargi la discipline du vers, et cela est bon; mais je ne l'ai pas supprimée! Pour qu'il y ait vers, il faut qu'il y ait rythme. A présent, on fait des vers à mille pattes! Ça n'est plus des vers, c'est de la prose, quelquefois même ce n'est que du charabia."[7] – A passage which shows yet once more the futility of dividing writers into categories. In most literary manuals, Verlaine is defined as a Symbolist.

The *avant garde* grew more and more disillusioned with him. Moréas and Ghil had both published Symbolist manifestoes; one of their group, Viélé-Griffin, asked Verlaine for a "declaration of principles" to support the new school. He refused. This was in 1887, and shows that his impatience with Symbolist ideas began fairly early. "Je n'ai pu tirer de ma conscience que cette conclusion: Tout est bel et bon qui est bel et bon, d'où qu'il vienne et par quelque procédé qu'il soit obtenu," he wrote Henri de Régnier. "Classiques, romantiques, décadents, symbolos, assonants ou com-

6 *CML*, II, 303.
7 *CML*, II, 1760.

ment dirai-je? obscurs exprès, pourvu qu'ils me foutent le frisson ou simplement me charment ... font tous mon compte ... Telle est ma théorie mûrement délibérée."[8] It was less a theory than an admission that he had got beyond the age of theories. His disciples began to drop away. Moréas concluded that he was an obstinate Parnassian, who had never progressed further than Baudelaire, with no influence on contemporary poetry, and the end of a line rather than a beginning; a man without ideas, theories, or a reasoned programme.[9]

Coming from a second-rater like Moréas (second-rate by comparison with Verlaine), such criticism appears remarkably brash. But it has some truth. Verlaine's importance in literature, whether French or universal, arises from neither his technical experiments nor his influence on later writers. The experiments were means of self-expression, vehicles for his genius, but not the genius itself. And, unlike Baudelaire, he did not found a line of poets and his influence, when it existed, was almost invariably bad. Verhaeren, Ghil, Viélé-Griffin, Gustave Kahn, Albert Samain, Moréas himself: at some time or other they all tried to imitate Verlaine, tried to be vague, suggestive, harmonious, and languorous. The results were poor. Their works now lie in the stacks of the Bibliothèque Nationale, that *pudridero* of so many theories and manifestoes, and a resurrection appears unlikely.

Verlaine provided a clue to the nature of his genius in 1882 when he replied to criticism from Charles Morice: "Laissez-moi rêver, si ça me plaît, pleurer quand j'en ai envie, chanter lorsque l'idée m'en prend."[10] At first this looks like pure Romanticism, something analogous to Musset's "Le seul bien qui me reste au monde est d'avoir quelquefois pleuré." But in one important way Verlaine differed from the Romantics. They were poets of emotion, he was a poet of sensation. "J'ose espérer," he wrote Mallarmé on November 22, 1862, when he sent him a copy of *Poèmes*

8 Martino, *Verlaine*, 196-97.
9 As quoted by Jules Huret, *Enquête sur l'évolution littéraire* (Charpentier 1891), 80. "Il tient trop à Baudelaire."
10 Martino, *Verlaine*, 188.

saturniens, "que vous y reconnaîtrez ... un effort vers l'Expression, vers la Sensation rendue."[11] *Vers la Sensation rendue*: there is a curious parallel to the phrase in the *Confessions* nearly thirty years later: "Ici, la sensation est si vague qu'elle n'en est plus sensation, mais caresse indéfinie, jouissance de néant meilleure que toute plénitude."[12] Was he analysing his own work? We might suppose so, for the passage defines very well the over-all impression of *Fêtes galantes, Romances sans paroles,* and much of *Sagesse.* In reality, he was discussing a childhood fever, alleviated by his mother's caresses. The phrase is interesting none the less; it sets forth so succinctly the effects he sought in his verse that it suggests yet another link, even if an unconscious one, between his memories of Elisa and the universe of illusion he sought to create in his poetry. The great Romantic poems ("Le Lac," "La Nuit de mai," "Tristesse d'Olympio," "Colère de Samson," even Baudelaire's "Le Cygne" and "Le Voyage") are rhetorical developments of personal feeling. The poet has suffered or enjoyed, and takes up the alexandrine like a trumpet. There is no rhetoric in Verlaine, only a series of devices for avoiding it. *Enjambement* was one device, used particularly at the end of the lines. Rhetoric is for strong nerves, not for a sensibility preoccupied with the past, eternally alive to the suggestions of memory. Verlaine dwelt in recollections of his first years; the escapades of his life and the beauties of his verse were both manifestations of the same wish-neurosis, the same desire for a *jouissance de néant meilleure que toute plénitude.* Hence his style, hence the eternal parallels between life and art: they were mutually nostalgic and even hallucinogenic. And hence too (since reality and illusion are very different things), his constant failure to adjust to ordinary living and the catastrophes that attended all his sentimental adventures.

They were not, essentially, very unusual adventures. It was normal, even banal, for a civil servant to marry an eligible girl. And there was no reason why, as a poet with a growing reputation, he should not welcome another who was young and obscure; nor,

11 *CML,* I, 929.
12 *CML,* II, 1117.

as a teacher, take an interest in one of his students. Thousands of civil servants, poets, and teachers have done as much. Yet every time, the perverse economy of his being turned normal into abnormal and the average into the disastrous. He tired of Mathilde when she was no longer a virgin; he fell in love with Rimbaud and drove him to exasperation; he tried to insulate his passion for Lucien with sham paternalism and fake religiosity. Had the boy not died the liaison would have ended in recrimination and ingratitude. Short of death, ingratitude was Lucien's only way of escape. And through all this certain factors remained constant: the mania for drink (that at least could always be bought across a counter), the child's obstinacy in pursuit of the unattainable, the child's refusal to face responsibility and disappointment. "Aime-moi, protège et donne confiance. Etant très faible, j'ai très besoin de bontés," he wrote Rimbaud in 1872. And twenty years later to Cazals: "Tu serais bien gentil d'être encore plus gentil ... Ne sois plus dur à qui est si doux ..."

His books were the direct and inevitable results of his temperament: artificial refuges, constructed according to the emotional habits he had contracted under the bell-glass of Elisa's affection. Each shows the persistence of memory in a man who never grew up, each is an attempt to adjust reality to the data memory supplies. All recreate in some form or other the never-forgotten paradise: ideal love (*Poèmes saturniens*); an eighteenth-century dreamworld (*Fêtes galantes*); harmonic suggestion (*Romances sans paroles*); union with God (*Sagesse, Bonheur*); life with Rimbaud or Létinois (*Parallèlement, Amour*); a flesh-padded universe of willing beauties (*Chansons pour Elle, Chair, Femmes, Hombres*). All the best poems spring from an involuntary nervous tremor, provoked by sensation; it cracks the glass of reality and the old obsession rises like a djin from a bottle. And always, behind the glimmering illusion, flows the chill wind of insecurity, the terror of time and death.

Verse of this kind, evolving from such capricious sources, inevitably has serious limitations, not the least of which is a disconcerting tendency to dry up, leaving the poet with no other resource than silence or uninspired labour. He is never free from the matrix of infancy, and even at its best, his work is often morbid and green-sick. At times he even distrusts his own genius: Verlaine sought to evade his more than once – as when he rushed into marriage, terrified by his passion for Lucien Viotti; or spent his year with Rimbaud lamenting the security he had lost; or again when, overtaken by disaster and locked in a cell, he alternated between exquisite inspiration ("Le ciel est par-dessus le toit") and the copious mediocrity of the *récits diaboliques*. Paralysed by subconscious trauma, he was not only powerless to face the present, but, at times, even to take advantage of his own sublime gifts: they half-frightened him. He was torn between opposites; he wanted illusion and reality, spiritual adventure with Rimbaud (iconoclasm, liberty, "amours de tigre," the flaming blue eyes and the demi-god's body) and also the bourgeois comforts of home, complete with hot tea, a good fire, and a natty little woman. That is to say, he wanted them all until he got them. Then, like Emma Bovary, he wanted something else. There was no end to his powers of self-deception. It would perhaps be an exaggeration to attribute all this to the childhood fixation. But that was the initial flaw, the minute fissure in the dyke which, enlarged by other pressures, admitted a whole sea of anarchic passion. He was never happy with either side of his nature: Mathilde bored him; Rimbaud filled him with guilt and remorse. Neither reconciled dream and action. Neither could, since the dream was so distorted by illusion as to correspond to nothing factual. This memory obsession is one of Romanticism's most poisonous and seductive legacies. The tough, classical centuries – the seventeenth, the eighteenth – had no past; they lived three-dimensionally. A fourth dimension, time, has since been included. It is no passive addition, like a new room in a house, but rather tends to control and even corrupt the other three, as though it were less a room that a hypogeum of badly embalmed corpses, wafting their stench throughout the building. There is a good deal of this kind of smell in Verlaine, unmitigated by any intellectual ventilation. His art belongs to the general reinterpretation of aesthetic values which set in with the waning of scientific positivism. It gave us Impressionist painting, the music of Debussy, Fauré, and Duparc, the poetry of Mallarmé, and the prose of Marcel Proust, not to mention the philosophy of Henri Bergson. Both Proust and Bergson were sensationists; Proust, certainly, was as much fascinated by the past as Verlaine himself. All three used sensation to unchain memory and put it to work in a creative or divinatory way. In more senses than one, Verlaine's poetry is another "recherche du temps perdu," a further example of "matière et mémoire."

But there was an essential difference: Proust and Bergson were less interested in sensation as an end than as a means; they used it to reach a better understanding of illusion and reality. Their aims were objective; they were intent on plumbing the mysteries of consciousness, personality, and the creative process. There was no such purpose in Verlaine. The lack of it was one reason for his break with the Symbolists. They wanted a programme, and he had none. He lived instinctively. In his deepest work (*Sagesse*) the ideas were not his own but those supplied by the Athanasian Creed. He wandered into unknown country almost by accident, and made no attempt to chart it. He never turned on reality the penetrating gaze of a Baudelaire or the fiery glance of a Rimbaud. His nature was submissive and masochistic – "feminine," as he told Cazals.

He was Baudelaire's disciple; he borrowed some of his ideas and techniques, but only those which heighten sensation, like the theory of *correspondances*. The two men had no other point of contact. The dark world of despair and unrest which yawns throughout *Les Fleurs du mal* was not for Verlaine, nor the refusal to accept half-answers, nor the heroic cynicism of "Le Voyage." In poems like "Il pleure dans mon cœur" and Baudelaire's "Spleen" ("Quand le ciel bas et lourd ..."), the situation is identical: the poet is alone, listening to rain falling on the city:

> Ô bruit doux de la pluie,
> Par terre et sur les toits!
> Pour un cœur qui s'ennuie
> Ô le chant de la pluie!

But there all similarity ends. Verlaine records a series of sensory perceptions: impressions play across the mind and end with no direct statement:

> C'est bien la pire peine
> De ne savoir pourquoi
> Sans amour et sans haine
> Mon cœur a tant de peine!

Baudelaire, however, develops his theme through a succession of powerful images, each creating an atmosphere of frustration and despair: the sky is a sombre lid, the earth a wet dungeon where Hope flits like a timid bat; rain is no gentle song, but a concrete and oppressive fact, the bars of a mighty prison. One poet gives us a tenuous prelude, as light and plaintive as the shower itself; the other a tragic sonata, with modern man helpless in the stony labyrinths of his cities.

We touch here, I think, on the main reason for Verlaine's popularity during his last years, and for the relative neglect into which he has fallen since. There is nothing "unpleasant" about his work. It is all charm, and, if one happens to be religious, positively comforting. It had an immediate appeal for the eighties and nineties: the content was smooth as a madrigal, and the technique just original enough to be thrilling. There were few unpalatable details or horrible similes, and no agonizing search for a higher truth. When Verlaine agonized he found truth at once, in the Church. Even in bed with his trollops or pursuing Cazals, he maintained that he was a Christian, something well suited to reassure any debauchee who read him. His age found his genius so apparent that it procured him a situation we can only call privileged. It was as though he said to his contemporaries: "Yes, I am disreputable, and worse; I live with pimps and whores, I drink like a fish, I have done time. But I am a poet and you shall adore me." And adore him they did: they bought his manuscripts, pensioned him, buried him, even looked after his slattern – for no other reason than that she had been his slattern. One thinks of Baudelaire during his last years: insulted by critics, snubbed by publishers, his Belgian lec-

ture-tour a failure, even his friends unable to take him seriously.
By comparison, Verlaine enjoyed an almost insolent triumph. In
1890 he was as old as Baudelaire when Baudelaire died, and his
fame was already secure. His very misfortunes were glamorous.
Not the prolonged, gnawing attrition of Baudelaire's end, but a
picturesque kermess.

It is this kermess impression we carry away from a study of the
man and his art. He had a prodigious lyric talent, and not many
poets can rival him for sheer virtuosity, not even Baudelaire or
Rimbaud. But it was the virtuosity of a child prodigy who never
ceased being a child prodigy. The more we read him, the more
we perceive that his achievements depended on this fundamental
immaturity. His shiftlessness, his tantrums, his inability to resist
seduction, and his raw sensitivity were all essential to his verse,
even his religious verse. Raw sensitivity is a prerogative of childhood; no amount of sophistication could have given birth to the
poignant sincerity of *Sagesse* or the alluring music of *Romances
sans paroles*. "Mes défauts ne sont que des excès de sensibilité" –
"Mon cœur est d'un enfant ... je suis naïf comme tout." He wrote
according to the dictates of a nervous erethism forever alert to the
half-felt and the intangible: perfume, sound, colour, light and
shade, remembered sexuality. Once involved with a subject demanding objectivity, he was beyond his depth and laboured in
vain. As far as such a thing is possible, he was a poet of the echo –
echoes of dead voices, silent music, joy realized through sadness.

It was a limited range; these are the qualities of frustration, with
nothing epic or tragic about them. The past lay across his talent
like a fallen column on a growth of acanthus:

> Pour soulever un poids si lourd,
> Sisyphe, il faudrait ton courage ...

And Verlaine was no Sisyphus. Even had he been, the obstruction
was too massive; he would have spent his forces in sterile effort.
There was no escape but the one he chose – illusion, the *affreux
soulagement* of sex and alcohol, the quest for self-oblivion in the
personalities of others. He was divided against himself, split into

"parallels" by the cumbrous burden. And since parallels never meet, there could be no fusion, no supreme revelation like *Les Fleurs du mal*. A sadder fate than Baudelaire's, because so totally unheroic. Yet defeat under such conditions was not absolute. It even had elements of victory. The crushed plant was not dead: year after year it sent up its shoots and its leaves, mysterious and indestructible; and with what exquisite foliage it bordered and concealed the unyielding stone!

Appendix

The case of Georges Verlaine

GEORGES VERLAINE PLAYS almost no role in his father's life, but as I worked on the foregoing pages, I often wondered what sort of person he was and what finally became of him. There seemed no way of finding out. He led one of those lives that leave few traces behind – a dim planet near a brilliant star, lapsing into darkness once the parent illumination was extinguished. Then one evening in 1965 M. Yvan Christ, the well-known authority on French art and architecture, told me that his maternal grandfather, Joseph Uzanne, had employed Georges for some years as his secretary, and that certain documents and letters still survived.[1] I was anx-, ious to see them, and a few days later they were put into my hands together with M. Christ's permission to print them if I thought fit. They have considerable interest. Dealing with a drunken crisis through which Georges passed in June 1904, they are a further revelation of the hereditary alcoholism of the Verlaine family.

According to Mathilde, Paul had little affection for his son, "une indifférence absolue," as she puts it: "jamais il ne l'embrassait ni le regardait."[2] She is perhaps too bitter, but it is true that when Georges was born (October 30, 1871) Verlaine was in all the violence of his passion for Rimbaud and had no time for children. He left Paris with Rimbaud on July 7, 1872, and appears to

---

1 Joseph Uzanne (1850-1937) was the brother of Octave Uzanne (1851-1931), the critic and bibliophile.
2 Mathilde, *Mémoires*, 182, 196.

have seen his son only twice after that: when he paid his two visits to the boy's sick-bed in 1878. Much later, during the winter of 1887-88, he sent Mathilde word from hospital that he was dying and asked to see Georges.[3] This was not the first time he had cried wolf about dying, and Mathilde was sceptical. She made inquiries through a medical friend and learned that the case was not serious. Verlaine, in fact, was to live another eight years. Georges remained at home.

Meanwhile, Mathilde had taken advantage of changes in the marriage laws as soon as they came into effect. On May 22, 1885, she turned her legal separation from Verlaine into complete divorce, and on October 30 of the following year married B. A. Delporte, a building contractor who was born in Belgium in 1852 and who also had been divorced. They lived for a while in Paris, then went to Brussels and finally Algiers, where they were divorced on May 12, 1905.[4] Mathilde died on November 13, 1914 in her boarding-house at Nice. As far as she could, she kept Georges in ignorance of the scandals of his father's life, especially the Rimbaud escapade. When she had to discuss the matter at all, she talked vaguely of Verlaine's drinking and of "incompatability." The boy grew up in the atmosphere of domestic ambiguity which is the lot of children in such circumstances. After leaving school, he spent a year in England to acquire the language, did his military service at Oran with the 2^e Chasseurs d'Afrique, and learned clock-making.[5] There is no evidence that his mother neglected him, but she had two children by Delporte and her new household was demanding. As far as Georges had a home, it was Delporte's, and a second husband seldom welcomes references to his predecessor. Paul Verlaine's name was mentioned as little as possible.

3 He was in the Hôpital Broussais from September 20, 1887, until March 20, 1888.

4 All these details are given by François Porché in his preface to Mathilde's *Mémoires*.

5 Georges Verlaine gave this information to Maurice Hamel, who used it in an article for *Comoedia*, 28 avril 1924, "Une visite au fils du divin Lélian: la modestie et la philosophie de Georges Verlaine."

But such a parentage could not be concealed forever. Verlaine was too famous. By the time he was twenty, Georges had read most of his father's works, and probably a number of the critical studies that had appeared.[6] It was impossible not to take some pride in being the son of a man who had written *Fêtes galantes*, *Romances sans paroles*, and *Sagesse*. In October 1895 (when he was twenty-four), he wrote Verlaine from Soignies, Belgium, asking to see him, and requesting money for a ticket to Paris. At the time Verlaine (as he says) was "dead broke"[7] and could send nothing, but several letters were exchanged. Then Georges fell silent. Verlaine, worried, wrote the mayor of Soignies, who replied that Georges "a quitté Soignies depuis trois ou quatre semaines, quelque peu malade. Après avoir passé vingt-quatre heures à l'hôpital de Braine-le-Comte, il est retourné chez sa mère, qui habite Bruxelles, avenue Louise, 451."[8] Verlaine then asked Count Carton de Wiart, whom he had met during his Belgian lecture-tour in 1893, to make inquiries. The Count went to 451, avenue Louise, but could find nobody there called Delporte. Verlaine was convinced that Mathilde was again hiding his son, and begged Wiart to continue the search. But he died himself on January 8, 1896, and Wiart did not find Georges until the 20th.

The reasons for the young man's silence were then explained. His health had been precarious for some years, and just after writing his father he suffered an attack of amnesia. "Il avait perdu la mémoire," Mathilde writes. "Lorsqu'on lui parlait il paraissait s'éveiller bursquement; il avait des gestes automatiques, une voix toute changée, et les allures d'un somnambule. Il fut transporté à l'hôpital. Traité par la suggestion, il guérit. Se sentant rétabli, et le moment étant venu de faire son service militaire ... il se rendait à Lille ... Malheureusement, on l'avait laissé partir trop tôt; n'étant pas complètement guéri, il fut repris d'un sommeil léthargique. Bien soigné, il se remit, mais le malade ayant intéressé les méde-

6 Louis Chauvet, "Paul Verlaine et son fils," *Le Figaro*, 29 juillet 1931.
7 *Ibid.*, "une crise pécuniaire assez carabinée," he wrote Wiart.
8 Quoted, *ibid.*

cins par la singularité de son état, il fut gardé en observation. On devait lui donner son congé de convalescence dans les premiers jours de janvier, mais on ne le laissa sortir que le 13, trop tard donc pour assister aux obsèques de son père." Georges himself confirmed this account: "J'étais prêt à partir pour Paris. C'est alors que j'ai été attent de crises de sommeil léthargique. Le dernier de ces sommeils a coincidé avec la mort de mon père."[9]

Verlaine was dead, but his son could never lack friends. His father's admirers were always ready to help him: "Après le décès de Paul Verlaine, son fidèle ami Edmond Lepelletier fut un véritable père pour mon mari," his wife later told an interviewer. "Il lui trouva une place, boulevard Saint-Germain, chez M. Uzanne, qui éditait les albums de vin Mariani."[10] This *vin Mariani* was a tonic mixture of wine and herbs; Georges' duties were of a secretarial order. Unfortunately, reflected glory was not the only thing he had inherited from his father. The *crises de sommeil léthargique* were doubtless a symptom of the Verlaine strain in his blood, but what particularly worried Uzanne was a morbid craving for alcohol. The young man worked in his employer's dining-room, and the Christ family still has the sideboard, fitted with a double door to protect the bottles it contained. "Je vous prie de fermer à clé tous vos placards, car je ne peux pas m'empêcher de boire," Georges used to say.[11] He could not see a bottle without emptying it, and lived in a perpetual state of mental absence. He never remembered a commission; he would listen attentively to instructions and then forget them at once.

Finally, on June 16, 1904 (he had been working for Uzanne

9 Mathilde's account is quoted by Lepelletier, *Paul Verlaine*, 539-40, Georges' by Louis Chauvet. There is some confusion. Mathilde seems to mean that the attack took place *before* Georges' military service, Georges that it occurred afterward. Perhaps there were two crises, one before and one after, and Mathilde confused them. Georges' service with the 2ᵉ Chasseurs should have taken place earlier than 1895.

10 Quoted by Paul Hauchecorne, "La Belle-fille de Verlaine," *Toute la vie*, 9 mars 1944. See also Lepelletier, *Paul Verlaine*, 420.

11 This is the tradition in the Uzanne family as Mme Marcel Christ, née Mary Louise Millon (Uzanne's step-daughter) still recalls it.

since about 1900), he suddenly disappeared. His employer learned the reasons from the newspapers:

Le Petit journal, 17 juin 1904 (column "Echos de partout"):

L'héritier d'un nom célèbre, M. Georges Verlaine, fils du poète Paul Verlaine – le pauvre Lélian – donnait depuis quelques jours des signes d'un dérangement cérébral assez accentué.

Son état a empiré au point que les personnes de son entourage ont cru devoir, hier, demander son internement, à la suite d'une crise violente qui l'avait pris au domicile où il résidait actuellement, dans le quartier des Epinettes.

La névrose est sœur de génie, dit-on – ou fille.

Le Matin, 17 juin 1904 (column "A travers Paris"):

Le fils de Verlaine. – L'infirmerie spéciale du Dépôt a recueilli hier un pensionnaire nouveau, dont le nom évoque bien des souvenirs. Georges Verlaine, le fils du poète, a été enfermé, à la suite d'une attaque de "delirium tremens."

Sous l'empire de l'ivresse, le malheureux jeune homme avait de véritables accès de folie. Comme il était atteint, hier, d'une crise plus forte encore que de coutume, sa maîtresse prévint le commissaire de police du quartier, M. Coston, qui a dirigé Georges Verlaine sur l'infirmerie spéciale.

L'Aurore, 18 juin 1904 (column "Faits divers"):

Le fils de Verlaine. – Georges Verlaine, le fils de l'auteur des *Poémes saturniens*, vient d'être envoyé à l'infirmerie spéciale, par les soins de M. Coston, commissaire de police. Le malheureux est âgé de trente-trois ans.

Georges Verlaine demeurait dans un hôtel meublé de la rue Gauthey.

Police Commissioner Coston's report on the arrest is still in the Paul Verlaine file at the Préfecture de Police (Archives et Musée). It is dated from the Mairie du xviiie Arrondissement, June 16, 1904, at 4:10 AM: "Commissaire Epinettes à Préfet Police: J'ai envoyé à l'infirmerie spéciale ce matin Verlaine Georges 33 ans demeurant 55 rue Gauthey qui ne serait autre que le fils du poète Paul Verlaine pauvre Lélian. Coston." The "maîtresse" mentioned by *Le Matin* was Alexandrine Henriette Stéphanie Corbeau, born in Paris on December 30, 1863; widow of Léon M. Corbeau (they had the same surname and may have been cousins). According to her own account, as she gave it to P. Hauchecorne, she met Georges in 1896, two weeks after his father's death. Since he was then undergoing treatment at the military hospital in Lille, her memory was doubtless at fault. They lived together at 55, rue Gauthey, Paris xvıı^e, for the rest of Georges' life; he married her on February 20, 1906. Edmond Lepelletier was present at the ceremony.[12]

The newspaper information was supplemented by a letter Georges wrote Uzanne from the asylum at Ville-Evrard, dated June 23, 1904: "Je n'ai pas besoin de vous raconter ce qui m'est arrivé. Les journaux ont été assez charitables pour amplifier à leur façon cette crise. Il est certain que l'alcool accumulé m'a monté au cerveau et a occasionné cette attaque. En me débattant j'ai cassé quelques objets, et me suis blessé assez sérieusement, j'étais couvert de sang. Je ne sais comment deux agents se trouvaient chez moi, j'étais trop étourdi. Ce que je me rappelle c'est qu'ils m'ont emmené à l'infirmerie du dépôt et de là on m'a transporté mourant à l'asile Sainte Anne où des soins énergiques m'ont remis. Avant hier j'étais beaucoup mieux, le docteur Magnan me fit suivre un régime anti-alcoolique, ... il m'a dirigé sur Ville-Evrard dans le service du docteur Legrain ... Pardon, Monsieur Uzanne, de vous avoir dérangé en vous quittant accidentellement, mais j'ai bien souffert et souffre encore beaucoup moralement pour bien des raisons, et ai compris trop tard vos bons conseils."

Uzanne had lost patience. He wrote Legrain, the doctor in charge at the Asile de Ville-Evrard, asking for information on the patient and announcing his intention to fire him. Legrain replied with humanitarian brevity: "Asile de Ville-Evrard, Neuilly-sur-Marne, le 28 juin 1904. Monsieur, Le malade dont vous me parlez est un simple buveur héréditaire. Son mal est curable à la condition qu'au dehors il soit bien entouré. Votre détermination de

12 Lepelletier, *Paul Verlaine*, 420, and Archives de la Mairie du xvıı^e Arrondissement, which I examined myself.

vous séparer de lui ne me paraît pas logique, eu égard à l'intérêt que vous dites lui porter, car c'est au moment même où il aura le plus besoin d'appui moral et matériel qu'il ne vous trouvera plus." Whether as a result of this letter or through simple kindness of heart, Uzanne changed his mind. He wrote Georges, enclosing some stamps, and received an answer dated June 30, 1904: "J'ai bien reçu votre lettre et les cinq timbres dont je vous remercie ... Je me trouve excessivement bien maintenant. Il y a du reste plus de quinze jours que je me trouve au régime, mais je crois que le docteur Legrain me gardera encore un peu. Si j'étais seul, je ne m'inquiéterais pas, mais vous savez qu'il faut que je gagne ma vie. C'est pour cette raison que je ne tiens pas à séjourner de trop ici, surtout que les œuvres de mon père ne me rapporte [sic] guère en ce moment, et il faut tout de même que le loyer soit payé ... Je n'ai pas besoin de donner ma parole d'honneur que je ne boirai plus d'alcool, je me sens trop bien en ne buvant que de la gentiane, du thé ou du lait."

These letters read very much like Paul's descriptions of his sojourns in hospital: there is the same good-humoured detail of hospital routine, the same repentance for past misconduct. Both father and son were model patients, and both got sympathetic attention from the doctors in charge. Georges had Magnan and Legrain, just as Paul had had Chauffart and Jullien. The great difference, of course, lies in the style. It was one of fate's minor ironies that Paul Verlaine's son, at thirty-three, wrote French like a retarded child.

Dr. Legrain's diagnosis – that the case was curable – appears to have been correct; at least Georges never again figured in the papers as in 1904. Through recommendations from Uzanne and Lepelletier, he obtained a position in the Paris métro, at the station Avenue de Villiers, where he punched tickets and supervised the quay. Until the end of his life he continued to be the son of Paul Verlaine. Every now and then some journalist in search of an article would look him up, and his bosses and fellow employees never forgot who he was: "Il ne faut pas lui faire de peine, c'est le fils de Verlaine."[13] He led a strange, muted existence – uneventful, rather melancholy – a sort of prolonged anti-climax to his father's riotous career. He took an interest in literature, even wrote some verse. It has no value. What has been preserved reads like very bad Verlaine:

> Un petit être se réveille,
> Sourit ou pleure, regardant
> D'un œil rond, la toute vermeille
> Fleur d'un sein. Puis il s'y suspend ...
> Maintenant nos corps vagabondent
> Ici-bas. Nos pensées abondent
> À notre souvenir en deuil.

In August 1926 he had an attack of uremia. His wife informed Uzanne in a characteristic scrawl (she seems to have been unable to spell her husband's name):

> Monsieur
>   je viens de recevoir un télegramme, pour me prevenire quon
> viens chercher mon Mari à la clinique pour le transporter a baujon
>   Donc Monsieur ne vous déranger pas je vous donnerez des
> nouvelles
>   Recevez Monsieur mon profond respect
> Me Verlainn

Georges died on August 31, 1926, and was buried in the Batignolles cemetery, in the family vault beside Captain Nicolas-Auguste and Elisa Dehée Verlaine, the grandparents he had never seen, and Paul Verlaine, the father he had scarcely known. "Un simple buveur héréditaire ..." Dr. Legrain's phrase comes very close to summing up the Verlaine family as we know it: Jean Verlaine and his fine of six florins for drunken cursing in 1742; Henry-Joseph bawling insults outside the church of Bertrix in 1804; Paul in a Brussels court in 1873 for shooting Rimbaud, and in 1885 condemned to a year in prison for attacking his mother; Georges carried off by police officers for insane violence while drunk in 1904. A hundred and sixty-two years – four different men in four different situations – yet the pattern is nearly identical.

13 Georges' own words to Maurice Hamel.

Bibliography

(Unless otherwise stated, the place of publication is Paris.)

I / WORKS BY VERLAINE

Œuvres complètes, 5 vols. Léon Vanier, ed. 1899; reissued subsequently by Vanier's successor, Albert Messein.

Œuvres complètes, 2 vols. (Club du Meilleur Livre 1959-60.) The definitive edition of Verlaine.

Œuvres poétiques complètes (Bibliothèque de la Pléiade 1966).

Œuvres libres de Paul Verlaine. Les Amies. Femmes. Hombres. Préface d'Etiemble (Au Cercle du Livre précieux 1961).

Correspondance de Paul Verlaine, 3 vols., publiée sur les manuscrits originaux avec une préface et des notes par Ad. Van Bever, Messein, 1922-29.

II / SECONDARY SOURCES

Adam, A. *Le Vrai Verlaine, essai psychanalytique* (Droz 1936).

Adam, A. *Verlaine* (Hatier 1953).

Adam, P. *Petit glossaire pour servir à l'intelligence des auteurs décadents et symbolistes* (Vanier 1888).

Aressy, Lucien. *La Dernière Bohème. Verlaine et son milieu* (Jouve et cie n.d.)

Bibesco, Prince A. *La Question du vers français et la tentative des poètes décadents.* (Lemerre 1893).

Bornecque, J. H. *Etudes Verlainiennes, les Poèmes saturniens* (Nizet 1952).

Bornecque, J. H. *Lumières sur les Fêtes galantes* (Nizet 1959).

Bornecque, J. H., *Verlaine par lui-même* (Editions du Seuil 1966).

Cazals, F. A. and Gaston Le Rouge. *Les Derniers jours de Paul Verlaine* (Mercure de France 1911).

Carco, Francis. *Verlaine* (La Nouvelle Revue Critique 1939).

Coulon, Marcel. *Au Cœur de Verlaine et de Rimbaud* (Le Livre 1925).

Coulon, Marcel. *Verlaine, poète saturnien* (Grasset 1929).

Cuénot, Claude. *Etat présent des études verlainiennes* (Belles Lettres 1938).

Delahaye, Ernest. *Verlaine* (Messein 1923).

Delahaye, Ernest. *Souvenirs familiers à propos de Rimbaud, Verlaine et Germain Nouveau* (Messein 1925).

Donos, Ch. *Verlaine intime* (Vanier 1898).

Fontainas, A. *Verlaine-Rimbaud, ce qu'on présume de leurs relations, ce qu'on en sait.* (Librairie de France 1931).

Ghil, René. *Traité du Verbe* (Giraud 1886).

Ghil, René. *Méthode Evolutive-Instrumentaliste d'une poésie rationnelle* (Savine 1889).

Huysmans, J. K. *A Rebours, Œuvres complètes de J. J. Huysmans.* tome VII (Crès 1929).

Kahn, Gustave. *Symbolistes et décadents* (Vanier 1902).

Le Febve de Vivy, L. *Les Verlaine* (Miette, Bruxelles 1928).

Lepelletier, Edmond. *Paul Verlaine, sa vie, son œuvre* (Mercure de France 1907).

Lemaître, Jules. *Les Contemporains*, IV (Société français d'imprimerie et de librairie 1897).

Lorrain, J. *Monsieur de Phocas* (Ollendorf 1901).

Martino, P. *Verlaine, nouvelle édition revue et corrigée* (Boivin 1951).

Mitchell, Bonner. *Les Manifestes littéraires de la belle époque* (Seghers 1966).

Moréas, J. *Esquisses et souvenirs* (Mercure de France 1908).

Morice, Ch. *Verlaine, l'homme et l'œuvre* (Vanier 1888).

Morice, L. *Verlaine, le drame religieux* (Nizet 1946).

Morice, L. *Verlaine, Sagesse, édition critique commentée* (Nizet 1964).

Mouquet, Jules. *Rimbaud raconté par Paul Verlaine* (Mercure de France 1934).

Nadal, O. *Paul Verlaine* (Mazenod 1948).

Nadal, O. *Paul Verlaine* (Mercure de France 1961).

Porché, F. *Verlaine tel qu'il fut* (Flammarion 1933).

Raynaud, E. *La Mêlée symboliste* (La Renaissance du Livre 1920).

Richer, J. *Paul Verlaine* (Seghers 1960).

Rimbaud, A. *Correspondance 1881-1891*, préface et notes de Jean Voellmy (Gallimard 1965).

Rimbaud, A. *Œuvres complètes* de Renéville Rolland et Jules Mouquet, eds. (Plêiade 1963).

Starkie, Enid. *Arthur Rimbaud* (New York, 1960).

Tellier, Jules. *Nos Poètes* (Lecène et Oudin 1889).

Underwood, V. P. *Verlaine et l'Angleterre* (Nizet 1956).

Vanwelkenhuyzen, G. *Paul Verlaine en Belgique* (La Renaissance du Livre 1945).

Verlaine, ex-Madame Paul (Mathilde Mauté). *Mémoires de ma vie* (Flammarion 1935).

Vicaire, Gabriel. *Les Déliquescences, poèmes décadents d'Adoré Floupette* (Byzance, chez Lion Vanné 1885).

Zayed, Georges. *Lettres inédites de Verlaine à Cazals* (Droz 1957).

Zimmermann, Eléonore M., *Magies de Verlaine* (Corti 1967).

III / PERIODICALS

Bornecque, J. H. "Les Dessous de *Mémoires d'un veuf.*" *Revue des Sciences humaines,* avril-juin 1952.

Bougard, P. "La Famille maternelle de Verlaine d'après les archives du Pas-de-Calais," *Revue des Sciences humaines,* avril-juin 1952.

Décadence, La. secrétaire de la rédaction, René Ghil 1886.

Décadent, Le. directeur, A. Baju, 1886-89.

Ermitage, L'. "Quel est votre poète?" février 1902.

Giraud, Albert. "Les Poètes baudelairiens." *La Jeune Belgique.* Bruxelles: avril 1888.

Kessler, Harry Graf. "Besuch bei Verlaine," *Insel-Almanach* 1965.

Martin, Auguste. "Verlaine et Rimbaud," *Nouvelle Revue française.* février 1943.

Rodenbach, G. "La Poésie nouvelle. A propos des décadents et des symbolistes," *La Revue bleue.* 4 avril 1891.

Verhaeren, E. "Paul Verlaine," *La Revue blanche,* 15 avril 1897.

Index